African Christian Mothers and Fathers

African Christian Mothers and Fathers

Why They Matter for the Church Today

Mark Ellingsen

CASCADE *Books* • Eugene, Oregon

AFRICAN CHRISTIAN MOTHERS AND FATHERS
Why They Matter for the Church Today

Copyright © 2015 Mark Ellingsen. All rights reserved. Except for brief quotations in critical publications or reviews, no part of this book may be reproduced in any manner without prior written permission from the publisher. Write: Permissions, Wipf and Stock Publishers, 199 W. 8th Ave., Suite 3, Eugene, OR 97401.

Cascade Books
An Imprint of Wipf and Stock Publishers
199 W. 8th Ave., Suite 3
Eugene, OR 97401

www.wipfandstock.com

ISBN 13: 978-1-60608-550-9

Cataloging-in-Publication data:

Ellingsen, Mark, 1949–

    African christian mothers and fathers : why they matter for the church today / Mark Ellingsen.

    xxxvi + 214 p. ; cm. —Includes bibliographical references and indexes.

    ISBN 13: 978-1-60608-550-9

    1. Africa—Church history. 2. Church history -- Primitive and early church, ca. 30-600. 3. Church history. I. Title.

BR190 .E44 2015

Manufactured in the U.S.A.   10/16/2015

For David Wallace

Dean

Colleague

and

Friend

through thick and thin

Contents

Preface | ix
Abbreviations | xi
Introduction: Ancient African Christianity and Why It Matters | xxiii

1 Anthony and Other Desert Fathers | 1
2 Mothers of the Desert | 20
3 Clement of Alexandria | 30
4 Tertullian | 48
5 Origen | 63
6 Commodianus | 78
7 Cyprian of Carthage | 82
8 Dionysius, Bishop of Alexandria | 95
9 Anatolius of Alexandria and Minor Writers | 100
    Theognostus of Alexandria | 101
    Pierius of Alexandria | 101
    Theonas of Alexandria | 102
    Phileas | 103
10 Lactantius | 104
11 Alexander of Lycopolis | 116
12 Peter of Alexandria | 119
13 Alexander of Alexandria | 122

CONTENTS

14 Arnobius | 125
15 Athanasius | 130
16 Macarius the Egyptian | 142
17 Caius Marius Victorinus | 155
18 Didymus the Blind | 165
19 Contemporaries of Augustine | 170
    Synesius of Cyrene | 171
    Optatus | 176
20 After Augustine | 180
    Cyril of Alexandria | 180
    Fulgentius | 190

Conclusion: Using Early African Theology Today | 198

Bibliography | 205
Index | 211

Preface

It's been too long coming, but ancient North African Christianity is starting to get its due in the academy, as we begin finally to appreciate that the Church would not be what it is today were it not for the contributions of African spirituality and (yes) for the contributions of Black men and women! Thanks to the work of Thomas Oden and his Center for Early African Christianity, study groups on the topic around the globe are beginning to form. But before Professor Oden and his colleagues came to their important insights, segments of the African-American and African churches have been aware of the importance of studying of this topic. Thus it is not suprising that a book like this, written by a son of Norwegian immigrants, has its origins in my teaching assignments at the largest and oldest accredited historic African-American seminary, the Interdenominational Theological Center. Its insights were further developed at a series of lectures given over a decade ago for the South Florida Center for Theological Education.

Given the rich resources that surround me in my setting and the historic Black denominations that support the seminary I serve, it is not surpising to note that I have many debts of thanks to offer for making this book happen. Nearly everyone associated with my intellectual home for the last twenty years (administrators, faculty colleagues, students) has had a hand in the book's development. And of course there is my wonderful wife, Betsey, who was up to her usual editorial tricks on this book, like all my previous eighteen volumes, not to mention all the love, encouragement, and good questions she provided. Brad Ost of the staff of my seminary's Woodruff Library did yeoman's work locating some obscure texts I badly needed. In all my years in the academy in several quality institutions, I have never worked with a more competent and assiduous librarian than Brad.

PREFACE

The editorial staff of Cascade Books displayed the competence that they are known for along with a lot of helpfulness when I needed it most.

Though each of those mentioned deserve a dedication, there is one person in my life that Betsey and I both feel should have this book for him. And so this volume is for my former dean (of Johnson C. Smith Seminary of the Interdenominational Theological Center), a valued colleague in the classroom for more than a decade in team-teaching, and dear, much appreciated friend, David Wallace. We come from different parts of the country, with different ethnic roots, life experiences, and denominational backgrounds, but that hasn't gotten in the way of things between us. Just made the friendship better. We clicked almost immediately since we first met over twenty years ago. Proud of his African-American heritage, but along with a pastoral and personal style that communicates to anyone privileged to know him that he's rooting for everyone (the kind of guy anyone would want for her pastor), this book on Christianity's African roots is exactly the volume I've wanted to present to him ever since we became friends (been waiting for some years to write just the right book for him). And it also gives me a chance publicly to thank his wife, Iris, for the years when in her role as a dean's wife she was kind enough to put in a good word on my behalf with students. Most of the time my friendship and collegial working relationship with Dave have just been a lot of fun. But true friendship is measured by sticking together through thick and thin, and there have been a few times when we've done that for each other too. And so this book is just a small way to say thanks to a great colleague who's also a true friend of mine.

Abbreviations

Alex. Alex.		Alexander of Alexandria
	Ep. Ar.	Epistles on the Arian Heresy and the Deposition of Arius [Epistolaie de Ariana haersi deque Arii depositiora] (n.d.)
Alex.		Alexander of Lycopolis
	Tract. Man.	Of the Manichaeans [Tractatus de Placitis Manichaeorum] (n.d)
An.		Anthony
	Ep.	Epistles [Epistoles] (n.d.)
Ana.		Anatolius of Alexandria
	Arith.	Fragments on the Books on Arithmetic [Fragmenta ex libris Arithmeticorum] (n.d.)
	Can. pas.	The Paschal Canon [Canon paschalis] (n.d.)
Arnob.		Arnobious
	Ad Gen.	Against the Heathen [Adversus Gentes] (n.d.)
Ath.		Athanasius
	Ag. Ar.	Four Discourses against the Arians [Τογ Αγτου κατα Αρειανων] (ca. 359)
	Apol. Ar.	Defence Against the Arians [Απολογητικος κατα Αρειανων] (339–47)

ABBREVIATIONS

Decr.	On the Decrees of the Council of Nicea [De Decretis] (346–56)
Ek. Pis.	Statement of Faith [Εκθεσις πιστεως] (n.d.)
Ep.	Epistles [Επιστολη]
Ep. Af.	Epistle to Africans [Των κατ' Αιγυπτον και Λιβην] (ca. 369)
Ep. Serap.	Epistles to Serapion [Επιστολη προς Σεραπωνα] (n.d.)
Exp. Ps.	Expositions on the Psalms [Expositiones in Psalmos] (n.d.)
Frag. Al.	Fragment from a Sermon to the Baptized [Fragmenta Alia] (n.d.)
Hist. Ar.	History of Arianism [Historia Arianorum] (c.358)
Jul. op. imp.	Against Julian: An Unfinished Work [Contra Julianus] (429–30)
Log. Eoan.	On the Incarnation of the Word [Λογος περι της Εςαναθρωνσεως του λογος, και της δια σωματος τος προς Ημας] (318)
Log. Hellen.	Against the Heathen [Λογ οσκατα Ελληνων] (318)
Synod.	On the Synods [De Synodis] (359–61)
V. Ant.	Life of Anthony [Του οσιου Πατρος Ημων Αντωνιου] (ca. 356–62)
Athenag.	Athenagoras
Leg.	A Plea for Christians [Πρεσβεια περι Χριστανων] (177)
Aug.	Augustine
C. Jul.	Against Julian: An Unfinished Work [Contra Julianus] (421–22)
Civ.	The City of God [De civitate Dei] (413–26)
Conf.	Confessiones (399)

ABBREVIATIONS

	Doctr. christ.	On Christian Doctrine [De Doctrina Christiana] (397–426)
	Ep.	Epistles [Epistulae]
	Ep. Joh.	Ten Homilies On the First Epistle of John [In Epistolam Joannis ad Parthos] (ca. 406/407)
	Grat. et lib. arb.	On Grace and Free Will [De gratia et libero arbitrio] (426/427)
	Nupt. et concup.	On Marriage and Concupiscence [De nuptis et concupiscentia] (318)
	Perf. Just.	On Man's Perfection in Righteousness [De perfection justitiae Hominis] (415)
	Vera relig.	On True Religion [De vera religion] (390)
Clem.		Clement of Alexandria
	Adum.	Comments On The First Epistle of Peter [Adumbrationes] (n.d.)
	Paed.	The Tutor [Παοδαγωτος] (n.d.)
	Prot.	Exhortation to the Greeks [Λόγος ὁ προτρεπτικὸς πρὸς Ἕλληνας] n.d.)
	Strom.	Stromata [Στρωματων] (194)
	Q.d.s.	Who Is the Rich Man That Is Saved? [Τις ο Σωζομενος Πλογσιος] (n.d.)
Comm.		Commodianus
	Instr.	Instructions [Instructiones] (ca. 240–ca. 250)
Cypr.		Cyprian of Carthage
	Bono. Pat.	On Works and Alms [Liber de Bono Patientiae] (256)
	Dem.	An Address to Demetrianus [Liber ad Demetrianum] (252)
	Domin. orat.	On the Lord's Prayer [De dominica Oratione] (252)
	Donat.	Epistle to Donatus [Epistola ad Donatum] (n.d.)
	Ep.	Epistles [Epistolae]

ABBREVIATIONS

De Exhort. Martyr.	*Exhortation to Martyrdom, Addressed to Fortunatus* [*Epistola ad Fortunatum de Exhortatione Martyrii*] (ca. 252/257)
Idol. Van.	*On the Vanity of Idols* [*Liber de Idolorum Vanitate*] (247)
Laps.	*On the Lapsed* [*Liber der Lapsis*] (251)
Laud. Mart.	*On the Glory of Martyrdom* [*Liber de Laude Martyrii*] (n.d.)
Mort.	*On the Mortality* [*Liber de Mortalitate*] (252)
Op. et Eleem.	*On Works and Alms* [*De Opere et Eleemosynis*] (254)
Quod Bapt.	*Concerning the Baptism of Heretics* [*Quod de Baptismo Tertium Est*] (258)
Unit. eccl.	*On the Unity of the Church* [*De unitate ecclesiae*] (251)
Zel. et Liv.	*On Jealousy and Envy* [*Liber de Zelo et Livore*] (256)

Cyprian and The Council of Carthage

Test. Ad. Jud.	*Three Books of Testimonies against the Jews* [*Testimonium Libri Tres Adversus Judaeos*] (248)

Cyr.	Cyril of Alexandria
Ad Acac.	*To Acacius of Melitene* [Πρὸς Ἀκάκιον] (n.d.)
Ad Eul.	*To Eulogius* [Ὑπομνηστικὸν Εὐλογίῳ] (n.d.)
Ad Joann.	*To John, Bishop of Antioch* [*Ad Joannem Antiochenum*] (433)
Chr. un.	*That Christ Is One* [οτι εις ο Χριστος] (n.d.)
Dial. Trin.	*Dialogues on the Trinity* [Περι Ατιας τε και Ομοουσιος Τριαδος] (n.d.)
Doct.	*Doctrinal Questons and Answers* [Ἐπίλυσις] (n.d.)
Ep. Cal.	*Letter to Calosirus* [πρὸς Καλοσίρον] (n.d.)
Ep Nest. 2	*Second Letter to Nestorius* [*Epistola IV*] (430)
Ep. Nest. 3	*Third Letter to Nestorius* [*Epistola XVII*] (430)

ABBREVIATIONS

Ep. Suca. 1	First Letter to Succensus [προς τον μακαριώτατυν Σούκενσον] (n.d.)
Ep. Suca. 2	Second Letter to Succensus [Ετερον ὑπομνηστικου ἀντιγραφὲν προς τὰ πεύγεις ἡμων παρὰ του αὐτου πρὸς τὸν αὐτὸν Σούκενσον] (n.d.)
Glaph.	Polished Comments [Γλαφυρως] (ca. 429)
Hag. Sum.	On the Creed [Τὸ ἅγιον συμβολον] (n.d.)
Hayaian.	Commentary on Isaiah [Εις τον Πριητην Ηηαιαν] (n.d.)
Inca. unigen.	On the Incarnation of the Only-Begotten [τερπι της ενανθρωπησεως του Μονογενους] (n.d.)
Luc.	Exposition of the Gospel of Luke [Εξητησις εις το κατα λογκαν Ευαγγελιον] (n.d.)
Matt.	Commentary on Matthew [Commentairum in Matthaeum] (n.d.)
Nest. Dus.	Against the Blasphemies of Nestorius [Των Νεστοριου Δυσφημιων] (n.d.)
Rect. fide	On the True Faith [De recta fide] (n.d.)
Rom.	Commentary on the Epistle to the Romans [Ερμηνεια εις την προς Ρωμαιους Επισταλην] (n.d.)
Tib.	Answers to Tiberius and His Companions [text in Coptic] (n.d.)
Didym.	Didymus the Blind
Spir.	On the Holy Spirit [Liber de Spiritu Sancto] (ca. 381)
Trin.	On the Trinity [De Trinitate] (381–92)
Zach.	Commentary on Zechariah [Εις τον Ζαχαριαν] (ca. 387)
Dion.	Dionysius of Alexandria
Ad. Bas.	The Epistle to Basilides [Επιστολη προς Βασιλειδην Επισκοπον] (n.d.)

ABBREVIATIONS

	Ad. Dion.	*Epistle to Dionysius, Bishop of Rome* [*Libris Ad Dionsium Romanum Potificem*] (n.d.)
	Ad. Sabell.	*The Books against Sabellius* [*Libris Adversus Sabellium*] (n.d.)
	Ap. Ekk.	*Exegetical Fragments* [Τεν Αρξην Εκκλησιαστου] (n.d.)
	Ep.	*Epistles* [*Epistolae*] (n.d.)
	Lib. et Nat.	*The Book on Nature* [*Libris de Natura*] (n.d.)
	Promiss.	*The Two Books on the Promises* [*De Promissionibus*] (n.d.)
Ep. Barn.		*Epistle of Barnabas* [Επιστολή Βαρνάβα] (100)
Eus.		Eusebius of Caesarea
	H.e.	*The History of the Church* [*Ecclesiastica historia*] (323–24)
Fer.		Ferrandus
	Fulg. Vita	*The Life of the Blessed Bishop Fulgentius* [*S. Fulgentii Episcopi Ruspensis Vita*] (n.d.
Fulg.		Fulgentius
	Ad. Mon.	*To Monimus* [*Ad Monimum Libri Tres*] (ca. 517–23)
	Ep.	*Epistles* [*Epistolae*]
	Fide ad Pet.	*To Peter on the Faith* [*De Fide Seu de Regula Verae Fide: Ad Petrum*] (n.d.)
	Rem. Pec.	*On the Forgiveness of Sins* [*De Remissione Peccatorum Ad Euthymum Ubri Duo*] (517–23)
Jer.		Jerome
	Com. Eph.	*Commentary on Ephesians* [*Commentaria in Epistolam ad Ephesias*] (387)
	Ep.	*Epistles* [*Epistolae*]
	Rufin.	*Apology Against Rufinus* [*Apologia Adversus Libros Rufini*] (402)

ABBREVIATIONS

Jerome and Gennadius

    Vir. Illus. — *Lives of Ilustrious Men* [*De virisi illustribus*] (480–92)

Lact. — Lactantius

    Ep. — *The Epitome of The Divine Institutes* [*Epitome institutionum divinarum*] (n.d.)

    I.D. — *A Treatise on the Anger of God* [*De ira Dei*] (n.d.)

    Inst. — *The Divine Institutes* [*Divininarum Institutionum*] (n.d.)

    M.P. — *Of the Manner in which the Persecutors Died* [*De mortibus Persecutum*] (n.d.)

    O.D. — *On the Workmanship of God, or The Formation of Man* [*De Opificio Dei*] (n.d.)

    P.D. — *A Poem on the Passion of the Lord* [*De Passione Domini*] (n.d.)

Mac. — Macarius the Egyptian

    Ep. — *The Great Letter* [*Epistola*] (n.d.)

    Hom. IInum. — *The Spiritual Homilies* ['Ομιλιαι Ιlνεγματικαι] (n.d.)

    Virt. — *Virtues of Our Righteous Father* (n.d.)

Mar. Vict. — Caius Marius Victorinus

    Ar. — *Against Arius* [*Adversus Arium*] (359–461)

    Can. Ar. — *Letter to Candidus the Arian* [*Ad Candidum Arrianum*] (n.d.)

    Homo. recip. — *The Necessity of Accepting Homoousios* [*De homoousio Recipiendo*] (n.d.)

    Hymn. — *Hymns* [*Hymnus*] (n.d.)

Optat. — Optatus

    Schis. Don. — *Against Dontatists* [*De Schismate Donatistarum Adversus Paramenianum*] (n.d.)

ABBREVIATIONS

Or.	Origen
Cels.	Against Celsus [Εις τομογσ κατα Κελσος] (cf. 176)
I Cor.	Fragment Commentary on 1 Corinthians [Codex Althous Laura 104] (n.d.)
Ex.	Homilies on Exodus [Εις την Εξοδον] (n.d.)
Gen.	Homilies on Genesis [Εις την Γενεσιν] (n.d.)
Heraca.	Dialogue with Heraclides [Ηρακλειδς] (n.d.)
Jer.	Homilies on Jeremiah [Homiliae in Jeremiam] (n.d.)
Joh.	Commentary on the Gospel of John [Κατα Ιοvvεv Εγαλλενιον Εξηγητικα] (n.d.)
Jos.	Homilies on Joshua [Homiliaen librum Jesu Nave] (n.d.)
Lev.	Homiles on Leviticus [Εκλογια εις Λεγιτικον] (n.d.)
Mart.	Exhortation to Martyrdom [Εις Μαρτυριον] (n.d.)
Matt.	Commentary on the Gospel of Matthew [Κατα Ματθαιον Εγαλλενιον Εξηγητικα] (246-48)
Orat.	On Prayer [Περι Ευχης] (n.d.)
Princ.	On First Principles [Περι Απξων] (n.d.)
Rom.	Commentary on Romans [Commentarium in Epistolam S. Pauli ad Romanos] (n.d.)
Pach.	Pachomius
Instruc.	The Instructions [Instructiones] (n.d.)
Pat. aeth.	The Wisdom of the Elders of Ethiopia [Paternican aethiopice] (n.d)
Praecept. et Inst.	Precepts and Instructions [Praecepta et Instituta] (n.d.)
Petr.	Peter of Alexandria
Act. Sinc.	The Genuine Acts of Peter [Acta Sincera Sancti Petri] (n.d.)

ABBREVIATIONS

	Ep. Can.	*The Canonical Epistle* [*Epistola Canonica*] (306)
	Frag.	*Fragments* [*Fragmenta*] (n.d.)
Ph.		Phileas
	Ad. Mil.	*Epistle to Miletius* [*Epistola ad Miletium*] (n.d.)
	Ad. Thum.	*Epistle to the People of Thumis* [*Epistola ad Thumitas*] (n.d.)
Phil.		Philo
	Maus. Kos.	*On the Creation* [περι τησ κατα Μωυσεα κοσμοπ-ουας] (n.d.)
Phot.		Photius
	Bib.	*Epistle to Lucianus* [*Bibliotheca*] (n.d.)
Plat.		Plato
	Phaed.	*Phaedo* [Φαιδων] (89–87 BC)
Plotin.		Plotinus
	En.	*Enneads* [Εννέαδες] (ca. 270)
	Katz. Kosmo.	*On the Creation* [Περι τησ καα Μαυσεα κοσμοπ-ουας] (n.d.)
	Poi. Herm.	*The Shepherd of Hermas* [Ποιμήν του Ερμά] (160)
Pontin.		Pontius
	Sanct. Caecili.	*The Life and Passion of Cyprian Bishop of Carthage* [*De Vita et Passione Sancti Cypriani*] (n.d.)
Socr.		Socrates Scholasticus
	H.e.	*Ecclesastical History* [*Historia Ecclesiastica*] (ca. 439)
Soz.		Salaminius Sozomen
	H.e.	*Ecclesiatical History* [*Historia Ecclesiastica*] (ca. 425)
Syne.		Synesius of Cyrene
	De. reg.	*On Kingship* [*De regno*] (n.d.)
	Epis.	*Epistles* [*Epistolae*]

ABBREVIATIONS

Hom.	*Homilies* [Ὀμιλια]
Hymn.	*Hymns* [*Hymnis*]
Insom.	*A Treatise on Dreams* [*De Insomniis*] (n.d.)
Prov.	*On Providence* [*De providentia*] (n.d.)

Tert.   Tertullian

Ad. Nat.	*To the Nations* [*Ad nationes*] (ca. 217)
Ad. Uxor.	*To His Wife* [*Ad uxorem*] (ca. 207)
Anim.	*A Treatise on the Soul* [*De anima*] (ca. 210)
Apol.	*Apology* [*Apologeticus Adversus Gentes Pro Christianis*] (ca. 198)
Bapt.	*On Baptism* [*De Baptismo*] (200–206)
Carn.	*On the Flesh of Christ* [*De carne Christi*] (ca. 207)
Castit.	*Exhortation to Chastity* [*De Exhortatione Castitatis*] (ca. 204)
Coron.	*On the Crown* [*De Corona*] (n.d.)
Cult. fem.	*On the Apparel of Women* [*De cultu feminarum*] (ca. 202)
Hermog.	*Against Hermogenes* [*Adversus Hermogenem*] (ca. 200–206)
Idol.	*On Idolatry* [*De Idolatria*] (n.d.)
Jejun.	*On Fasting* [*De jejunio*] (ca. 208)
Jud.	*An Answer To the Jews* [*Adversus Judaeos*] (ca. 198ff.)
Marc.	*The Five Books Against Marcion* [*Adversus Marcionem*] (207)
Monog.	*On Monogamy* [*De Monogamia*] (ca. 208)
Nat.	*To the Nations* [*Ad Nationes*] (ca. 217)
Orat.	*On Prayer* [*De oratione*] (c. 192)
Pat.	*On Patience* [*De Patientia*] (ca. 202)
Poenit.	*On Repentance* [*De Poenitentia*] (192)

Praescrip.	*The Prescription Against Heretics* [*De praescriptione Haeriticorum*] (n.d.)
Prax.	*Against Praxeas* [*Adversus Praxean*] (ca. 208)
Pudic.	*On Modesty* [*De Pudicitia*] (ca. 220)
Res.	*On the Resurrection of the Flesh* [*De Resurrectione Carnis*] (ca. 208)
Scap.	*To Scapula* [*Ad Scapulam*] (n.d.)
Scorp.	*Scorpiace* (ca. 205)
Spect.	*On the Spectacles* [*De Spectaculis*] (ca. 198–200)
Test. anim.	*The Soul's Testimony* [*de testimonia animae*] (n.d.)
Virg. vel.	*On the Veiling of Virgins* [*De virginibus velandis*] (ca. 204)
Theog.	Theognostus of Alexandria
Hyp.	*Hypostases* [*Hypotyposeon*] (n.d.)
Theoph.	Theophilus of Alexandria
Ad Pal.	*Letter of Theophilus to the Bishops of Palestine and of Cyprus* [*Seu Theophili Synodica ad Episcopas Palaestinos, et ad Cyprios*] (400)
Pros.	*The Prosphonesus of Theophilius When the Epiphanies Happened to Fall on a Sunday* [Προσφονεσυσ] (385)

Collections in which English Translations of These Works Appear

ANF	*Ante-Nicene Fathers.* Edited by Alexander Roberts and James Donaldson. 1885–87. 10 vols. Reprint, Peabody, MA: Hendrickson, 1995.
AP	*The Sayings of the Desert Fathers* [*Apophthegmata Patrum*]. Translated by Benedicta Ward. Rev. ed. Kalamazoo, MI: Cistercian, 1984.

ABBREVIATIONS

CSL	*Cyril of Alexandria: Select Letters*. Edited by Lionel R. Wickham. Oxford: Clarendon, 1983.
FC	*The Fathers of the Church*. Washington, DC: Catholic University of America Press, 1947–97.
HM	*The Lives of the Desert Fathers* [*Historia monachorum in Aegypto*]. Translated by Norman Russell. Kalamazoo, MI: Cistercian, 1981.
LCC	*The Library of Christian Classics*. 26 vols. Louisville: Westmister John Knox, 1953–2011.
Mash. Senk.	*The Book of the Saints of the Ethiopian Orthodox Church* [*Mashafa Senkesar*]. Edited by E. A. Budge. 4 vols. Cambridge: University of Cambridge, 1928.
NPNF	*Nicene and Post-Nicene Fathers*. Second Series. Edited by Philip Schaff and Henry Wace. 14 vols. Reprint. Peabody, MA: Hendrickson, 1994.
OAD	*Optatus: Against the Donatists*. Translated and edited by Mark Edwards. Liverpool: Liverpool University Press, 1997.
Pach. Koin.	*Pachomian Koinonia*. Vol. 3. Translated by Armand Veilleux Kalamazoo, MI: Cistercian, 1982.
PM	*Pseudo-Macarius: The Fifty Spiritual Homilies and The Great Letter*. Translated and edited by George Maloney. New York: Paulist, 1992.

Introduction

Ancient African Christianity and Why It Matters

WITH THE BOOMING GROWTH of Christianity in Africa and the increased awareness of the impact of the African-American church on American society as a whole, the question of the roots of early Christianity in Africa has become a broader academic and ecumenical concern. Why does it matter for the Church today if we come to this awareness?

The task of recovering African roots has already begun in earnest, notably with the establishment of the Center for Early African Christianity.[1] My aim in this book is not only to reiterate points made by previous authors demonstrating the role early North African Christianity played in influencing the Church in its earliest centuries, but also to highlight very specifically what and how the Church can use these insights today.

In an earlier book, *The Richness of Augustine*, I not only reiterated some of the well-known points regarding how St. Augustine has and continues to impact the Church. I also demonstrated in that book his African ethnicity and heritage.[2] Consequently, the focus of this volume will be on earlier theologians of ancient North Africa or on two of Augustine's lesser-known contemporaries and two of the next generation, one a first-generation admirer. Since virtually all of them have had a greater impact on Eastern Christianity than on the West (which is Augustinian), in general I will use

---

1. See Oden, *How Africa Shaped the Christian Mind*; see also Jenkins, *The Lost History of Christianity*.

2. Ellingsen, *The Richness of Augustine*.

Augustine as a dialogue partner with those on whom we focus. We may find that the insights of these other great early African theologians have a contribution to make to Protestantism and Catholicism, both because on some points they concur with Augustine and because these traditions' fixation on Augustine have led us to ignore some of their important insights.

Each chapter will introduce the theologian(s) identified in the chapter's title, followed by an analysis of their thought on the following theological issues: (1) Theological Method; (2) God and Trinity; (3) Christology; (4) Holy Spirit; (5) Creation and Providence; (6) Human Nature; (7) Sin; (8) Atonement; (9) Salvation/Justification; (10) Christian Life/Sanctification; (11) Church and Ministry/Polity; (12) Sacraments; (13) Eschatology; and (14) Social Ethics. In some chapters attention will not be devoted to these doctrines, only because the theologian(s) considered did not address this particular issue. In any case, it is obvious that this way of considering each historical figure allows for this book to function as an introduction to theology text, especially for those readers looking for African input or an African orientation in their own study of theology.

The North African Ethos of Early Christianity

Before undertaking our study we need to clarify our context—the culture and church life of early African Christianity in the first centuries. North Africa in the centuries immediately before and after the New Testament era was a multicultural society (especially in the regions around Egypt and to its west). This section of North Africa was part of the Roman Empire. This had been the case since 30 BC when Cleopatra, the last of the Ptolemaic royal house, committed suicide. Egypt and the immediate environment, extending west to what is today Algeria and was then called Maghrib, was fertile economic territory, producing one-third of all corn consumed in the Roman Empire, a thriving craft industry, and a tax base that the empire exploited (especially taxing Egyptians and Jews).[3]

Greeks were longtime residents of Egypt (long before Roman immigration), having settled there as early as the seventh century BC. Egypt (known by its inhabitants as Kemet [Black], for in ancient times Egyptians had black hair and black skin) had been under foreign domination since the tenth century BC. In 331 BC Alexander the Great had founded the

---

3. See Patrick, *Traditional Egyptian Christianity*, ix; Isichei, *History of Christianity in Africa*, 13ff.

great city of Alexandria on the Mediterranean coast.[4] Perhaps as much as 12 percent of the Egyptian population in the first century was Jewish. They had likely been there as diaspora communities since the eighth century BC, as both Isaiah (30:1–7) and Jeremiah (44) refer to them, in part with criticism for compromising the purity of the Hebraic faith.[5]

In Alexandria, the first vanguard of the Church was converts from the Jewish community, which had been thoroughly Hellenized (immersing themselves fully in Greek language and culture).[6] Greek speakers became Christian in Egypt long before the indigenous Copts.[7]

Religion and government were closely aligned in ancient Egypt. Egyptian religion and culture were obsessed with life after death. In that sense ancient Egyptian religion may have had great impact on the rise of the later monotheistic faiths of the ancient Near East. Related to this commitment was the affirmation of something like a body-soul dualism. Egyptians taught that the body had a double, called *ka*, which survived the death of the body. Later Egyptians began to develop a moral notion that one would be rewarded and punished in the afterlife for what one did on Earth. This cult of immortality centered in worship of a specific god, Osiris, identified with the Nile. And as early as the fourteenth century BC the Pharaoh Ikhnaton and the upper classes opted for a kind of monotheism, preaching Aton as the sole deity.[8]

In keeping with ancient forms of Egyptian religious life, the early Egyptian version of Christianity was very legalistic, ascetic, and otherworldly, in the sense of drawing on a dualism like that of Greek philosophy.[9] This dualism may explain why the dualistic heresy of Gnosticism also made strong inroads in Egypt and the Egyptian church.[10] The most extensive collection of Christian Gnostic literature in the early Church was discovered in Nag Hammadi in Egypt. Thus it seems not off base to call Africa (especially Egypt) the cradle of Christian Gnosticism.

---

4. Isichei, *History of Christianity in Africa*, 13.

5. Ibid., 16; Shaw, *Kingdom of God in Africa*, 23.

6. Shaw, *Kingdom of God in Africa*, 27.

7. For this assessment, see Latourette, *History of Christianity*, 1:77.

8. Brinton et al., *Civilization in the West*, 11; Atiya, *History of Eastern Christianity*, 20ff.

9. Plat. *Phaed.*, VI, XIV.

10. Shaw, *Kingdom of God in Africa*, 28.

ANCIENT AFRICAN CHRISTIANITY AND WHY IT MATTERS

We have no firm historical or biblical evidence regarding the initial planting of the Church in Egypt. The tradition credits St. Mark as the founder of Christianity in Africa, specifically in Alexandria, where he was the first bishop. And indeed, the very first postbiblical history of the Church, the *Church History* of Eusebius of Caesarea, written in the first third of the fourth century, asserts Mark's role as the evangelist of Egypt.[11] Acts 18:24-25 also refers to an Apollos, a native of Alexandria who had been well instructed in the Way.

As for Ethiopia, there is of course the traditional claim that Christianity was established in the region as a result of the ministry of the Ethiopian eunuch (a significant member of the Ethiopian royal court) converted by Philip (Acts 8:27-39). But the first hard historical evidence we have suggests that it was established in the fourth century by two young shipwrecked Phoenician Christians, Frumentius (ca. 300-ca. 380) and Aedesius. They seem to have been taken in by the Abyssinian royal house (rulers of the Kingdom of Axum) and eventually, while tutoring the young crown prince, soon to be King Ezana, converted him and the royal house to Christianity.

This particular section of modern-day Ethiopia, the Kingdom of Axum, had become a trading center with the Greek-speaking ancient world. This early orientation to Greek culture is important in understanding Ethiopia's eventual adoption of Christianity. But earlier religion dynamics in the kingdom need to be considered. The earliest religion in the region seems to have involved the veneration of the gods Mahrem (Mars), Astar (the heavens), Beher (the sea), and Medr (the earth). Oral tradition claims that Judaism was introduced at the time of Solomon (through Memelik, the offspring of the union of King Solomon and the Queen of Sheba). There is historical evidence of an immigration of Semitic people to biblical Sheba around 600 BC.

A tribe of Jews, the Falashas, remain in the land to this day, though in diminishing numbers. They know only the Pentateuch, not the Talmud, and do not speak Hebrew. Their liturgy is in Agaw, an ancient Cushite tongue.[12]

These dynamics may or may not have made it easier for the ancient Ethiopians to accept Christianity. At any rate, Frumentius was later consecrated bishop by the famed archbishop of Alexandria, Athanasius (ca. 296-373), whose theology we shall consider later in the book. Only the royal house of the Kingdom of Axum had been converted at this stage,

---

11. Eus. *H.e.*, II.16 (*NPNF*² 1:116).
12. See Isichei, *History of Christianity in Africa*, 15, 17.

and the Church did not spread far beyond Axum. It was a mission of Syrian monks (the so-called Nine Saints) in the next century that brought the Gospel to the Ethiopian masses. These monks established monasteries that henceforth shaped Ethiopian church life around these institutions. To this day, Ethiopian church leaders and the church's theology are drawn from monasticism.[13] With the subsequent Arab invasion of Africa, by the tenth century Axum was not as influential, and the real center of Ethiopian power and influence shifted to the south with kings from the Amharic line claiming to descend from Solomon.

Further to the west, we can consider the foundation of an early Latin-based Western church in North Africa. Carthage had been founded by Phoenicians in the seventh century BC. Romans conquered the city in 146 BC. The region between it and Egypt (modern-day Libya) had long been multi-cultural. After the Roman conquest, the region became populated by Roman immigrants. Perhaps because they were settlers, they more quickly embraced Christianity than their kin on the Italian peninsula. Romans and Jewish residents became the first Christians in the region. Only later did the Gospel take root among the Punics (offspring of the first Phoenician settlers) and the indigenous population (Black people who are ancestors of the modern Berber tribe).[14]

Cultural Trends in Ancient North Africa

To understand the daily life of the first Christians of North Africa, we need to recognize how thoroughly the cultures of Egypt and the western part of North Africa reflected the Greek and Roman civilizations that had settled in these regions. Rome may have been ruling in both Egypt and in African lands to the west at the time of Christ, but they were two very different cultures.

In Egypt, Roman conquest of the region transpired in 30 BC (almost a century after Carthage and the region of present-day Algeria). Little changed in Egyptian life as a result of Rome's conquest. Hellenization, the impact of Greek culture on the people, was still very much in play. This explains why the dominant language (and style of theology) of this region (and Ethiopia) has been Greek.

13. Ibid., 32–33, 17; Shaw, *Kingdom of God in Africa*, 62ff.

14. Latourette, *History of Christianity*, 1:77; Isichei, *History of Christianity in Africa*, 33–34; Oden, *Early Libyan Christianity*, 88ff.

Traditional Egyptian culture had been oligarchical, with a small priestly and noble class overseeing a larger group of peasants. But like the culture of the Roman colonists, there was social mobility. The Hellenizing tendencies embedded by this time in Egyptian culture were further sharpened after the Roman Empire was divided into East and West, with Egypt falling under the rule of the Byzantine Empire in AD 395. Of course, the change in general cultural life creating modern Egypt came about with the invasion of the Moslems in AD 640. Since that time Egypt has become part of the Arab world, with Arabic as the language of the streets, while the Christianity that survived retained its Greek and indigenous African flavor as a counter-cultural community in the Arab world.

Meanwhile, in the western part of North Africa (present-day Algeria, Libya, and Morocco—known in the Roman era as the Maghrib), Roman civilization had completely come to dominate the culture. Like Egypt, it had become a multicultural society, including Roman immigrants, the children of Phoenician immigrants (Punics), and Black Africans (who, as already noted, were ancestors of the modern Berber tribe).

The ready way in which this region was Romanized is hardly surprising in view of the significant economic prosperity the Maghrib region enjoyed from the time of its association with the empire, a prosperity it would continue to enjoy until the fourth century.[15] Many former Roman soldiers were given land grants and became colonists. Local African notables and whole townships were given Roman citizenship, some rising to the heights of power in the empire. In this context, it is understandable why Christianity, as it became the religion of the empire, would become readily accepted in the region.[16]

So thoroughly Romanized was northwestern African that its Roman citizens, like St. Augustine, regarded native dialects of non-Romanized people as "Punic."[17] If you wanted to go anywhere in society, you had to speak Latin and adopt Roman ways. Again St. Augustine is a good example

---

15. Brown, *Augustine of Hippo*, 19–20.

16. Isichei, *History of Christianity in Africa*, 15, 33–34.

17. For a good example of Augustine's apparent use of the term "Punic" in this broader sense, see his *Ep. Joh.*, II.3 (*NPNF*[1] 7:470): "Isti autem qui multum amant Christum, sice honorant Christum, ut dicant illum remanisse ed duas linguas, latinam, et punicam, id est afram." For fuller analyses making these points, see my *Richness of Augustine*, 9, 168; Brown, *Augustine of Hippo*, 22; Frend, "Note on the Berber Background," 188–91; Courtois, "Saint Augustin et le Problème de la Survivance du Punique." This data, as we shall see in a later chapter, is crucial for establishing Augustine's African ethnicity.

of this, as we will note the likelihood of his Black Berber or at least Punic Phoenician background. But he and perhaps all of the church leaders on whom we shall concentrate in this book never learned any of the other languages spoken in the region in which they grew up. Berber and Punic were the languages of the countryside and the lower-class laborers. Even a lower-middle-class family like Augustine's spoke only Latin at home.

What was daily life like in Romanized North Africa, Egypt, and Ethiopia? In a word, daily life was very *public*, all on display, nothing under the covers, not even sex. It was all debated, complained about in public. Men in this patriarchal society lived out of doors, disclosing in public the most intimate details of their lives. Reputation was coveted above all else. Such concern about reputation entailed that the public sphere was very fragile. Africans developed impressive public-speaking skills not just to praise but also to debunk their peers. In small towns such jousting could lead to long, rancorous feuds.

Although Roman entertainments, like chariot races and gladiator fights with wild animals, had been exported to Africa, rhetoric was the most typical form of entertainment. The rhetoric was emotional and moving (perhaps a bit akin to African-American rhetoric in the United States). Speakers were encouraged to weep and to make others weep.[18]

Men in these regions could be prickly, but also ferociously loyal to each other. Lifelong friendships and close extended family relationships were a way of life.[19] The patriarchy of these societies is especially apparent in western North Africa, the home of Augustine. He reports that women were frequently beaten by their husbands.[20] The educational system was rigid, often enforced with beatings. Part of the reason for such discipline was that the unruly behavior of some students mandated it. Augustine himself lamented the educational system of Carthage, noting that students often broke in on an instructor's lecture and seemed largely undisciplined.[21]

---

18. Brown, *Augustine of Hippo*, 37.
19. Ibid., 31–32.
20. Aug. *Conf.*, IX.IX.19 (*NPNF*[1] 1:136).
21. Ibid., V.VIII.14 ; I.IX.1–14 (*NPNF*[1] 1:84, 49).

Early North African Christianity

What was the Christianity that emerged in ancient North Africa like? With some notable exceptions, we will see that it tended to be legalistic, ascetic, and otherworldly.

Other features of early Christianity on the African continent probably owed to the indigenous, pre-Christian religions of the region. These religions were ecstatic, involving dancing, dreams, and trances.[22] Such rites of ritual power, including magic and casting spells, maintained themselves in early African Christianity. This is evident in the literature available about the earliest desert monks, manifesting in the practice of magic at least in early Egyptian Christianity.[23]

In this connection, St. Augustine reports his devoutly Christian mother's reliance on visions. Her belief in magic and sacrifice, venerating the deceased, said to be typical of African Christians, was also reported.[24] Use of amulets to heal apparently was very common among Christians in Augustine's home region, and he was critical of the practice.[25]

Of course this was not a totally charismatic piety, because very early in the lives of these churches they established a set liturgy. But this liturgy has a mysterious, lively, magical dimension to it. They are not mere rituals.

One other aspect of early North African church life demands our attention, because this feature was so influential on other developments. I refer to the city of Alexandria and its vibrant intellectual life. Founded by Alexander the Great, the city, a key trading center on the Mediterranean Sea, served as capital of Egypt during this period. It was a cosmopolitan, multicultural city. Appropriately enough, given Alexander's love of Greek culture, it had become a center of Greek intellectual life. It had a famous library.

To live in the city as an intellectual entailed that you were going to be in dialogue with ancient Greek philosophy. The substantial Jewish community in the city was thus influenced. A great philosopher, Philo (ca. 20 BC), emerged just prior to the Christian era. In the best traditions of Greek thought he tried to make sense of the apparently unsophisticated Hebrew Scriptures by allegorizing them, reinterpreting them in light of the concepts

---

22. Brown, *Augustine of Hippo*, 32–33, 196.

23. See Russell, *Lives of the Desert Fathers*, 74; Meyer and Smith, *Ancient Christian Magic*.

24. Aug. *Conf.*, III.XI.19–20; VI.XIII.23; VI.II.2 (*NPNF*[1] 1:66–67, 99, 90).

25. Getty, *Life of the North Africans*, 143ff.

of Greek philosophy.²⁶ His impact on the formation of early African Christian theology is incalculable and undeniable, especially on the Catechetical School of Alexandria. For there a Christian version of Philo's approach to Jewish thought developed—a kind of Method of Correlation suggestive of the modern approaches of Friedrich Schleiermacher, Paul Tillich, and Feminist Theology.

The Way Ahead

With this background on early North African Christianity and the culture of the region in hand, we can close with an overview of where we are headed. Although we will begin out of chronological order with a consideration of the earliest monks and nuns of the African desert, we will then proceed in the next chapters chronologically with the important early North African theologians, starting with Clement of Alexandria in the late second century through Cyril of Alexandria and Fulgentius, who actually lived in the first generation after Augustine. We have not included Minucius Felix or Julius Africanus, as there has been dispute about their African roots (though they were clearly trained in North Africa).²⁷ As we shall observe, perhaps several of the pre-Augustinian Fathers considered, and Synesius of Cyrene, a contemporary of Augustine, likewise should not have been included in the analysis. Because he is not African, John Chrysostom has not been selected for consideration, even though his theology has been and continues to be widely studied in the traditional theological curriculum of the Ethiopian Orthodox Church.

Another African theologian of this era, Fortunatianus, Bishop of Aquileia of the fourth century, is also omitted. Jerome tells us about him and his not extant commentaries on the Gospels, but we know little else about him, save the impact of his writings on semi-Arian heretical tendencies of Liberius, Bishop of Rome.²⁸ It seems fair, then, to omit Fortunatianus from consideration due to his apparent rejection of the divinity of the Holy Spirit.

---

26. Phil. *Maus. Kos.*

27. For an argument against the African character of Julius Africanus, see Gelzer, *Sextus Julius Africanus*, 4, 5. On the other hand, Oden has argued for Julius's African ethnicity (*Early Libyan Christianity*, 128ff.).
In *Vir. Illus.*, LVIII (*NPNF*² 3:374), Jerome identified Minucius Felix as a Roman advocate.

28. Jer. *Vir. Illus.*, XCVII (*NPNF*² 3:380).

At this point, though, we should consider accounts of several early African martyrs as well as give some attention to *The Epistle of Barnabas*, *The Shepherd of Hermas*, and *The Didache*. These early anonymous treaties appear in ancient manuscripts written in Coptic (the language of the early church in Egypt), and this has led many interpreters to assume they may have been products of the early African church.

The Epistle of Barnabas

The epistle is an anonymous work that was traditionally ascribed to St. Barnabas, the Christian who introduced Paul to the disciples (Acts 9:27; 12:25). Because the document relies so heavily on allegorical interpretation of Scripture, reinterpreted in the categories of Greek philosophy, and since that was primarily being done by Christians in Alexandria in the first century, most scholars believe it is rightfully considered an African Christian document. We might call it a forerunner of the Alexandrian School of Theology. The epistle was critical of many of Christianity's Jewish roots, but legalistic in the style of much early African Christianity.[29] And yet the document does refer to Christ dwelling in our hearts (XVI, VI) and also to the remission of sins (V).

The Shepherd of Hermas

Manuscripts of this apocalyptic work have been found in Ethiopian, so it clearly had an influence on early African Christianity. Though likely edited, it was written by Hermas, a second-century former Christian slave, later wealthy merchant, and brother of the pope. Its primary concern was the problem of what to make of sins committed after baptism. The document grants the possibility of repentance for sins after receiving the Sacrament, or at least a second chance (II.IV.III.1). However, the possibility of seeing God is said to be dependent on preserving purity and holiness (II.IV.IV.1). Also the document claims that it is possible to do more than God's commandment requires, and so to gain merits (III.V.III.3).

Interesting Christological and ecclesiological nuances appear in the work. The Holy Spirit is identified with the Son of God (III.IX.I.1). This is coupled with a concern about the unity/harmony of the Church

---

29. For the document's legalistic propensities, see *Ep. Barn.*, XVIII-XX (*ANF* 1:48–49).

(I.III.V.1; III.IX.XVII.4). A possible problematic cultural dimension appears in this document as well as in *The Epistle of Barnabas*. In both, evil is identified with black.[30]

The Didache

This document is probably the oldest manual of Christian worship. Because it is an anonymous work, we cannot be certain of its origins, but the fact that at least one ancient version of this document appears in Coptic entails that we can be sure of its use in early African Christianity. The document commences with a Manual of Conduct about lifestyle standards (not unlike *The Epistle of Barnabas*). Patience, humility, abstinence, and goodness are urged. Some very common practices in modern Christian worship have origins in *The Didache*. Baptism in the Name of Father, Son, and Spirit is mandated (VII). Weekly celebration of the Eucharist is reported as standard practice, and the rite is identified as a sacrifice (XIV). There are suggestions in the document that the Sacrament is only a symbol, as its prescribed Thanksgiving Prayer refers only to "spiritual food and drink" without reference to Christ's bodily presence (X).

Martyrs

In the late second and early third century the church in North Africa was plagued by persecutions initiated by various Roman emperors. Consequently, some of the great martyrs of the Church were African. So seriously did many African Christians take martyrdom, believing that one was not a true follower of Christ unless one was willing to die for it, that the Church in North Africa was actually twice divided on this issue—in disputes between those who had confessed their faith in face of persecution (the confessors) and those who had fled such persecution (the lapsed).

The first occasion transpired as a result of the empire-wide persecution of the Roman ruler Decius (249–51). It seems that the savage persecution in the regions of Alexandria and Carthage had cost many lives but that some Christians, including the Bishop of Carthage, Cyprian, had fled.[31]

---

30. *Poi. Herm.*, III.VIII–IX (*ANF* 2:46); cf. *Ep. Barn.*, XX (*ANF* 1:149).

31. For an account of the persecution in Alexandria, including the martyrdom of women such as Apollonia and Ammonarium, see *The Works of Dionysius*, Ep. III (*ANF* 6:98–100).

After the persecution, he and the Church had offered forgiveness to the lapsed. Confessors, led especially by a Roman presbyter, Novatian, objected to this compromise of the purity of the Church's membership. We will further examine how this controversy was resolved in the chapter devoted to Cyprian of Carthage.

The other occasion in which these tensions over a willingness to endure martyrdom flared was as a consequence of the persecution initiated by Diocletian (303–5). The controversy began in Carthage in 311 with the election of a new bishop, Caecilian. In his service of installation he allowed the participation of several leaders to whom the confessors objected. They responded by electing Donatus as their bishop. A strong leader, his movement continued to thrive as a rival to the Church catholic until the seventh century. The movement plagued Augustine, and so we shall examine it again subsequently. The movement may have gained some impetus as a protest of the poorer classes in North Africa (as most of the confessors were poor) or as a vehicle of the Black Berbers' protest against Roman domination of the Church. In any case, the fact that indigenous ancient Christianity no longer exists in this region of western North Africa, that the Arab conquest effectively obliterated it, may be a function of the fact that the Donatist heresy divided the Church so thoroughly as to render it impossible to contend with the social and military pressures that the Arab conquest imposed on the region.

In this connection, the martyrdom of one African married woman, Vibia Perpetua (181–203), and her slave Felicitas, who was pregnant, in the early third century, is of special theological relevance because its account (perhaps written by Tertullian) reflects several important theological emphases relevant for our understanding of early African theology. It seems that Perpetua was a catechumen. An empire-wide persecution had been initiated by a new emperor, Septimius Severus. Arrested in Carthage, she and her slave were eventually thrown to wild beasts to meet their fate.

The account makes clear that Perpetua's father tried to counsel her to renounce her faith in order to be saved. But she defied him, even receiving Baptism while in prison (I.2; II.1), a truly bold action in view of the patriarchy of western North Africa in her lifetime. When baptized, the Spirit instructed her not to request anything from the baptismal waters except endurance of punishment (I.2). Elsewhere Tertullian elaborates on this point, regarding martrydom as a kind of "second baptism."[32] Much in the spirit of the book of

---

32. Tert. *Bapt.*, XVI (*ANF* 3:677).

Revelation, Perpetua reports various visions and direct communication with God about her martyrdom (I.2). (Note the strong doctrine of the Holy Spirit. The text speaks of her being entranced with the Spirit [VI.3]. We must ask if these emphases might associate her with Montanism.)

Also theologically relevant is the way in which the author depicts Perpetua's martyrdom in terms of a struggle with the devil (III.2; VI.3-4)—most suggestive of the Classic View of the Atonement that characterizes the thinking of most of the early African Fathers. Stripped of her clothing in early gladiatorial confrontation, she held her own, claiming, "I became a man" (II.2). It is not clear from the context if at this point she merely was reporting that she was treated like a male gladiator or if this statement is related to her rebellion against the role of women in her context.

Given the preoccupation of the account with the work of the Holy Spirit, it is not surprising to discern a strong affirmation of grace in Perpetua's witness. To her father, she affirms a strong doctrine of Providence, claiming that "whatever God wills shall happen. For know that we are not placed in our own power, but in that of God" (II.1). She is said by Tertullian to be a true spouse of Christ, a darling of God (a construal of Justification as Union With Christ) (VI.1). He speaks of her as a great woman who, feared as she was by the unclean spirit, would not have been martyred had she not willed it—guiding her executioner's hand to her throat (VI.4).

In a sense the theological convictions of these martyrs were not characteristic of early African theology. As we proceed in examining the major pre-Augustinian theologians of Africa, we will see that the themes characteristic of the anonymous treatises already examined (Threefold View of Ministry, strong Sacramentology, a High Christology, law-driven visions of the Christian life, and strong doctrine of the Holy Spirit) more typically surface in their thought. To that sort of analysis we now turn.

A Note on Greek Texts

The Greek text used in most of the footnotes did not have a clear script for kappa (κ), employing something like a chi (χ) where kappa would be more appropriate. The text has been followed in the citations throughout the book even in cases where a kappa would be more appropriate. Thus proper Greek would demand that kappa (κ) should appear rather than a chi (χ) as the text employed, and so the quotations have maintained the irregular style/spelling in the case of such Greek words like και and καιρος.

1

Anthony and Other Desert Fathers

The Establishment of Christianity led to a serious backlash in Africa. The days of martyrdom were over! And the Church was no longer comprised only of committed members. The energy and commitment previously devoted to martyrdom focused in new directions. For some giants of the faith of ancient North Africa, talents were directed to theological reflection. Others directed their high levels of commitment instead to monasticism, which functioned as a kind of substitute martyrdom. As a result, hundreds of faithful men and women flocked to the desert.

The Constantinian establishment also led the Church to accommodate itself to Roman culture. This often manifested itself in new attitudes to wealth, including the desire to build elaborate churches after the fashion of Roman architecture. Monasticism, then, was also a kind of reaction to the wealth of the Church and its new well-being. As a result, for many monks, exile to the desert was a way of renouncing this wealth-seeking way of life along with a protest against lax membership standards of the new imperial church. The protest was not isolated. Hundreds of Christians fled to the African desert both in protest and out of commitment to finding a way to a closer walk with God. Roman tax policy may have been a contributing factor. There was no income tax or tax on urban property. But a "head tax" was imposed, especially impacting the agricultural sector, mandating that everyone in rural areas needed to engage in public works projects or send a worker to take his place. Sometimes the fiscal burden was so high that there were incentives to flee, and so fleeing the world for monastic life had further incentives.[1]

There were pre-Constantinian roots to the movement and its associated lifestyle. There were biblical precedents in Paul's references to the freedom of the single life (1 Cor 7:32f.) coupled with Jesus's claim that in the kingdom "they neither marry nor are given in marriage" (Matt 22:30). Jesus's directive to "go and sell your possessions, and give the money to the poor" in order to achieve perfection (Matt 19:21) was also a shaping precedent for the movement.

The intellectual ethos of the day also contributed to the emergence of monasticism. Stoic doctrine had held that passions were the true enemy of wisdom. Greek philosophy generally regarded the self as imprisoned in the body. Several religions in the Mediterranean basin included sacred virgins and celibate priests.[2] Some scholarly speculation exists now that Gnosticism may have been related to the monastic movement, especially in a connection between the Gnostic Nag Hammadi library and Pachomius's Cenobitic community, which we will soon consider.[3]

Though monasticism emerged in several regions of the Roman Empire, the greatest growth of monasticism was in the Egyptian desert. Paul and Anthony (both of whose lives were depicted in works by Jerome and Athanasius, respectively) are said to be the first monks (not perhaps chronologically, but the first of the famed monks). The word *monk* derives from the Greek word *monachos*, meaning "solitary." Early monks like Paul and Anthony sought solitude, away from the distractions of society that made it difficult to practice Christian life. Solitary monks were called "Anchorites."

---

1. For similar analyses, see Schaff, *History of the Christian Church*, 3:154–55; Harmless, *Desert Christians*, 10.

2. Among examples of the practice of asceticism in this region include the Nazarites of the Hebrew faith (Num 6:1–21) and the warnings against pursuing riches issued in the seventh- or sixth-century BC Egyptian document *The Instruction of Amen-Em-Opet*, xi.10. Regarding the higher expectations laid on Egyptian priests, see Sauneron, *Priests of Ancient Egypt*, esp. 10. Regarding veneration of virgins, something like a cult of the Virgin Mary is presupposed in ancient Egyptian religion with the goddess Isis (Aset to the Egyptians), who as the mother of Pharaoh played a crucial role in ancient Egyptian piety.

3. See James Robinson, "Introduction," in Robinson, *Nag Hammadi Library*, 19–21.

The Life and Impact of Anthony

Though not the very first monk, he is reported to have received instruction in the monastic life from an older man who had lived such a lifestyle since his youth, Anthony was the man who through his fame transmitted through the oral tradition effectively made monasticism a truly catholic phenomenon.[4] Born in Egypt in AD 251, the uneducated son of well-to-do peasant parents, he is reported to have lived until the age of 105.[5] Athanasius reports to have been the holy man's servant/disciple.[6] Athanasius claims he had an extraordinary beautiful face.[7] He also raved about Anthony's intelligence, even though he had not been formally educated.[8]

Anthony's life in the desert was characterized by conflict with demonic powers.[9] (A Classic View of the Atonement underlies much of his theology.) He is said to have influenced not just numerous men to practice monasticism, but also many women to remain virgins for Christ.[10] Athanasius reports how the great monk's fame was spreading all over the Roman Empire during his lifetime.[11]

Anthony's own theological convictions reflect the theological profile of many of his early African Christian spiritual heirs. Motivated as he was by hearing Matt 19:21 to practice monasticism,[12] it seems that Anthony was motivated by a desire to earn eternal life (for Jesus promises eternal life to those who give all they have to the poor in that pericope). He called for discipline and avoiding sin, returning to our natural condition that leads to virtue.[13] But on the other hand, he reported a vision that testified to the centrality of the theme of the forgiveness of sin.[14]

---

4. Ath. *V. Ant.*, 3 (*NPNF*² 4:196).

5. Ibid., 1–2, 89 (*NPNF*² 4:195–96, 219); Benedicta Ward, "Foreword," in Ward, *Sayings of the Desert Fathers*, xviii, 1.

6. Ath. *V. Ant.*, 71 (*NPNF*² 4:215).

7. Ibid., 67 (*NPNF*² 4:214).

8. Ibid., 72–80 (*NPNF*² 4:215–17).

9. Ibid., 5, 22–25, 28, 52 (*NPNF*² 4:196–97, 202–3, 210); also see Pelikan, *Emergence of the Catholic Tradition (100–600)*, 135–37. For Christ's conquest of the devil, see Ath. *V. Ant.*, 24, 28 (*NPNF*² 4:202–3).

10. Ibid., 88 (*NPNF*² 4:219).

11. Ibid., 93 (*NPNF*² 4:221).

12. Ibid., 2 (*NPNF*² 4:196).

13. Ibid., 18–21 (*NPNF*² 4:201); Anthony, 2–3, in *AP* 2.

14. Ath. *V. Ant.*, 64 (*NPNF*² 4:213).

There is some indication that a kind of spiritual pride existed among the monks, reflecting the consequences of legalist, works-oriented strands of piety we have just observed in Anthony. Some felt that because their life was holier than the clergy, they, not the bishops, should determine Christian teaching. One ancient document recording the sayings of early monks, the *Wisdom of the Elders of Ethiopia*, speaks of bishops going on the way to hell along with lazy monks.[15] In another document a monk named Apphy is reported to have suffered in his spiritual life after becoming Bishop of Oxyrrynchus, for in that office he comes to depend less on God and more on human beings.[16]

The Monastic Style of Life

Life in the African desert was harsh, testing the limits of natural life. By the second generation of monks, the old style of nomadic hermit life was less evident. The monks and nuns had their own housing—sometimes two-roomed cells and even in villages. Stone huts with roofs of branches often functioned as the cells. Reed mats served as beds. Some participants in the movement had gardens, but most earned a living by weaving baskets and mats. They practiced devotional exercises while working. Some avoided sleep, lest Christ be coming.

The diet in the desert tended to be bread with some fruit and vegetables. Rags were the preferred clothing. Because of the suspicion of possessions, even ownership of books was thought to lead to pride, the Bible tended to be taught and studied through memorization. Wise anecdotes were often exchanged.[17]

The emphasis on monastic life as one of total renunciation raised problems regarding the status of children. Caring for one's own children or even practicing monasticism with a grown son was criticized.[18] In a few cases a charge is issued by an Abba to a novice to sacrifice his child as a spiritual test.[19]

Because many of the monks and all of the women of the desert were lay people, the movement tended to be anti-clerical. As a result,

---

15. *Pat. Aeth.*, 102.
16. Apphy, in *AP*, 35–36; cf. Sisoes, 15–16, in *AP* 215–16.
17. Benedicta Ward, "Introduction," in Russell, *Lives of the Desert Fathers*, 20ff.
18. Carion, in *AP* 117–18.
19. Sisoes, 6–13, in *AP* 213–14.

Communion was celebrated less frequently among the Anchorites. But this was not the case with those monks who were priests, who celebrated the Sacrament frequently.[20]

The aim of the monks was not asceticism as an end in itself, but charity. Anthony reportedly returned to the city to relieve those dying of the plague. The monks themselves placed a great emphasis on hospitality. Life was geared toward regular, disciplined prayer, often by using the Psalms.[21]

The monastic ideal was not a sub-human existence, but an angelic mode of existence.[22] They commonly placed themselves under a spiritual father. The emphasis on charity as a way of life took the form of not judging. One ancient monk would not hear of or see sin. Moses the Negro claimed to be so full of sin that he could not judge a brother.[23] It was reportedly revealed to Isaac the Theban that one should not judge the neighbor before God has.[24]

The Spread of Monasticism and Its Distinct Paradigms

At least three types of early African monasticism developed, roughly corresponding to the three geographical locations in which each style dominated.[25] Lower Egypt tended to be the native area for the hermit life as practiced by Anchorites like Anthony. Upper Egypt was home to another style, "Cenobitic Monasticism." This is a communal style of monasticism. Monks like Pachomius, who organized an early community in Tabennisi, and his sister Marie did not leave a legacy of preserved sayings, accounting for why our focus will be on the wisdom and theology of the earlier Anchorite monks. More on Cenobitic Monasticism shortly.

In the regions of Nitria and Scetis, respectively west and south of the Nile Delta, a third monastic paradigm developed. Here a unique kind of asceticism developed. These were regions that were meeting places between the world and the desert, where visitors like John Cassian (a fourth-century compiler of wise sayings of the monks) could easily come into contact with the traditions of the African desert. Here a monasticism more under

---

20. Ward, "Introduction," in Russell, *Lives of the Desert Fathers*, 26.

21. Ammonas, 4, in *AP* 26; *Pat. Aeth.*, 78; cf. Benedicta Ward, "Foreword," in *AP* xxiv; Ward, "Introduction," in HM 26.

22. Ward, in *AP* xxiii.

23. Moses the Negro, 2, in *AP* 138–39; see notes 113, 115.

24. Isaac the Theban, 1, in *AP* 109–10.

25. Ward, in *AP* xviiff.

the influence of Greek culture could evolve. Prime examples of this style include Macarius the Great, Macarius of Alexandria, Moses, Pambo, and Abraham.

Finally a number of Egyptian monks migrated to Syria where yet a more radical ascetic monasticism evolved. These monks pushed the physical limits to the utmost, with practices like living for long periods on the top of a pillar or reportedly dwelling in nakedness were evident. A primary example of this monastic style was the fifth-century monk Simeon Stylites.[26]

Sometimes in Egypt this extreme asceticism was practiced. One monk, Zacharius, who had been raised in the desert by his father Carrion and was later consulted by famed monks like Macarius and Moses the Negro, claimed the work of the monk was to do violence to oneself.[27] Violence was also practiced in a community led by Shenoute of Atripe. Pambo (303–373) retained perpetual silence and did not smile.[28] Pior, a contemporary and acquaintance of Anthony, is reported to have walked while eating so his soul would feel no bodily pleasure in eating. Another early monk of the desert, Paul, had the brethren bow before him as he handled snakes.[29]

Cenobitic Monasticism

Cenobitic or Communal Monasticism was also indebted to Africa, as we noted in referring to the role of Pachomius and Marie in initiating this monastic style. Both had been raised by pagan parents in the late third century. Pachomius himself had been converted to Christianity as a result of kindnesses shown him by Christians.[30]

Much like monastic life in all its forms, for Cenobitic monks and nuns daily life included both work and devotion. But the exaggerated poverty practiced by some Anchorites was not the Cenobitic way. There was also a concern with instruction in reading and biblical literacy through memorization.[31] The basic rule of communal life was mutual service and absolute

---

26. Ibid., xviii–xix.

27. Zacharius, 1,3, in *AP* 67–68.

28. Pambo, 13, in *AP* 197; cf. James Timbie, "The State of Research on the Career of Shenoute of Atripe," in Pearson and Goehring, *Roots of Egyptian Christianity*, 264.

29. Pior, 2, *AP* 199; Paul, 1, in ibid., 204.

30. *First Greek Life of Pachomius*, 4 (*Pachomian Koinonia*, 1:300); Pearson and Goehring, *Roots of Egyptian Christianity*, 273ff.; Harmless, *Desert Christians*, 118.

31. Pach, *Praecept. et Inst.*, 139 (Harmless, *Desert Christians*, 127, 144).

obedience to superiors. Superiors were expected to serve those under them. Yet ultimately Abbas (those above the superiors of each community) did have absolute authority. The Rules of the community addressed good order down to the smallest details.[32] The life-denying character of the daily life of the community has led some scholars to speculate that the Gnostic Nag Hammadi Library might have been Pachomian. But the evidence does not seem to make the case for such a provocative conclusion, in view as we shall see of the lack of express Gnostic heretical teachings in his corpus.[33]

In this connection the actual writings of Pachomius are relevant. It is true that he urged humility to his community.[34] But he spoke of sin as concupiscence (not unlike Augustine did later) and also of salvation by grace, contending that God would drive away evil and wayward thoughts.[35] We are to put on Christ, he contends.[36] These commitments all contributed to the African Father's overall agenda of responding to an angel's call that "the Lord's Will is to minister to the race of men and to unite them to Himself."[37] This stress on uniting the whole of humanity stands in marked tension with the solitude nurtured by the Anchorite model of Monasticism.

We have already noted that women were involved in the movement. In the next chapter we will focus on their leaders and the theological profile of the women of the desert.

Out of Africa

The spread of the monastic ideal transpired first through local oral traditions, but in the long term primarily through bishops and scholars who saw great value of the monastic witness for the daily life of the Church, a development that tamed down the early monastic movement's anti-clericalism. Among those propagating it included Athanasius (who as we

---

32. Pach, *Praecept. et Inst.* (Harmless, *Desert Christians*, 131).

33. For a similar conclusion, see Harmless, *Desert Christians*, 161–63. For an openness to possible cross-fertilization of Gnosticism and the Pachomian heritage, see Chadwick, "Pachomius and the Idea of Sanctity," 17–18.

34. Pach. *Instruct.*, 1.4 (*Pachomian Koinonia*, 3:13–14).

35. Ibid., 1.9, 30, 53 (*Pachomian Koinonia*, 15, 26, 37); cf. Aug. *Perf. Just.*, XIII.31 (*NPNF*[1] 5:170).

36. Pach. *Instruct.*, 1.39 (*Pachomian Koinonia*, 3:31).

37. *First Greek Life of Pachomius* (*Pachomian Koinonia*, 1:23); cf. Harmless, *Desert Christians*, 119, 142.

shall see was the great champion of the formulations of the Council of Nicea and the Creed which bears its name) and Jerome (who translated the Bible into Latin—the Vulgate). Augustine (inspired by Athanasius's *Life of St. Anthony*) established a semimonastic community for his followers, which later inspired the creation of the Augustinian Order. In Europe a pillar in the further spread and popularization of the monastic life was fourth-century Hungarian Martin of Tours, who among other monks was drafted in the episcopacy, from which position he propagated the monastic ideal.

To be sure, the early monasticism of Africa we consider in this book is not the same as the Western monasticism with which the majority of readers of the volume will be familiar. But there would likely be nothing like monasticism as the Church catholic has known it over the centuries had there not been the early African monastic movement in which monasticism as we know it is rooted.

Early African monasticism was not as communally centered as in the West. For only in early African monasticism do we find the Anchorite model of the solitary monk or nun practiced. Also the African renunciation of all material comforts and the tension between monks and the episcopacy does not characterize the West. We have already observed the tensions with the episcopacy in the claim by the *Wisdom of the Elders of Ethiopia* that speaks of bishops going on the way to hell along with lazy monks.[38]

The Theology of the Desert Fathers

If we are to evaluate the early African monasticism regarding what it might teach the Church today, we need to close with a survey of what the monks taught theologically. This will help put their dedication and renunciation of the ways of the world in perspective. We begin with what can be said of the monks' theology collectively, and then focus on the theological profiles of several of the most famous ancient monks. We rely especially on the most ancient collection of wise sayings of the monks, the *Apophthegmata Patrum* (*Sayings of the Desert Fathers*), probably first recorded in the fourth century and then arranged in the sixth century alphabetically according to the name of the monk to whom a statement was attributed.

---

38. See note 15.

Collective Trends

To be sure, the desert monks of Africa were not teachers or scholars. In fact, they tended to place an economy on words. Anthony and Isaac of Cells commended silence, as the best way to teach. In fact in Anthony's view, talk about secular matters unlooses an ass that distracts.[39] But thanks to the alphabetical collection of the *Sayings of the Desert Fathers*, we do have access to some pregnant theological talking points.

The monks clearly tried to put God at the center of life (in contrast to most of us who in the post-Kantian mode tend to discern everything from the perspective of our own experience).[40] Their Theological Method then was typically Orthodox—using the Word of God, not experience or philosophy, as the starting point for theological reflection. Several examples help provide this focus on God's Presence as the heart of early African monastic spirituality.

Abba Nisterus the Great is recorded as advising, "A monk ought to ask himself every night and every morning, 'What have we done that is as God wills and what have we left undone of that which He does not will? He can do this throughout his whole life."[41]

In the same spirit, the monk Alonius noted, "If a man does not say in his heart, in the world there is only myself and God, he will not gain peace."[42]

Many other examples of this focus on God (and corresponding Theological Method) can be cited.[43]

Of course, the influence on monasticism of the great African theologian Origen, whom we consider in a later chapter, left its imprint on some monks. Thus like their mentor, some monks like Poemen did employ allegorical modes of interpreting the Bible.[44]

At the same time there is a striking sense of sin evident among the monks. Matoes taught that the nearer one draws to God the more he sees

---

39. Anthony, 18, in *AP* 5; Isaac of Cells, 2, in *AP* 99–100.

40. For this analysis, see Ward, "Foreword," in *AP* xiii–xiv; Kant, *Critique of Pure Reason*, 41–62, 87–89, 257–75.

41. Nisterus, 5, in *AP* 155: "... ὅτι ὀψείλει ὁ μοναχὸς καθ᾽ ἑσπέραν καὶ πρωίας λόγον ποιεῖν, τί ὧν θέλει ὁ θεὸς ἐποιήσαμεν, καὶ τί ὧν οὐ θέλει οὐχ ἐποιήσαμεν; καὶ οὕτως τραχτεύοντες ἑαυτῶν τὴν πᾶσαν ζωήν."

42. Alonius, 1, in *AP* 35: "Ἐὰν μὴ εἴπῃ ἐν τῇ χαρδίᾳ αὐτοῦ ἄνθρωπος, ὅτι Ἐγὼ μόνος χαὶ ὁ Θεός ἐσμὲν ἐν τῷ χόσμῳ, οὐχ ἕξει ἀνάπαυσιν."

43. Agathon, 6, in *AP* 21; Daniel, 3, in *AP* 52; John the Dwarf, 41, 44, in *AP* 95.

44. Poemen, 30, 60, in *AP* 171, 175.

himself a sinner.⁴⁵ Prefiguring the doctrine of Original Sin as developed by Augustine, some monks like Longinus held that even passionate desire negates our sinlessness. Again we find the monks combating temptation, passion, and lust, which are portrayed as sin in a manner Augustine would later develop.⁴⁶ But this strand of thinking was mitigated by others like Cyrus of Alexandria who held that it was not sinful to think of fornication.⁴⁷ Given this weaker view of sin characteristic of traditions that teach a role for works contributing to salvation/justification, it is not surprising to find the monks frequently teaching a role for works in saving us.

Anthony's disciple and successor Ammonas claimed that a monk is saved by rigorous isolation in his cell and by having a sense of one's own unworthiness. Isaac priest of Cells claimed that as we keep God's Commandments God will send grace.⁴⁸ An angel even informed the monks that their not judging others and confessing their sins merit inclusion in the book of life.⁴⁹

These affirmations seem to echo a kind of legalistic understanding of Christian faith, not unlike the Pelagianism with which Augustine and the whole Church would later contend.⁵⁰ But we find other comments more suggestive of the Eastern or Roman Catholic visions of Justification (involving salvation as a cooperation of grace and works).⁵¹ An (anonymous) early monk of Nitria (in Egypt) calls us to put ourselves in subjection to the grace of Christ through poverty and charity. A similar claim was made by Athanasius in his Life of St. Anthony. In another text he has Anthony refer to God as "our fellow-worker."⁵²

We also find remarks in the texts most suggestive of an affirmation of justification by grace at several points. An ordained monk Corpes is reported to have exhibited profound modesty about the holiness of his life,

---

45. Matoes, 4, in *AP* 143.

46. Abraham, 1, in *AP*, 34; Joseph of Penephysis, 3, in ibid., 102; Cyrus, in ibid., 118-19; Longinus, 5, in ibid., 123; Poemen, 34, in ibid., 172. For Augustine's thinking on the subject, see note 35 above.

47. Cyrus of Alexandria, in *AP* 118-19.

48. Ammonas, 1-6, in *AP* 25-27; Isaac, Priest of Cells, 11, in *AP* 101.

49. Paphnutius, 1, in *AP* 202.

50. Pelagius, *Pro libero arbitrio* (418).

51. Christoforos Stavropoulos, "Partakers of Divine Nature," in Clendenin, *Eastern Orthodox Theology*, 183-92; *Catechism of the Catholic Church* (1994), 1993.

52. Omega, 13, in *AP* 248; Ath. *V. Ant.*, 19 (*NPNF*² 4:201).

claiming that "there was nothing wonderful about his own achievements,"[53] an affirmation that implies that it is only by grace that we can be saved or live a holy life. Anthony is also reported to have taught that we are not to trust in our own righteousness. He also taught that we are to be ourselves with God (presumably because we have nothing to prove).[54]

An even clearer affirmation of salvation only by God's grace, not by our works, is evident in *The Wisdom of the Elders of Ethiopia* regarding a Desert Father Agaton:

> About discretion and patience. They told how some men, having heard of Abba Agaton's reputation, came to him with the intention of testing his discretion and patience, to see if he could be made angry.
>
> They said to him, "Are you Agaton? We have heard what a great fornicator you are!"
>
> He gave thanks and said to them, "That is quite correct, that's just what I am!"
>
> Again they said, "Are you the Agaton who is such a slanderer and calumniator of men?"
>
> "Yes," he said, "that's who I am."
>
> Then they said to him, "Are you not Agaton the heretic?"
>
> At this he answered and said, "No, I am not! A heretic I have never been!"
>
> And he was angry!
>
> So they inquired further and said to him, "Tell us why you willingly bore what we said at first, but our last remark you will not tolerate at all?"
>
> He replied, "I took what you said first, because it was good for me to do so; but were I to declare myself a heretic, I would be separating myself from the Lord!"
>
> Hearing this statement, they marveled at him and went away edified.[55]

Although the monks were not systematic theologians, that did not keep some of them from engaging in theological disputes. Athanasius claimed that Anthony opposed the Arians.[56] We can also see in some of the early monks' reflections the origins of a Monophysite Christology that characterizes the historic African churches (the Ethiopian Orthodox and the Coptic

---

53. Corpes, in *HM* 82.
54. Anthony, 6, in *AP* 2; ibid., 32, in *AP* 8.
55. *Pat. Aeth.*, 71.
56. Ath. *V. Ant.*, 69–70 (*NPNF*[2] 4:214–15).

churches). Many of the monks were caught up in a later dispute over the validity of Origen's thought, the majority opposing his views, for reasons a later chapter on that great African Apologist will make clear.[57] The monk Olympius broke with the consensus of the Fathers on Theological Method by expressing an openness to learning certain truths from other religions.[58]

Having considered some of the common convictions of the early Desert Fathers, let's conclude now with a survey of the theology of some of the most famous monks of the African desert.

Anthony

We have already described Anthony's life and background. Perhaps we should add to his devoutness and appreciation of his interpersonal talents, his working of miracles such as successfully praying for water in the desert as well as healings (typical of the other Desert Fathers).[59] Athanasius made it clear that these miracles happened not by Anthony's own command, but by his calling on Christ's Name. When miracles did not happen it was not the Will of God, he reports.[60]

This has implications for Anthony's view of Providence. References are made in what Athanasius wrote about Anthony to the fact that God loves humankind and Who works when He will.[61] God's preservation of him from martyrdom for the good of the Church is another example of a strong doctrine of Providence in Anthony's (and perhaps Athanasisus') thought.[62] God is said to "allow" certain temptations.[63] While grappling with the question of how God may be said to be just in view of the fact of the disparity between rich and poor, in view of the death of some who are young, Anthony advises that it is not to our advantage to know these

---

57. Lot, in *AP* 121; "Editorial Expositions," in *AP* 54, 122.

58. Olympius, 1, *AP* 160, in marked contrast to Anthony in Ath. *V. Ant.*, 78 (*NPNF*[2] 4:216).

59. Ath. *V. Ant.*, 4, 14, 48, 54, 71 (*NPNF*[2] 4:196, 200, 209, 210, 215); cf. John of Lycopolis, 6–11, in *HM* 53–54; Theon, 1, in *HM* 68; Elias, 2, in ibid., 69; Corpes, 1, in ibid., 82; Amoun, 3–4, in ibid., 111; John in Dioclos, in ibid., 117.

60. Ath. *V. Ant.*, 38, 48, 56, 84 (*NPNF*[2] 4:206, 209, 211, 218).

61. Ibid., 40, 32, 49 (*NPNF*[2] 4:207, 205, 209).

62. Ibid., 46 (*NPNF*[2] 4:208–9).

63. Anthony, 23, in *AP* 6.

matters, that it is better to attend instead to ourselves.⁶⁴ He offered a similar argument on behalf of his affirmation of the Word of God's Incarnation in a human body. (Note the language of Christ's Two Natures.) This reality and the Cross, he argued, are a more beautiful confession of faith than the Roman attribution of adultery and seduction of boys by the gods.⁶⁵

Anthony is said to have experienced depression. He seems to have found that he could best deal with it by manual work and prayer.⁶⁶ If its precepts are kept we will be saved, we are advised.⁶⁷ This is either a use of the Commands of God to guide us in Christian living (the so-called Third Use of the Law), or it is another example of a failure to appreciate the role of grace in saving us?⁶⁸

We have also identified the richness (or confusion) regarding his position on the relation between grace and works in Justification. Of course, this is a characteristic typical of almost all the pre-Augustinian African theologians. It is a characteristic of Eastern thought to this day, which raises for us whether this way of construing our salvation is a vice or a virtue for us today. Thus on one hand Anthony says that he no longer feared God, but loved Him, implying that God is the One Who has attended to our sin.⁶⁹ He teaches the role of the Holy Spirit instructing us in purity, leading us back to God.⁷⁰ But then the venerable monk noted that we do need to fear God, hating this world so that we might be worthy of Him.⁷¹ God, it is said, will not have mercy on those who do not make an effort.⁷² And elsewhere he adds that the Spirit only comes to one who is prepared to receive it.⁷³ Yet in the tradition of Eastern thinking and its failure to pin down whether our response or grace supersedes, Anthony claims that life and death lie with the neighbor, that if we gain a brother we have gained God.⁷⁴ In connection

---

64. Ibid., 2, in *AP* 2.

65. Ath. *V. Ant.*, 74 (*NPNF*² 4:215).

66. Anthony, 1, in *AP* 1–2; Ath. *V. Ant.*, 4 (*NPNF*² 4:196).

67. Ibid., 3, in *AP* 2.

68. For more examples of teaching rubrics that are said to be able to guide and save us, see Ath. *V. Ant.*, 55 (*NPNF*² 4:210–11).

69. Anthony, 32, in *AP* 8: "Εἶπεν ὁ ἀββᾶς Αυτώνιος: Ἐγω οὐχέτι ψοσοῦμαι τὸν Οεὸν, ἀλλ᾽ ἀγαπῶ αὐτόν."

70. An. *Ep.*, 11:38—12:2; 2:27–28.

71. Anthony, 33, in *AP* 8.

72. Ibid., 16, 20, in *AP* 4, 5.

73. An. *Ep.*, 2:7, 27–29; 3:31; 4:11–14.

74. Anthony, 39, in *AP* 3.

with his teachings overlapping with traditions of the Eastern church, Athanasius even attributes to Anthony a comment that is most suggestive of deification.[75] Related to these commitments is Anthony's apparent belief (like Origen) that all beings originated from one source, evident in his claims that "whoever does evil to his neighbor does evil to himself" and his claim that to love God is to love one's own soul.[76]

Regarding the Christian life (Sanctification), Anthony predictably had a life-denying view, correlating with the dualistic Anthropology of the various worldviews embedded in ancient Egypt. Thus to Anthony is attributed the claim that we should devote more time to the soul than to the body.[77] We may as well give up the things of the world now, for we will leave them behind anyway when we die. He speaks of life as a daily death.[78] We will not sin if we live as though dying daily, he claims.[79] There is also an element, as we would expect, of construing the Christian life as a struggle with Satan.[80] We can expect temptations, he claimed, and will need to encounter them in order to be saved.[81] This theme of a struggle with Satan manifests in Anthony's construal of Christ's Atoning Work as an overcoming of Satan (the Classic View of the Atonement).[82] He also refers to Christ as the Physician.[83]

Anthony believed that we can make progress in the Christian life as we live this way. And yet he taught that we are deeply mired in sin. As he put it, "Hate the world and all that is in it . . . despise the flesh, so that you may preserve your souls."[84]

Striving for perfection is possible in Anthony's view, as long as the soul keeps understanding in its natural state.[85] This process is also facilitated, in his view, by humility and the practice of solitude.[86] There is an

---

75. Ath. *V. Ant.*, 74 (*NPNF*² 4:215).
76. An. *Ep.*, 6:57–63; 6:92; cf. Or. *Princ.*, II.VIII.3 (*ANF* 4:288).
77. Ath. *V. Ant.*, 45 (*NPNF*² 4:208).
78. Ibid., 19 (*NPNF*² 4:201).
79. Ibid.
80. Ibid., 9, 11, 12, 21, 22, 23, 30, 31, 51, 52 (*NPNF*² 4:198, 199, 201–2, 204, 210); Anthony, 12, 22, in *AP* 3, 6.
81. Anthony, 5, in *AP* 2.
82. Ath. *V. Ant.*, 24, 28, 78 (*NPNF*² 4: 202, 203, 216).
83. An. *Ep.*, 3:15–24; 2:9–10.
84. Anthony, 33, in *AP* 8.
85. Ath. *V. Ant.*, 34 (*NPNF*² 4:205).
86. Anthony, 6, 11, in *AP* 2, 3.

eschatological urgency in Anthony's reflections, a sense that life is short and the past is gone.[87]

Later in his career, not just at the outset of his entrance into a monastic vocation, Anthony concerned himself with the poor, even preaching on this issue. Monks like Nilus and Nisterius joined him in this commitment.[88]

With respect to Theological Method we would expect Anthony, like most of the Desert Fathers, to operate with an Orthodox approach, subordinating our reason and experience to the Word of God, as the starting point for theological reflection. Thus in view of his previously noted comments about the inability of reason to penetrate all the mysteries of faith, Athanasius attributes to him the observation that when one has a strong faith, proof by reasoning is useless.[89] This evidences itself in Anthony's critique of the other religions of the empire.[90] As Athanasius wrote, Anthony's witness was heard throughout the Church, and as we shall see his theological convictions echo in many who follow, just as he embodied much that was already evident before his time in the ancient Church of North Africa.[91]

Macarius

Who Macarius was is somewhat of a mystery. In a later chapter we will examine the theology of fifty sermons attributed to Macarius the Great, also known as Macarius the Egyptian (300–390). Influenced by Anthony, this former camel-driver was ordained as a priest, whose life was impeccable except for enduring a false accusation of impregnating a woman.[92] Sometimes this Anchorite monk has been confused with another monk who practiced extreme asceticism, Macarius of Alexandria (296–393). But there is much historical-critical controversy over whether the sermons are in fact the work of the Egyptian monk, or rather the work of a Syrian author with links to the Cappadocian Fathers.[93] Because of this dispute, it seemed

---

87. Ath. *V. Ant.*, 17, 19 (*NPNF*² 4:200, 201).

88. Ibid., 17, 30 (*NPNF*² 4:201, 204); Anthony, 24, in *AP* 6; for other monks with this commitment, see Nilius, 4; Nisterius, 4, in *AP* 153, 154–55.

89. Ath. *V. Ant.*, 77ff. (*NPNF*² 4:216f.).

90. Ibid., 75, 76 (*NPNF*² 4:216); cf. ibid., 94 (*NPNF*² 4:221).

91. Ibid., 93 (*NPNF*² 4:221).

92. Macarius, 1, in *HM* 108; Macarius, 4, *AP* 127–28.

93. George A. Maloney, "Introduction," in Maloney, *Pseudo-Macarius*, 6ff. Also see Socr. *H.e.*, IV.XXIII (*NPNF*² 2:107).

wiser to deal with the utterances of one who was unambiguously engaged in African monasticism in this context, and treat the disputed texts in a separate chapter.

Macarius is reported to have engaged in various healings.[94] We have already noted that the performance of miracles was accomplished typically by the monks and by religious leaders of other African religions. Indeed, another monk, Paul the Simple, was said to have the grace to discern the stage of souls merely by looking at people's faces.[95]

There was a profound and attractive humility in Macarius's ministry in this regard. He was so humble that he did not even claim to be a monk, just to have seen them.[96] He only spoke to those who castigated him. Indeed, he is said to have taken no pleasure in conversation.[97] If he ate with his brethren he fasted the next days accordingly in order to balance what he had eaten.[98] His emaciated body he attributed to the fear of God.[99]

Regarding theology, many of the themes characteristic of the other Desert Fathers are in evidence—including a preoccupation with sin and understanding the Christian life as a struggle with Satan.[100] He would have us weep for our sins.[101] And much like other African monks, his humility was emphasized in contending that it is humility that conquers Satan.[102] Again there is no unambiguous affirmation of grace in saving us and facilitating the Christian life.

Given the monks' preoccupation with Sanctification it is not surprising to find Macarius add further comments about the Christian life, saying little about other doctrines save how we are saved (Justification/Deification) and Eschatology. He urges the faithful to take no account of praise or blame, for then one can be saved.[103] This emphasis on works makes sense in view of the association of the African Father's affirmation of something like deification (our becoming God-like), a characteristic treatment of Jus-

---

94. Macarius, 7, 8, 13–15, in *AP* 128–30.
95. Paul the Simple, in *AP* 205.
96. Macarius, 2, in *AP* 125, 126.
97. Ibid., 31, 41, in *AP* 134, 138.
98. Ibid., 10, in *AP* 129.
99. Ibid., 12, in *AP* 130.
100. Ibid., 11, 27, 35, in *AP* 129–30, 133, 136.
101. Ibid., 27, in *AP* 133.
102. Ibid., 11, in *AP* 130; cf. Mius, 2; Tithoes, in *AP* 150, 236–37.
103. Macarius, 23, in *AP* 132.

tification and Sanctification by the Eastern church.[104] About Macarius it is written, "They said of Abba Macarius the Great that he became, as it is written, a god upon earth, because, just as God protects the world, so Abba Macarius would cover the faults which he saw, as though he did not see them; and those which he heard, as though he did not hear them."[105]

In accord with deification (for God is perfect) he taught the doctrine of perfection, or at least its possibility.[106] As deification includes a role for works in saving us, so we are judged in that manner (Eschatology). Thus Macarius posited degrees of punishment in hell.[107]

Other aspects of the Macarian vision of Christian life follow from these commitments of humility and the denial of the world's ways, along with a God-like spirit of forgiveness. In correcting others, he urged, we must not get carried away in anger, lest we lose ourselves in trying to save them. Nor should we remember wrongs done to us.[108] Yet he would have us separate from those with bad reputations.[109] To these points, Macarius also adds a Social Ethical insight. As we are to not be caught up on praise, so riches are to be deemed as no different than poverty.[110] The godly existence to which Macarius directs us echoes many of the visions of his monastic brothers. It will echo again, we shall observe, in the sermons attributed to him.

Moses the Negro

Also known as Moses the Robber as a result of his supporting himself through criminal theft after being released as a slave, this Black man become a monk late in life and was ordained as a priest. Advised by Macarius, he was martyred by barbarian invaders. There is a troubling account about his ethnicity. He was castigated as a Black man on at least one occasion, and questions himself as a human being, even wondering if he should be

---

104. See note 51.

105. Macarius, 32, in *AP* 134: "Ἔλεγον περὶ τοῦ ἀββᾶ Μαχαρίου τοῦ μεγάλου, ὅτι γέγονε χαθώς ἐστι γεγραμμένον θεὸς ἐπίγειος, ὅτι ὥσπερ ἐστιν ὁ θεὸς σχεπάζων τὸν χόσμον, οὕτως γέγονεν ὁ ἀββᾶς Μαχάριος σχεπάζον τὰ ἐλαττώματα, ἃ ἔβλεπεν ὡς μὴ βλέπων, καὶ ἃ ἤχουεν ὡς μὴ ἀχούων."

106. Ibid., 33, in *AP* 135.

107. Ibid., 38, in *AP* 137.

108. Ibid., 17, 36, in *AP* 131, 136.

109. Ibid., 29, in *AP* 133.

110. Ibid., 20, in *AP* 131.

allowed to meet other men.¹¹¹ It is unclear whether this episode bespeaks a racism (which is anachronistic, given the fact that the ancient Egyptians were dark-skinned and black-haired, and the fact that the name they called Egypt, *Kemet*, means Black). But on the other hand, many Christians in this era were inclined to envision demons as Ethiopians or as Black.¹¹² Racism as we know it is post-slavery (an ideology developed to justify slavery). And yet we must ask if European diminution of African Blackness is only a function of ethnic rivalry.

Theologically, many of the same themes we have already observed emerge in Moses's comments. In a remark we previously noted, humility is evident in his interaction with another monk about whose sin a council of monks was preoccupied. His own sins, Moses claimed, ran behind him, so that he could judge no one.¹¹³ The key to the Christian life, he contends, is seeing ourselves as sinners, or God would not hear us.¹¹⁴

This awareness of sin has implications for Sanctification, it seems. In a remark filled with stunning wisdom Moses notes that when you bear your own faults you stop paying attention to whether anyone else is good or bad.¹¹⁵ Moses's remarks make it seem that our salvation is dependent on what we do. But then in a manner like the other monks, the relation between grace and works is not so neat. The African monk contends that peace is forever by the grace of God.¹¹⁶ But this proclamation does not remove the ambiguities about how grace relates to works typical of Pre-Augustinian and Eastern thought. These ambiguities are further evidenced in the African Desert Father's claim that keeping God's Commandments will lead to protection from barbarians.¹¹⁷ Moses the Negro's theological insights are clearly in line with the consensus we have observed among the first monks.

What Matters for the Church Today

Of course we cannot but be inspired by the faith, humility, and lives of self-denial of the Desert Fathers. But there are important theological lessons to

---

111. Moses the Negro, 3–4, in *AP* 139.
112. *Pat. Aeth.*, 35; Ath. *V. Ant.*, 6 (*NPNF*² 4:197).
113. Moses the Negro, 2, in *AP* 138–39.
114. Moses the Negro, "Instructions," 3, in *AP* 141.
115. Ibid., 7, in *AP* 142.
116. Ibid., in *AP* 143.
117. Moses the Negro, 9, in *AP* 140.

learn from them. There is a diversity (should we term it a "catholicity) in the monks' thought in addition to what they hold in common. Most share commonalities regarding a Theological Method that is Orthodox, a sense of the Christian life as a struggle with evil, a Classic View of the Atonement, and a focus on Christian living (Sanctification, even a striving for perfection), with little express attention to Social Ethics (save a concern for the poor). But we have identified a diversity in the desert over whether Sin is something we can resist by willing it and over the relation between God's grace and works with regard to how we are justified or saved. These are trends that we will see reflected in much of pre-Augustinian African Christian thought.

2

Mothers of the Desert

AFRICAN CHRISTIAN WOMEN ALSO flocked to the desert, for the same reasons that the Abbas did. But at least one other dynamic was involved. Life in the desert represented a liberation from the Roman patriarchy (at least to some extent). We cannot understand the leadership of and freedom experienced by African Christian women in the desert, though, apart from the influence of Gnosticism and the sort of patriarchy which characterized Roman North Africa.

Gnosticism was a clear dialogue partner for the early African church in the development of its views on women. Women were given a prominent role in Gnostic churches. Tertullian raved against these developments, contending that "the very women of these heretics . . . are bold enough to teach, to dispute, to enact exorcisms, to undertake curses, it may be even to baptize."[1]

Even the patriarchalism of Egypt was modified somewhat after the Roman conquest by the Roman version of patriarchy. Women had begun to achieve equal rank, at least in family and in ability to carry on its financial transactions. Of course public speaking and public places were the sole prerogative of men. Private spaces like the household were the proper sphere for women's activities.[2]

These dynamics entailed that women's roles were not narrowly circumscribed in these societies. Like in Egypt, household management was

---

1. Tert. *Praescrip.*, XLI (*ANF* 3:263): "Ante sunt perfecti catechumeni, quam edocti. ipsae mulieres haereticae, quam procaces! quae audeant docere, contendere, exorcismos agere, curationes repromittere, forsitan et tingere."

2. Torjesen, *When Women Were Priests*, 11–12.

an executive position. It involved the direction of both women and men servants and laborers, production and distribution of what was produced in the fields and by craftsmen of the household. In holding the responsibility for the distribution of these products, these women householders often traveled, bought, sold, and negotiated contracts. In accumulating such wealth, sometimes without a husband, successful women in Roman Empire societies early in the Christian era functioned not unlike today's Chambers of Commerce luminaries, representing the interests of their communities. Often like men they contributed to the welfare of such communities by providing financial assistance to worthy causes, making recommendations to officials, and providing protection for political leaders.[3]

Of course, the Church tended to take its cue from social convention in the first centuries (just as it does today). Mindful of its precarious status in the Roman Empire, the first Christians looked to members with social status to be patrons. Likewise, the early church as a household church naturally looked to women for leadership, as women were often the heads of their households.[4] These dynamics in the New Testament period are illustrated by Paul as he hails Prisca, who with her husband risked their lives for him and in whose house the church in Rome met (Rom 16:3–5). Mary, the mother of John Mark, is said to have presided over a house church in Jerusalem (Acts 12:12–17), as well as other women leaders in Col 4:15 and Acts 16:14–15.

Study of ancient inscriptions indicate that likewise women played prominent leadership roles in the synagogues of the era. It is hardly surprising, then, that as Christians adopted Jewish models of worship (a male priesthood), women would not continue to be considered for leadership positions.[5]

Women in the African Church

Given these trends in the Roman Empire and the Church as whole, it is not surprising to find evidence of women in church leadership positions in Africa or at least evidence of women exerting a significant impact on the Church in that region. For example, one unidentified wealthy woman in Alexandria became a patron of a promising young scholar, Origen, whose

---

3. Ibid., 12.
4. Ibid., 12–13; cf. 126–27.
5. Ibid., 19ff.

contributions we will explore in a subsequent chapter.⁶ A fourth-century Egyptian papyrus refers to a Christian woman named Kyria as a teacher. (In other regions like Bythinia and Cappadocia there is even evidence of women actually functioning as presbyters/priests.)⁷

Such a leadership role for women in the Church began to change, though, as soon as Christianity became more credible in the Roman Empire. These dynamics transpired not just in North Africa but everywhere in the empire. More hierarchical (episcopal) models of leadership were adopted. By the fourth century this monarchial model of leadership was reflected in church architecture. The Church was now truly a public institution. And as such it could no longer readily countenance women's leadership since good Roman wisdom relegated women to the private sphere, excluding them from public life.⁸

Examples of these dynamics abound. We have already noted Augustine's comments about the patriarchy that characterized Roman North Africa. He reports how his mother Monica bore many acts of unfaithfulness by her husband (Augustine's father). Monica, it seems, had the wisdom to know that a woman should not resist a husband in anger. Many of her female friends did not follow suit and as a result, Augustine reports, carried marks and blows disfiguring their faces. He writes, "my mother—talking lightly but meaning it seriously—advised them [other married women] against their tongues: saying that from the day they heard the matrimonial contract read to them they should regard it as an instrument by which they became servants; and from that time they should be mindful of their condition and not set themselves against their masters."⁹

There are reports that the wife of Amoun of Nitria (295–353), one of the great founders of Egyptian monasticism, lived with him in ascetic celibacy for eighteen years after their marriage. Eucharistus the Secular and his wife Mary reportedly lived together in celibacy as witness to monks of

---

6. Eus. *H.e.*, VI.II.13 (*NPNF*² 1:250).

7. Torjesen, *When Women Were Priests*, 114–15.

8. Ibid., 155–58.

9. Aug. *Conf.*, IX.IX.19 (*NPNF*¹ 1:136): "Denique, cum matronae multae quarum viri mansuetiones errant, plagarum vestigia, etiam dehonestata facie gererent, inter amica colloquia illae arguebant maritorum vitam, haec earum linguam, veluti per jocum graviter admonens, ex quo illas tabulas quae matrimoniales vocantur, recitari audissent, tanquam instrumenta quibus ancillae facte assent, deputare debuisse; proinde memores conditionis, superbire adversus dominos non opotere."

their great virtue. Carion, a married Egyptian, left his family to become a monk, and his wife sent their son to live with him.[10]

Abba Bessarion tells the story of a woman who impersonated a Desert Father.[11] Abba Eudemon reports that Abba Paphnutius, father of Scetis, would not let this monk stay with him and his colleagues, because the face of a woman could not dwell there on account of temptations.[12] We can only conclude that this action was occasioned by Paphnutius's perceived feminine features in Eudemon's visage. In the *Wisdom of the Elders of Ethiopia*, a story is told of a monk who avoided a group of virgin nuns. When the leader of the convent learned this, she shouted that the monk could not have been a real monk or he would not have even noticed that she and her sisters were women.[13]

Given such sexist-patriarchal tendencies in the early African church, Gnostic egalitarianism, its use of women as ministers and teachers, was quite obviously most controversial in catholic circles on the continent.[14] Not surprisingly, Tertullian and Origen, as we shall observe in subsequent chapters, opted for patriarchal practices regarding leadership in the Church and their attire (positions very much in line with Pauline directives). Other examples can be cited. Anthony is said to have been tempted by the devil taking the form of a woman. And a Mother of the Desert, Mary the Egyptian, also saw the devil in this way.[15]

In view of this patriarchal background, it is hardly surprising that in the bulk of the book we will be examining the theology of African Church Fathers, not Mothers. Given these realities, the fact that women fled to the desert was a clear testimony to female strength and autonomy, a kind of recovery of earlier cultural and ecclesiastical sensibilities. It is to an examination of the theology of the most prominent women of the desert that we now turn.

---

10. On Amoun, 1–2, in *HM* 111; Eucharisticus the Secular, in *AP* 60; Carion, 2, in *AP* 117; cf. regarding the ascetic union of Amoun of Nitria and his wife, see the editor's introduction in Ward, *Sayings of the Desert Fathers*, 31.

11. Bessarion, 4, in *AP* 41.

12. Eudemon, in *AP* 64.

13. *Pat. aeth.*, 29.

14. Torjesen, *When Women Were Priests*, 158; see note 1 above.

15. Ath. *V. Ant.*, 23 (*NPNF*² 4:202); Budge, *Book of Saints*, 3:786.

The Theology of the Mothers of the Desert

No discussion of African Christian Mothers can neglect Perpetua, whose theology we have already considered, and Marie, the sister of Pachomius, who herself founded the woman's wing of Cenobitic Monasticism. She founded three monastic communities for women, numbering over three thousand, on the model of her brother's male communities. Unfortunately as we previously observed, the Cenobitic traditions have not left us much in the way of preserved sayings. Fortunately, though, we find the oral sayings of a number of Desert Mothers which offer us helpful insights into the theology of women of the early African church.

Theodora

This great woman of the desert is said to have been the wife of a tribune (an elected official in the Roman Empire). In her life in the desert she achieved a notable depth of poverty. She made a profound impact on the faithful of the desert in her life, evidenced by the fact that a significant number of Desert Fathers consulted her for advice.[16]

Characteristic of the monks, Theodora noted that the present age is filled with many trials. Evil weighs down the soul. This struggle with evil is chastened, though, with the confidence that all things can be made profitable.[17] Granted this is a comment made by Archbishop Theophilus, but she seems to have endorsed it.

The same stress on what we are to do manifests in a Law or works-oriented approach to Sanctification and even Justification. Thus the Desert Mother speaks of a commandment compelling her to keep her mouth shut, even when insulted.[18] Likewise she wisely adds that a teacher ought not desire domination or be a fool for flattery, but be patient.[19] Her most legalistic statement transpires when she claims that we can only be saved by humility. But she was not as extreme as some Desert Fathers like Macarius who sought to avoid conversation; she claimed that one can hear secular conversations without forfeiting concern for God by remaining attuned to God.[20] This self-

---

16. "Editor's Introduction," in *AP* 82.
17. Theodora, 1, 3, in *AP* 82–83.
18. Ibid., 4, 2, in *AP* 83.
19. Ibid., 5, in *AP* 83–84.
20. Ibid., 6, 8, in *AP* 84; cf. see chapter 1, note 97.

conscious focus on God and the claim that all things can be made profitable is indicative of the mixing of God's gracious activity and human works that we have already observed in the Desert Fathers and will continue to observe in virtually all the pre-Augustinian African theologians (with the possible exception of some of the other Desert Mothers). This point (affirming God's role in illuminating our works and lifestyle) is also evident in Theodora's (biblically rooted) claim that the Risen Christ is the pledge and prototype, not just the examples of the resurrected life of the Christian.[21]

Athanasia

Born of rich parents in the city of Manuf, upon their death Athanasia transformed her home into a dwelling place for monks. Her story is a witness to Justification by Grace.[22]

It seems that certain evil men had corrupted Athanasia's mind and induced her to commit sin. Monks heard this and out of gratitude for all she had done for them and in order to save her soul they sent John the Short to go to her and show affection. He wept for her. In order to make repentance she asked to go away with the monk wherever he would go. Sleeping apart he awoke at midnight and noted a pillar of light shining on Athanasia. He saw an angel bearing away her soul; she was dead. God had accepted her repentance. She had been saved, despite her sin.

Eupraxia

The Mother of the Desert belonged to a race of kings. Her father died while she was an infant. Her mother took her to a house of virgins when she was six years old and lived this way her entire life.[23] Despite these influences the decision to become an Amma was her own. We learn how the six-year-old Eupraxia asked the virgins why they led the life they lived. Their answer, that they did it for Christ's sake, made a deep impression. In response to her question of where Christ is the Mothers showed her a picture of Him. She responded by bowing and kissing the feet of the picture. Then she

---

21. Theodora, 10, in *AP* 84.
22. *Mash. Senk.*, 4:1182–84.
23. Ibid., 1184–85.

asked to be received as a Desert Mother, and her own mother left them in the Ammas' care.

The accounts concerning Eupraxia witness to the characteristic monastic vision of Justification as involving grace and works, in no particular order. It seems that Eupraxia fought the spiritual life continually, fasting every eighth day. In a manner characteristic of most Desert Mothers and Fathers, she was frequently tempted by Satan, in her case enduring various accidents and injuries.

Eupraxia energetically fought these temptations. She is said to have served the virgins faithfully by performing household duties. Reportedly she never laid on the ground, but to the marvel of all stood upright, sometimes for forty days. God was made manifest in her hands, signs, and wonders. She also was gifted with the ability to perform healings. She learned to read and write from her dear friend, the virgin Iyalaya.

At age thirty Eupraxia reprtedly died. Her friend saw deacons bringing her to the royal palace of the Heavenly Bridegroom where there is never-ending joy. Her own disciplined life and the grace of Christ the Bridegroom had overcome her sin.

Mary the Egyptian

Born of Christian parents in Alexandria, we only know of Mary's personal life through accounts of her spiritual trials and highs. The characteristic idea of monastic life as a struggle clearly reflects in reports of Mary's life. But we also gain insights regarding Christology, Mariology, the Eucharist, and perhaps salvation by grace.[24]

It seems that Mary had been seduced by Satan to love fornication. She paid for a trip to Jerusalem by prostitution. Yet she prayed for forgiveness, especially first by petitioning Mary whom she terms the Mother of God. (The Alexandrian Christology which referred to Mary as Mother of God and maintained that whatever is said of one of Jesus's Natures is attributable to the other seems affirmed here.) Hearing a voice to go to the desert of the Jordan, she willingly complies in order to find rest and salvation. The fact that in death her body was protected by a lion suggests that she was saved, certainly by grace, but also perhaps by the work she did in going to the desert.

Inspired by forgiving grace it seems that Mary was gifted with the ability to divine the name of one of the desert monks following through her

24. Ibid., 3:784–87.

region. An account of the Desert Father Zosimus bringing her the Eucharist, for she desired Christ's Body and Blood, is significant for two reasons. On the one hand, we see that not all the faithful of the desert rejected the Sacraments in their piety. Also we observe here the affirmation of the Real Presence of Christ in the Communion elements, after the fashion of the consensus of early African theology, as well as the characteristic Eastern and Coptic view of the rite.

Sarah

We don't know much about this Amma's life except that like most of the other Desert Mothers and Fathers she waged spiritual warfare, in her case a warfare with fornication for thirteen years.[25] We also find a grace-oriented vision of the Christian life portrayed in her witness.

Sarah notes that she never prayed that her temptation should cease, just that she would have strength.[26] Finally she gives full credit to Christ (to grace), never to herself, in overcoming the spirit of fornication.[27] Here it seems we find Justification By Grace is affirmed.

A grace orientation often can give courage to live boldly. For example, Sarah is recorded as saying, "If I prayed God that all men should approve of my conduct, I should find myself a penitent at the door of each one, but I shall rather pray that my heart may be pure towards all."[28]

Don't worry so much about what others think of you. You are free to care for others.

Through service, Sarah adds, we serve God: "She also said, 'It is good to give alms for men's sake. Even if it is only done to please men, through it one can begin to seek to please God.'"[29]

There is one dimension of Sarah's comments that might be a bit disturbing to modern Western eyes. She claimed that according to nature

---

25. Sarah, 1, in *AP* 229.
26. Ibid.
27. Ibid., 2, in *AP* 230.
28. Ibid., 5, in *AP* 230: ". . . Ἐὰν εὔξωμαι τῷ Θεῷ, ἵνα πάντες οἱ ἄνθρωποι πληροφορῶνται εἰς ἐμὲ, Εὑρεθήσομαι εἰς τὴν Θύραν ἑχάστου μετανοοῦσα. ἀλλὰ μᾶλλον εὔζομαι τὴν χαρδίαν μου ἁγνὴν εἶναι μετὰ πάντων."
29. Ibid., 7, in *AP* 230: "Εἶπε πάλιν, ὅτι χαλόν ἐστι χαὶ δι'ἀνθρώπους ποιεῖν ἐλεημοσύνην. Εἰ γὰρ χαὶ δι'ανθρωπαρεσχίαν, ἀλλ'Ἔρχεται παλιν εἰς Θεοῦ ἀρίσχειαν."

she was a woman, but not according to her thoughts. Of course she was responding to other monks who were testing her conceit deliberately by contending that they had come to see her, a mere woman.[30]

Patriarchal propensities of ancient Roman, if not North African culture are clearly manifest at these points. Likewise it is evident when she mocked other monks, claiming, "It is I who am a man, you also are a woman."[31]

Syncletica

Little is known biographically of this influential Mother of the Desert. Besides the usual witness to Christian life as a struggle and the need for legal guidelines in living it (especially stimulating humility), we also gain insights into her Theological Method in the sayings about her.

Typical of the other monks and nuns we have considered, Syncletica claims that Christian life is an ongoing struggle with the devil, who is always seeking to seduce us.[32]

The Law orientation in her reflections are apparent in her claim that behavior is as important as words when teaching, that it is good not to get angry at people. We are to hate the sickness, but not the sick person.

In Syncletica's view, because prayer joined to fasting drives away evil thoughts, the life of poverty was seen as a good thing.[33] But a sense of proportion in fasting (depending on age and quantity of food in breaking fasts) is advocated.[34]

A concern with humility reflects in this famed Amma's comments. She urges us to seek to avoid praise, for we cannot be surrounded by worldly honor and still bear fruit.[35]

Indeed, she claims, just as a ship cannot be built without nails, so one cannot be saved without humility.[36] Our actions or mental convictions seem to determine salvation.

We find Syncletica also teaching lessons on Theological Method. In a manner implicit in the storytelling tradition of virtually all the monks and

---

30. Ibid., 8, in *AP* 230.
31. Ibid., 9, in *AP* 230.
32. Syncletica, 7, 18, in *AP* 231–32, 234.
33. Ibid., 3–5, in *AP* 231.
34. Ibid., 9, in *AP* 233–34.
35. Ibid., 21–22, in *AP* 234.
36. Ibid., 26, in *AP* 235.

nuns, she aims to have her hearers identify with the characters of the Bible's stories.[37]

Does What They Said Matter?

Overall the theological emphases we have identified are similar to what we observed among the African Desert Fathers. Christian life is portrayed by them as much as their male counterparts as a struggle with the devil. This preoccupation (the focus on Sanctification) sometimes to Protestant ears may sound like Pelagian works-righteousness. But here Perpetua's witness to the sovereign God and the witness to God's unconditional grace by Sarah, Athanasia and perhaps by Mary the Egyptian seem to be significant exceptions. There is not a clear indication that the experience of being female in African made a significant difference in the theology of these African women, except that save it seems at some points they needed to deny who they were. In that sense the early Church was clearly not free of patriarchy. But in view of the general theological agreement we find between them, if we like the theology of the Desert Fathers, we cannot but admire and appreciation the thought of the African Christian Mothers.

37. Ibid., 13, 25, in *AP* 233, 235.

3

Clement of Alexandria

TITUS FLAVIUS CLEMENS (150–215), known as Clement, may not have been an ethnic African. There is some uncertainty about whether he was born in Alexandria or in Athens. He was clearly a wanderer in search of truth, no less so than his primary mentor, Pantaenus. But inasmuch as he is associated with Alexandria in a way that his mentors were not (though they taught in Africa) it seems like tradition's association of him with Africa makes a significant, viable point.

Originally a pagan philosopher, Clement became a Christian in adulthood and traveled to seek out the greatest Christian teachers, which meant going to the Catechetical School in Alexandria to study with its master, Pantaenus. We have not included this great Stoic philosopher who converted to Christianity and died while on a mission to India, because Clement suggests that his beloved mentor was a native of Sicily, referring to him as the "Sicilian bee."[1] (Athenagoras, another master of the Alexandrian school, is likewise not considered due to his identification as an Athenian.[2]) Nevertheless the modeling both did of relating philosophy to the faith made a deep impression on this brilliant student of theirs, as Clement operated with a Method of Correlation (relating the Word to philosophy, with philosophy functioning as the starting point or framework for understanding faith).

---

1. Clem. *Strom.*, I.1 (*ANF* 2:301, 342–43); cf, Eus. *H.e.*, V.X.1 (*NPNF*[2] 1:224–25). For the theology of Pantaenus, see *ANF* 8:776–77.

2. For Athenagorus, see *Leg.* (*ANF* 2:129).

With this sort of Methodological approach to theology, Clement has been identified as an Apologist. He clearly dedicated his career to win pagans to faith. In seeking to correlate the Word of God to philosophy there were occasions when he deemed worldly intellectual trends as giving testimony to faith.[3] From 189 to 202, Clement led Alexandria's catechetical school, making a great impact on the Church in Africa and elsewhere. This happened in no insignificant way through one of his star students, Origen, whose thought we shall examine subsequently.[4] He fled Alexandria in 202 as a result of a persecution of Septimus Severus, spending his final years in Antioch.

Clement's primary dialogue partner was Greek philosophy. This is hardly surprising given the Greek character of Alexandria's social ethos. The language and literature of the Clementine corpus, like most of the great early theologians, was Greek.[5] But no less was Clement engaged in dialogue with Gnosticism, a dualistic worldview which as we have noted was highly influential in post-piblical North Africa. Perhaps as an Apologist, Clement agreed with Gnostics that "knowledge" (*gnosis*) is the chief element in religious perfection. Yet unlike the Gnostics, for him the only true *gnosis* was presupposed in the Church's faith, and the source of reason and revelation was deemed to be found in Christ (Logos), that it is given by God.[6]

Biblical Authority and Theological Method

In Clement's view, philosophy and the Word of God are dialogue partners (his Method of Correlation). The Word of God "suits and conforms Himself to reason, to persons and places."[7] But the former is very much the junior partner. Philosophy, he says, is "a kind of preparatory training to those who attain to faith through demonstration."[8] What we seem to have

---

3. Clem. *Prot.*, V–VI, I (*ANF* 2:190–92, 171).
4. Eus. *H.e.*, VI.VI (*NPNF*² 1:253).
5. Alexander Roberts and James Donaldson, "Introductory Note," in *ANF* 2:165–66.
6. Clem. *Strom.*, II.VI, XI; V.1; VI.VII (*ANF* 2:349–50, 358, 445, 494).
7. Clem. *Paed.*, II.IV (*ANF* 2:249): "Ὁ γὰρ Λόγος ὁ τοῦ Κυρίου ἐνοιχείτω ἐν ὑμῖν πλουσίως, ὁ Ἀποστολός ψησιῶ. Ὁ δὲ λόγος οὗτος συναρυβζεται χχι συσχηματίζεται χαιροῖς, προσώπης, τόποις."
8. Clem. *Strom.*, I.V (*ANF* 2:305): "Προπαρασχευάζει τοίνυν ἡ φιλοσοφία, προοδοποιοῦσα τὸν ὑπὸ Χριστοῦ τελειούμενον." Cf. ibid. (*ANF* 2:307); ibid., VII. III (*ANF* 2:528).

here with Clement is a Method of Correlation, later developed by modern theologians like Friedrich Schleiermacher and Paul Tillich.[9]

Philosophy or some prior set of intellectual categories does not provide the content of Christian faith (as we shall see Origen to some extent held), but affords us with the tools into which the content of the Gospel is to be interpreted.

Opting for this sort of Method of Correlation approach does not for Clement entail a denial of biblical authority. Prophets are the organs of the divine voice, he contends.[10] Consequently the Scriptures are not just inspired. They are said to be the infallible criterion of faith.[11]

Of course, the great early African Apologist did not read the Bible literally, but allegorically, though he did not deny its literal sense.[12] Yet Scripture's meaning is veiled by parables. He speaks of different senses of Scripture.[13] The allegorical approach operates with a critical principle regarding Scripture. In keeping with his dialogue with Gnosticism, Clement identifies his critical principle (the heart of Scripture) as Christocentric, operating with the supposition of harmony in the covenant delivered by Christ.[14] Another interesting point about Scripture he makes pertains to its use. The Bible presents us with applications necessary for the attainment of piety, he contends. And these successful applications establish the Bible's truth.[15]

The correlation between Scripture and Platonic philosophy entails several other important Methodological commitments. We have already noted his dialogue with Gnosticism. Consequently he speaks of a true Gnosticism, interpreted in a Christian way.[16] Faith is said to be the foundation of all knowledge.[17] In a manner most suggestive of Tertullian, Clement went so far as to claim that since the Word of God has come we

---

9. Schleiermacher, *Christian Faith*, 1:12–17, 76ff.; Tillich, *Systematic Theology*, 1:3–8, 59–66.

10. Clem. *Strom.*, VI.XVIII (*ANF* 2:520).

11. Ibid., II.II,IV (*ANF* 2:349).

12. Clem. *Paed.*, XI (*ANF* 2:202–3); Clem. *Strom.*, II.XVIII; I.XVIII (*ANF* 2:368, 340–41).

13. Clem. *Strom.*, VI.XV; I.XVIII (*ANF* 2:509, 340).

14. Ibid., VI.XV (*ANF* 2:509).

15. Clem. *Prot.*, VIII (*ANF* 2:193–94).

16. Clem. *Strom.*, III.XII; IV.XXII; VII.Iff. (*ANF* 2:396ff., 434, 523ff.).

17. Ibid., II.IV (*ANF* 2:349–50).

need not go in search of human learning from Athens. God, he claims, is not an object for science.[18]

On the other hand, he could state that because philosophy prepares us for faith, it must have some truth.[19] It teaches righteousness.[20] In fact, Clement claims at one point that the truth of philosophy is the result of a revelation of God. In the same vein he claims that philosophers got their ideas from the Hebrew prophets.[21] Indeed, he adds, Christians can draw on all human knowledge, taking from each branch its contribution to truth.[22] But faith (the Word), it is still claimed, is the foundation of all knowledge.[23] These remarks suggest that Clement might operate with something like the modern Method of Critical of Correlation—initiating theological reflection with God's Word which both revises our philosophical conceptions but is itself shaped by philosophical analysis.[24]

Clement proceeds to add that philosophers love Wisdom, and so they love the Creator and Wisdom of all things, Who is Christ. For all truth is one.[25] Consequently it follows for Clement that we have some access to truth through reason. He writes, "It is man's very nature to be on intimate terms with God." If we know ourselves, we know God.[26] In fact, Clement adds, Jews, Greeks, and Christians know the same God, though not in the same way. Christians alone know Him spiritually.[27] Plato certainly has his place here. The great Greek philosopher is praised for describing the nature of God as the cause of all things, yet is not fully known. He is also said to provide insights into the Trinity.[28]

---

18. Clem. *Prot.*, X (*ANF* 2:203); Clem. *Strom.*, XXV (*ANF* 2:438).

19. Clem. *Strom.*, I.XIII; CI.XV (*ANF* 2:313, 508).

20. Ibid., I.VII (*ANF* 2:308).

21. Clem. *Prot.*, VI (*ANF* 2:191); Clem. *Strom.*, I.XXI (*ANF* 2:324).

22. Clem. *Strom.*, VI.X (*ANF* 2:498).

23. Ibid., II.IV (*ANF* 2:349–50).

24. Tracy, *Blessed Rage for Order*, esp. 43–56.

25. Clem. *Strom.*, VI.VIII (*ANF* 2:493); ibid., I.XIII (*ANF* 2:313).

26. Clem. *Prot.*, X (*ANF* 2:200) (appearing only in Latin version): "Est enim alioqui a natura homini insitum, ut ei quedam sit cum Dei conjunctio." Cf. Clem. *Paed.*, III.1 (*ANF* 2:271).

27. Clem. *Strom.*, VI.V (*ANF* 2:489).

28. Clem. *Prot.*, VI (*ANF* 2:191–92); Clem. *Strom.*, V.XIV (*ANF* 2:468).

Assessment of African Culture and Religion

The Methodological convictions discussed have implications for how Clement assesses the value and contributions of African culture. In a manner that foreshadows modern Afrocentric scholarship, he had much to say about the indebtedness of Greek philosophy to ancient African culture. He writes,

> And Plato does not deny that he procured all that is most excellent in philosophy from the barbarians, and he admits that he came into Egypt.[29]

> ... the best of the philosophers, having appropriated their most excellent dogmas from us, boast, as it were, of certain of the tenets which pertain to each sect being culled from other Barbarians, chiefly from the Egyptians—both other tenets, and that especially of the transmigration of the soul. For the Egyptians pursue a philosophy of their own.[30]

In fact, Clement adds, Plato learned geometry from the Egyptians.[31] There is even a suggestion that the Egyptians are the oldest people, as some claim the land to be that "first gave birth to the gods of men." (But then elsewhere he claims that the Jewish race is the oldest.)[32] Clement even cites a text in Plato that implies that great philosopher's acknowledgment of the origins of Greek philosophy being in other cultures.[33]

These pro-African comments could be taken as suggestive of Clement's African/Egyptian ethnicity, as he proudly celebrates the contributions of his native culture. But elsewhere he is more critical of North African cultural artifacts.

Clement seems acquainted with pre-Christian Egyptian cultural and religious practices. He disapproved of the Egyptian practice of handclapping

---

29. Clem. *Strom.*, I.XV (*ANF* 2:315): "Πλάτων δὲ οὐχ ἀρνεῖται τὰ χάλλισευ, εἰς φιλοσοφιαν παρὰ τῶν Βαρσάρων ευπορεύεσθαι εἰς τε Αιγυπτον αψικέσθαι ὁμολογει."

30. Ibid., VI.IV (*ANF* 2:488): "Εὔροιμεν δ'ἄν χαι ἄλλο μαρτύριον εἰς βεσαιωσιν τοῦ τὰ χάλλιστα τῶν δογμάτων τοὺς ἀρίστους τῶν ψυοσόφων, παρ ἡμῶν σψ— ετερισαμένους, ὡσεὶ διαυχεῖς τῶν χαι παρὰ τῶν ἄλλων Βαρζάρων ἀπηνθισθαι τῶν εἰς ἐχάσυην αἵρεσιν συντεινόντων τινὰ ῥάιστα δὲ Αιγυπτίων τά τε ἄλλα χαι το περι τὴν μετενσωμάτωσιν τῆς ψυχῆς δογμα. Μετίασι γὰρ οἴχιαν τινὰ φιλοσοψιάν Ἀιγυπειοι." Cf. ibid., VI.VI (*ANF* 2:493).

31. Clem. *Prot.*, VI (*ANF* 2:191–92).

32. Ibid., I (*ANF* 2:173); cf. Clem. *Strom.*, I.XV (*ANF* 2:316).

33. Clem. *Strom.*, I.XXIX (*ANF* 2:341).

at festivals in harmony with drums, claiming it creates a theater for drunkenness.[34] He transferred these attitudes to Christian worship, only permitting in a most qualified way the use of musical instruments.[35]

Regarding Egyptian religion he noted that priests were not allowed to feed on flesh, that none might touch fish.[36] Other details of the Egyptian pantheon of gods are provided, including its hierarchical character.[37] The heathen gods and their practices are absurd, Clement claims. As such he was critical of Egyptian shrines and their ornatmentation.[38] But he was also critical of Roman and Greek gods. These people are the real atheists, he asserts, not Christians. He does add, though, that Egyptian worship of gods is no worse than the Roman religion.[39] In a comment with deep contemporary significance for how theology is done, Clement adds that as heathen make gods like themselves, so Ethiopian gods are said to be Black and apes.[40]

In view of these critiques Clement appeals for the abandonment of ancient cultural practices. There is no reason not to abandon these customs, the eminent Apologist argues, any more than for discontinuing use of the milk of our nurses in adulthood.[41]

God and Trinity

Like many other Christians of the first century, Clement needed to defend the faith from charges of promoting atheism, since Christians did not worship a god who was seen in an image. He vigorously defended the Christian refusal to make an image of God.[42] Religion and aesthetics cannot be confused, he argued.[43] But he did concede that there is some truth in the poets, just as there is some truth in Reason.[44]

---

34. Clem. *Paed.*, II.IV (*ANF* 2:248).
35. Ibid. (*ANF* 2:249).
36. Clem. *Strom.*, VII.VI (*ANF* 2:532).
37. Clem. *Prot.*, IV (*ANF* 2:185); Clem. *Strom.*, V.VII (*ANF* 2:454).
38. Clem. *Prot.*, II (*ANF* 2:174–75); Clem. *Paed.*, III.II (*ANF* 2:272).
39. Clem. *Prot.*, II (*ANF* 2:175–77, 182).
40. Clem. *Strom.*, VII.VI (*ANF* 2:528–29).
41. Clem. *Prot.*, X, XI (*ANF* 2:197, 202, 205).
42. Clem. *Strom.*, VII.1 (*ANF* 2:524); Clem. *Prot.*, IV (*ANF* 2:186).
43. Clem. *Prot.*, IV (*ANF* 2:188).
44. Ibid., VII (*ANF* 2:192–93).

Related to these convictions is Clement's contention that words are inadequate to describe the Being of God.[45] The great Apologist does insist, though, that God is love, a theme he emphasizes.[46] He speaks of God's great love to man, as a mother hen flying to her young that has fallen out of the nest.[47]

Greek philosophical assumptions seem to undergird much of Clement's views on this locus. God, he claims, is free of anger and impassable.[48] This is a sovereign God in Clement's view.[49] He is everywhere present and knows all things.[50] In His eternity, future, past, and present, are given in one instant.[51] Regarding the Trinity, Clement comes close to asserting something like it. He speaks of the Son as the energy of the Father. And he contends that God brought our love into being by giving His own (His Word) to all, so all was common. On this basis all should be shared in common and the rich should not have an undue share.[52]

Christology and Atonement

In Clement's view, the Word is the source of our being. He is both God and human.[53] In speaking of Christ, Clement claims that the Spirit is incarnate in His flesh.[54]

The flesh that Jesus assumed is construed by Clement as capable of suffering.[55] (There are some hints in these comments of the beginnings of the development of Alexandrian Christology and its concept of the *communicatio idiomatum*.) In the same spirit, Clement asserts that Christ was not handsome (a view shared by Tertullian and Origen).[56]

45. Clem. *Strom.*,V.XII (*ANF* 2:464).
46. Clem. *Prot.*, I,II (*ANF* 2:173, 178).
47. Ibid., X (*ANF* 2:197).
48. Clem. *Strom.*, IV.XXIII; II.XVI (*ANF* 2:437, 363).
49. Ibid., IV.XV (*ANF* 2:508).
50. Ibid., VII.VII (*ANF* 2:533).
51. Ibid., I.XIII (*ANF* 2:313).
52. Clem. *Paed.*, II.XIII (*ANF* 2:268).
53. Clem. *Prot.*, I (*ANF* 2:173).
54. Clem. *Paed.*, I.VI (*ANF* 2:220).
55. Clem. *Strom.*, VII.II (*ANF* 2:524).
56. Clem. *Paed.*, III.1 (*ANF* 2:272); cf. Or. *Cels.*, VI.LXXV (*ANF* 4:607); Tert. *Jud.*, XIV (*ANF* 3:172).

The eminent Apologist flirted with Docetism. He claims that true Gnostics (Christians) are subject to affections that exist for the maintenance of the body, such as hunger, thirst, etc. But in the case of Christ, it is ludicrous to think that His Body demanded it, Clement asserted. He did not eat because of bodily need, and is said to have been untroubled by pain and pleasure.[57]

Clement did criticize Marcion. The Tradition of the Church is older than the heresies, Clement argued, in support of his preference.[58]

Regarding the Work of Christ, the great Apologist opted for the Classic View of the Atonement. God in Christ is said to have conquered death, but is also portrayed as our Teacher.[59] But to this he adds a universal thrust, teaching that Christ is the Savior of all.[60] He emphasizes this point by going so far as to claim that Christ preached the Gospel to the righteous in Hades, those classed as having lived under faith. He is said to preach to those who departed before His advent.[61]

Creation and Anthropology

In speaking of God as the demiurge of all things, Clement essentially taught creation out of nothing.[62] Clement's dialogue with Gnosticism did not entail that he gave this worldview a free ride. He was especially critical of it when its proponents vilified created existence.[63] God is said to be in control of particular events.[64] But He does not wish to be involved in evil, though He is said to foretell the evil of suffering by the faithful.[65]

Regarding human nature, the great Apologist viewed our nature as constituted for fellowship with God.[66] We are a sweet savor to Him.[67] He

   57. Clem. *Strom.*, VI.IX (*ANF* 2:496).
   58. Ibid., VII.XVII (*ANF* 2:554–55).
   59. Clem. *Prot.*, I (*ANF* 2:172); Clem. *Paed.*, II.VIII (*ANF* 2:257). The reference to Christ as Teacher appears in Clem. *Prot.*, I (*ANF* 2:173).
   60. Clem. *Strom.*, VII.II (*ANF* 2:524).
   61. Ibid., VI.VI (*ANF* 2:490–91, 492).
   62. Clem. *Prot.*, IV (*ANF* 2:190).
   63. Clem. *Strom.*, VI.VII (*ANF* 2:493).
   64. Ibid., I.XI (*ANF* 2:312).
   65. Ibid., IV.XI (*ANF* 2:423).
   66. Clem. *Prot.*, X (*ANF* 2:200).
   67. Clem. *Paed.*, II.VIII (*ANF* 2:254).

posits our creation in the image of God, equated with reason. The most beautiful thing in man is said to be his mind.[68] Clement embraces a Greek-philosophical body-soul dualism when describing human nature. In that sense, human beings are the universe in miniature, making melody on this instrument to God.[69] But the African Father also insists that humans are created social and just.[70]

Justification and Sanctification: Deification

Clement characterizes faith as knowledge (in accord with his dialogue with Gnosticism).[71] Many methods of salvation are employed by God, he contends. Sometimes He admonishes, and sometimes He pities.[72] This dual emphasis on both grace and works in saving us is a consistent theme in Clement's soteriology. He speaks of two paths of salvation, works and knowledge (faith).[73]

There is but a single covenant in Clement's view, eternal, but benefitting people in different ways.[74] Tied to this, we find the great Apologist teaching predestination, at least implying it when he claims that before the foundation of the world we were destined to be in God, preexisting in His eyes.[75] Predestination is expressly taught.[76] Christ is also said to have been predestined.[77] But there is a suggestion that we can reject salvation; this frees God of blame.[78] On the other hand, Clement was open to the idea that when Christ descends into hell He preached to those who had not heard of His Coming (1 Pet 3:19–20).[79]

---

68. Clem. *Prot.*, X (*ANF* 2:199); Clem. *Paed.*, III.III (*ANF* 2:276).
69. Clem. *Prot.*, I (*ANF* 2:172); Clem. *Strom.*, II.XI; IV.III,V (*ANF* 2:359, 411, 413).
70. Clem. *Strom.*, I.VI (*ANF* 2:307).
71. Ibid., II.XI (*ANF* 2:358–59).
72. Clem. *Prot.*, I (*ANF* 2:173).
73. Clem. *Strom.*, IV.VI (*ANF* 2:416).
74. Ibid., VI.XIII (*ANF* 2:504).
75. Clem. *Prot.*, I (*ANF* 2:173); Clem. *Strom.*, IV.VII (*ANF* 2:417).
76. Clem. *Strom.*, VII.II (*ANF* 2:524).
77. Ibid., VI.IX (*ANF* 2:497).
78. Clem. *Prot.*, I (*ANF* 2:174); Clem. *Strom.*, I.I (*ANF* 2:300).
79. Clem. *Strom.*, VI.VI (*ANF* 2:490–92).

Clearly there is a grace emphasis here. Thus Clement teaches that Christians have been made righteous by Christ.[80] Christ saves us by His mercy, not by works of righteousness.[81] Sins are forgiven by God as if we had not done them, Clement says.[82] Salvation by grace alone is taught. For God is said to be revealed without price.[83] Christ freely bestows life on us. It is said to be monstrous for us to reject salvation.[84]

Even Justification by Faith, not by works, is expressly taught. The teaching of piety is a gift, Clement remarks. Faith itself is grace.[85] God supplies us with good even before we ask.[86] But faith is said to be necessary for repentance to transpire.[87] This grace orientation has implications for minimizing differences in who we are, even gender differences in the patriarchal society in which Clement lived. Thus he contends that there is no distinction between men and women in matters of salvation.[88]

The dual emphasis of grace and works that we have previously observed surfaces in the Apologist's affirmation of free choice (along with predestination).[89] Thus we are not saved against our will. Grace cannot penetrate those with an impure heart.[90] We must prepare ourselves to receive grace.[91] God saves those who turn to Him; we must be willing.[92] The Law is said to train up to piety. It can make some righteous. Sometimes Clement notes that it makes us fearful.[93] But the Command of the Lord is said to be the fountain of life.[94]

---

80. Clem. *Prot.*, XII (*ANF* 2:206); cf. Clem. *Strom.*, IV.XVI (*ANF* 2:428).
81. Clem. *Prot.*, I (*ANF* 2:172).
82. Clem. *Strom.*, IV.XXIV (*ANF* 2:437).
83. Clem. *Prot.*, X (*ANF* 2:198).
84. Ibid., XI (*ANF* 2:204); cf. ibid., I (*ANF* 2:174).
85. Clem. *Strom.*, I.VII (*ANF* 2:308).
86. Ibid., VII.VII (*ANF* 2:536).
87. Ibid., II.VI (*ANF* 2:353).
88. Clem. *Paed.*, I.IV (*ANF* 2:211).
89. Clem. *Strom.*, I.VI (*ANF* 2:353); cf. ibid., VI.VIII (*ANF* 2:496).
90. Ibid., VII.II,VII (*ANF* 2:524, 534); Clem. *Q.d.s.*, XV (*ANF* 2:595).
91. Clem. *Prot.*, IX (*ANF* 2:196); Clem. *Q.d.s.*, XXI,XLI (*ANF* 2:597, 603).
92. Clem. *Strom.*, VI.VI; VII.II (*ANF* 2:492, 524).
93. Ibid., I.XXVII (*ANF* 2:339); cf. ibid., II.VII; IV.IV (*ANF* 2:354-55, 411).
94. Ibid., II.XVIII (*ANF* 2:367).

There is no avoiding the fact that for Clement we must be worthy of grace.[95] Indeed, we may purchase love though our own resources.[96] Whoever endures to the end will be saved, he claims.[97] Christ's saving agency is said at these points to consist in His teaching us to live well.[98] Consequently Clement is very critical of those who repeatedly fall into sin and repent.[99]

Tied with this teaching of free will is a weaker view of sin. Probably reacting in part to Gnostic determinism, Clement claims that actions that are not the result of free will are not imputed to us.[100] Philanthropy and love are said to be natural affections.[101] On the other hand, at least at one point Clement prefigures the doctrine of Original Sin as he claims that even wishing to sin is sin. And yet only Gentiles, not Christians, are said to submit to concupiscence.[102] Sin, he claims, is an activity, not an existence.[103] And yet much like Augustine's view of Original Sin, Clement does refer to sin as desire.[104]

The integration of salvation by grace while asserting a role of works is made evident in Clement's apparent affirmation of deification. He writes, "yea, I say, the Word of God became man, that thou mayest learn from man how man may become God."[105]

In knowing God, Clement says elsewhere, we are made like God. In this form, we are beautiful, an unchanging beauty unlike passions.[106] We are assimilated to God.[107] In this sense we become knowledge itself. Love joins us to God.[108] Faith and works are needed to save, Clement contends; he even rejects salvation by faith alone at one point.[109]

---

95. Ibid., VI.X (*ANF* 2:538–39).
96. Clem. *Prot.*, IX (*ANF* 2:196).
97. Clem. *Strom.*, IV.IX (*ANF* 2:422).
98. Clem. *Prot.*, I (*ANF* 2:173).
99. Clem. *Strom.*, II.XIII (*ANF* 2:360–61).
100. Ibid., II.XIV (*ANF* 2:361).
101. Ibid., II.IX (*ANF* 2:357).
102. Ibid., IV.XII (*ANF* 2:424, 425); cf. ibid., VII.XII (*ANF* 2:543).
103. Ibid., IV.XIII (*ANF* 2:426).
104. Ibid., II.XIII (*ANF* 2:361).
105. Clem. *Prot.*, I (*ANF* 2:174) (in the Latin version): "Verbum, inquam, Dei homo factum, ut tu quoque ab homine discas, qua arto homo fier Deus possit." Cf. Clem. *Paed.*, I.XII (*ANF* 2:234).
106. Clem. *Paed.*, III.1 (*ANF* 2:271).
107. Clem. *Strom.*, II.XII (*ANF* 2:377).
108. Ibid., IV.VI (*ANF* 2:416); cf. ibid., IV.XVIII (*ANF* 2:429).
109. Ibid., VI.XIV (*ANF* 2:505).

In the same spirit the language of cooperation with God appears elsewhere. We are said to be drawn by the Father in order to become worthy, that the Holy Spirit inspires the faithful.[110] God is said to save those who turn to Him (works precede grace). He persuades the willing.[111] Predestination seems based on what we will do and love.[112] Elsewhere Clement claims that we must prepare ourselves to receive grace,[113] reiterating his claim that we may purchase love through our own resources.[114] We must be worthy of grace.[115] Alluding again to deification, Clement states that the godly man is destined to become divine, to arrive at final perfection.[116]

The Christian Life

Given this view of the role of works in Justification, it is not surprising that Clement would portray the Christian life in terms of obedience to the commandments.[117] He calls for imitating God through holy service, for imitating Christ.[118] In fact, he says that the Gospel commands us to put ourselves (slaying the old being) to death.[119] We are rescued from all passion.[120] This ethic of self-sacrifice leads the great Apologist to praise martyrdom.[121] For him this martyrdom is about love and confession.[122]

From these commitments it is only logical that Clement would offer detailed descriptions of the shape of Christian life. This includes, on his account, strictures on the use of costly household utensils; on eating certain kind of delicacies, hearty and undisciplined laughter, walking too fast, sneezing, and talking too much; on how to exercise, wear one's hair,

---

110. Ibid., VII.VII; V.XIII (*ANF* 2:536, 465).

111. Ibid., VI.VI; VII.I (*ANF* 2:492, 524).

112. Ibid., VI.IX (*ANF* 2:497).

113. See note 91 above.

114. Clem. *Prot.*, IX (*ANF* 2:196).

115. Clem. *Strom.*, VII.X (*ANF* 2:539).

116. Ibid., VII.I, II (*ANF* 2:524); cf. ibid., V.I; II.VII (*ANF* 2:446, 355).

117. Ibid., VII.IX; I.XXVII (*ANF* 2:538, 339); Clem. *Paed.*, III.XII; I. I (*ANF* 2:292–94, 209).

118. Clem. *Strom.*, I.I (*ANF* 2:301).

119. Ibid., VII.III (*ANF* 2:526–28).

120. Ibid., VI.IX (*ANF* 2:497).

121. Ibid., IV.IV, IX (*ANF* 2:411, 422).

122. Ibid. (*ANF* 2:412, 422).

and sleep; and on women's apparel.[123] Only women, not men, were to wear shoes, for women are tender and easily hurt. They should be entirely covered.[124]

Clement also advocates celibate relationships in marriage.[125] He warns against the love of money. Frugality is the Christian way to love, he asserts.[126] These ways of construing Christian life could reflect the influence of monasticism (perhaps Gnosticism) or even Stoicism on Clement's thought.[127] They are said to be ways of safeguarding the Word's power to bring us away from the external things of the body.[128] At least in the case of dietary structures, these practices also nurture health.[129] Poverty is advocated along with other rigorous rules for the practice of Christian life.[130] For example, Clement advocates light sleeping in order that we might get up in the night to thank God and sex for procreation only.[131]

Clement of Alexandria was also an early advocate of the doctrine of Christian perfection, calling readers to strive for it.[132] He depicts perfection as being with the Lord or as submission to Him.[133] To be sure, we cannot be perfect as the Father is, he claims. But we can strive for perfection by living blamelessly in obedience to the Gospel.[134] Much in the spirit of John Wesley's idea of perfection as a process, he refers to striving for perfection as best we can while still abiding in the flesh.[135] He equates perfection with

---

123. Clem. *Paed.*, II.I-VII; IIXI-XII; III.II,X,XI (*ANF* 2:237ff., 252, 264ff., 272, 283, 284-86, 288); cf. Clem. *Strom.*, VII.XIIff. (*ANF* 2:546ff.).

124. Clem. *Paed.*, II.XII; III.XI (*ANF* 2:267, 290).

125. Clem. *Strom.*, VI.XII (*ANF* 2:503).

126. Clem. *Paed.*, II.III; III.VII (*ANF* 2:248, 280-81).

127. See the discussion of this matter by Maier, "Clement of Alexandria and the Care of the Self," 737-38. Maier finds Clement more rigorous than the Stoics in seeking to put to death all desire.

128. Clem. *Paed.*, II.1 (*ANF* 2:237); Clem. *Strom.*, IV.V (*ANF* 2:413).

129. Clem. *Paed.*, II.1 (*ANF* 2:238).

130. Clem. *Strom.*, IV.V (*ANF* 2:413); Clem. *Paed.*, III.III (*ANF* 2:275ff.). Regarding rigorous rules for the practice of the Christian life, see notes 123-26, 129 above.

131. Clem. *Paed.*, II.IX-X (*ANF* 2:258, 259-63).

132. Clem. *Strom.*, II.VII; IV.XVIII,XXI; V.I; VI.VII; VII.II (*ANF* 2:355, 429, 433, 446, 494, 525).

133. Ibid., VII.X (*ANF* 2:539).

134. Ibid., VII/XIV (*ANF* 2:549).

135. Ibid., IV.XXI (*ANF* 2:433); cf. John Wesley, *Brief Thoughts On Christian Perfection* (1767), 2.

being Gnostic (part of his ongoing dialogue with Gnosticism).[136] In much the same spirit as in a dialogue with Gnosticism, he construes Perfection as passionlessness.[137] This also relates to Clement's concern that we crucify our sin.[138] In the same spirit he advocates martyrdom.[139] These commitments fit his claim that the Christian life involves divesting oneself of passions. He actually praises the Stoics in this connection.[140]

In one interesting, uncharacteristic discussion, Clement describes perfection as a kind of spontaneous behavior, more like a habit than obedience.[141] We do good, he asserts, only out of love, not for hope of reward. The perfect one does not seek to do good for his or her own advantage.[142]

In line with his monastic-like stress on simplicity in the Christian life, Clement claims that true beauty is love. He contrasts this with how Egyptians often sought to make themselves beautiful.[143] (Is this an important Word for today, an antidote to media pressures to seek beauty and to equate worth with it?)

Clement's last word on the Christian life is a helpful way to look at life, to see our faith as all-inclusive. Since God is always with us, he says, the true Gnostic (the Christian) may pray while cultivating fields, sailing, living everyday life.[144] As it was said in the African-American community: "Ain't no difference 'tween prayin' and ploughin.'"

Church

Clement maintained that the ancient catholic Church is alone in collecting the unity of the one faith.[145] For him the Church is not a place but the assemblage of the elect.[146]

---

136. Clem. *Strom.*, IV.XXI (*ANF* 2:433).
137. Ibid., IV.XXII; VII.XI (*ANF* 2:434-35, 541).
138. Ibid., VII.XI,XII (*ANF* 2:541-42, 543). Also see note 119.
139. Ibid., IV.IV (*ANF* 2:411).
140. Ibid., IV.V,XXIII; VI.IX,XIV (*ANF* 2:412, 437, 497, 505. But see note 127 above.
141. Ibid., VII.VII (*ANF* 2:536).
142. Ibid., IV.XX (*ANF* 2:434).
143. Clem. *Paed.*, III.I-II (*ANF* 2:271ff.).
144. Clem. *Strom.*, VII.VII (*ANF* 2:533).
145. Ibid., VII.XVII (*ANF* 2:555).
146. Ibid., VII.V (*ANF* 2:530).

Insofar as the Church collects all the saved Clement effectively taught that there is no salvation outside the Church.[147] This is related to his view of the Church as a nurturing Mother (we all need mothers) and a true Virgin.[148] Given his general stress on works and living the Christian life, it is not surprising that Clement had high expectations of the clergy. He insists that they must be righteous.[149] But he also taught the priesthood of all believers. Priests are said to be those who live purely.[150]

Sacraments

With Clement we can observe a high view of the Sacraments. Grace is remitted in these rites, he claims.[151] We are actually born again in baptism.[152] In accord with his concern with good works and in line with sentiment of his era, Clement taught that to be baptized was to break with the pagan way of life.[153]

Regarding the Eucharist, it is true that Clement distinguishes the Blood of Christ's flesh and the spiritual blood by which we are anointed. (A symbolic view of the Eucharist is suggested.) Wine is said to be the symbol of sacred blood.[154] But then he contends in a way as to suggest Christ's Real Presence and in line with the concept of deification that to drink Christ's Blood is to become a partaker of His immortality, as the Spirit is the energetic principle of the Word.[155]

Eschatology

In addition to his openness to the salvation of all, Clement posited degrees of glory in heaven.[156] The grades of offices in the Church are imitations of

---

147. Ibid., VII.XVII (*ANF* 2:555).

148. Clem. *Paed.*, I.VI (*ANF* 2:220).

149. Clem. *Strom.*, VI.XIII (*ANF* 2:504).

150. Clem. *Adum.* (*ANF* 2:572); Clem. *Strom.*, IV.XXV (*ANF* 2:438).

151. Clem. *Paed.*, I.V (*ANF* 2:215).

152. Ibid., I.VI (*ANF* 2:215, 216); Clem. *Strom.*, IV.XXV (*ANF* 2:439).

153. Clem. *Strom.*, II.XIII (*ANF* 2:361).

154. Clem. *Paed.*, II.II (*ANF* 2:245). For a similar assessment of Clement's teaching at this point, see Schaff, *History of the Christian Church*, 2:244.

155. Clem. *Paed.*, II.II (*ANF* 2:242).

156. Clem. *Strom.*, VI.XIIIf. (*ANF* 2:504ff.).

the heavenly glory. This is determined by the worth of one's belief.[157] Clement advocated a Realized dimension of Eschatology, claiming that those called to the Kingdom should walk worthy of the Kingdom.[158]

Social Ethics

Clement strongly objected to efforts men made to embellish their appearance with grooming, for in so doing they are said to act like women. He criticizes men acting effeminately by use of perfume.[159] The man who would be beautiful must adorn himself with the most beautiful thing he has, the mind.[160]

Luxury deranges everything, as it leads to decadent and lecherous living. It is better to have inexpensive things than costly ones, he claims.[161] We noted earlier how he commends frugality.[162]

Of course, Clement does not forbid wealth as long as it is not achieved unjustly and insatiably. There is nothing enviable about not having money.[163] Riches are a useful instrument. When used rightly they serve justice; they can be beneficial to one's neighbor.[164] One becomes poorer by not sharing wealth. Thus Clement adds that when making entertainment, the poor should be invited, for God cares for the poor.[165]

In this spirit, Clement advocates that all things be held in common. He writes, "God brought our race into communion by first imparting what was His own, when He gave His own Word, common to all, and made all things for all. All things therefore are common, and not for the rich to appropriate an undue share."[166]

---

157. Ibid., VI.XIII,XIV (*ANF* 2:505, 506).
158. Clem. *Paed.*, III.XI (*ANF* 2:291).
159. Ibid., III.III; II.VIII (*ANF* 2:275, 254-55).
160. Ibid., III.III (*ANF* 2:276).
161. Ibid.; Clem. *Prot.*, XII (*ANF* 2:206).
162. See note 126 above.
163. Clem. *Strom.*, III.VI (*ANF* 2:279-80); Clem. *Q.d.s.*, III, XI (*ANF* 2:591-92, 594).
164. Clem. *Q.d.s.*, XIV (*ANF* 2:595); Clem. *Paed.*, VI (*ANF* 2:279).
165. Clem. *Paed.*, II.1, IV (*ANF* 2:238, 248); Clem. *Strom.*, IV.VI (*ANF* 2:415).
166. Clem. *Paed.*, II.XIII (*ANF* 2:268): ". . . ἀλλ' οὐ πάντα συμψερετ. Παρήγαγς δὲ τὸ γένος, ἡμῶν ἐπι χοινωνιᾳ ὁ θεός, αὐτὸς τὸν ἑαυτοῦ πρότερος μεταδους χαὶ χοινὸν πᾶσιν ἀνθρώποις τὸν ἑαυτοῦ ἐπιχουρήσας Λόγον, πάντα ποιήσας ὑπὲρ πάντων. Κοινά ουν τὰ πάντα χαὶ μὴ πλεονεχτουντων οι πλούσιοι."

God dispenses food to all ungrudgingly, Clement asserts. His gifts are for the common good.[167] On wealth he writes elsewhere: "Riches are then to be partaken of rationally, bestowed lovingly, not sordidly, or pompously; nor is the love of the beautiful to be turned into self-love and ostentation."[168]

Righteousness is the true riches.[169]

Despite these commitments, Clement did not condemn slavery.[170] He expresses pity for boys in slavery and also laments prostitution. Yet he was open to the evil institution.[171]

Clement did demonstrate some consistency with his position on wealth; he warned against slaveholding to the point of having a bloated household. Having slaves can soften slaveholders, he contended, by feeding their basic appetites.[172]

Regarding male-female relationships, Clement displayed some openness to women's roles in his patriarchal context. He noted Christ's outreach to women. They can philosophize equally with men, Clement asserts.[173] But women were not to paint their faces to ensnare men or to dye their grey hair. Of course men too were to abide by certain strictures. They were not to be clean-shaven and should not shave their hair, unless it was curly.[174] The African Father spoke against ostentation in furniture and utensils, which along with use of oil he associates with effeminacy.[175] Indeed, although as we have seen Clement conceded that women might philosophize equally with men, men are said to be preferable at all things to women, unless men become effeminate.[176]

He also contended that Christians are a peaceful race. War is a work of the devil, he claimed.[177] Yet Clement was not an outright pacifist. He was

---

167. Clem. *Strom.*, II.XVIII,XIX (ANF 2:366, 369).

168. Clem. *Paed.*, III.VI (ANF 2:279): "Πλούτου τοίνυν μεταληπτίον αξιολόγως, καὶ μεταδοτίον ψιλανθρώπως οὐ Βαναύσως, οὐδὲ ἀλαζονικῶς οὐδὲ εχτριπιέον τὸ ψιλόχαλον εις ψιλαυτίαν χαὶ ἀπειροχαλίαν."

169. Ibid., (ANF 2:280).

170. Clem. *Strom.*, IV.VIII (ANF 2:420-21); Clem. *Paed.*, II.V (ANF 2:279).

171. Clem. *Paed.*, III.III (ANF 2:276).

172. Ibid., (ANF 2:275-76); ibid., III.IV (ANF 2:277-78).

173. Clem. *Prot.*, I.IV (ANF 2:211-12); Clem. *Strom.*, IV.VIII (ANF 2:420).

174. Clem. *Paed.*, III.XI (ANF 2:287-88); cf. ibid., III.III (ANF 2:275).

175. Ibid., II.III,VIII (ANF 2:247, 254).

176. Clem. *Strom.*, IV.VIII (ANF 2:420).

177. Clem. *Prot.*, III (ANF 2:183).

open to Christian participation in war, even exhorting Christians in the Egyptian army to be good soldiers.[178]

Contemporary Relevance

In many respects Clement seems a most relevant voice for today. We have already noted how his Theological Method prefigures several prominent modern theologians. His vision of a reality permeated by God's Word and its rationality and his vision of the Christian life as a striving for perfection, a giving up of worldly impediments, are visions that still inspire today.

---

178. Ibid., XI,X (*ANF* 2:204, 200).

4

Tertullian

QUINTUS SEPTIMIUS FLORENS TERTULLIANUS (160–250), known as Tertullian, was born of pagan parents in Carthage.[1] There are some traditions suggesting he may have been of the Berber tribe (and so as others of that background in that era, been Black), though the upper-class character of his background makes that less likely. He became a lawyer of considerable repute, converting to Christianity around 193 AD. He was the first of great theologians to work in Latin.[2] His work involved responding to common criticisms levelled against the faith in his day. But in his view it was ultimately the practice of the Christian life that rendered faith credible. This linked with his profound veneration of the saints and Martyrs: "The blood of Martyrs is the seed of Christians," he wrote.[3]

Jerome claims that Tertullian was a priest, though there is much controversy about this. There are three distinct periods in his theological development: (1) his Catholic period (197–206); (2) a Semi-Montanist period (206–212); and (3) his Montanist era (212–220). We will focus on the

---

1. Eus. *H.e.*, II.II.4 (*NPNF*² 1:106).

2. For this assessment of his significance, see Schaff, *History of the Christian Church*, 2:819. Regarding the possibility of Tertullian being Berber and so Black, see Surhone, Timpledon, and Marseken, *Tertullian*; Wilhite, *Tertullian the African*. The Berber influence on Tertullian's home region as a whole, though not in his home of Carthage, has been noted by Chadwick, *Early Church*, 89–93. For an example of Tertullian distinguishing himself from being Roman, as he refers to Rome as "that city of yours," see his *Ad. Nat.*, I.XIV (*ANF* 3:123).

3. Tert. *Apol.*, L (*ANF* 3:55): "Plures efficitmur, quoties metimur a vobis; semen est sanguis Christianorum."

first two periods, both because we want to examine what he has to offer the catholic heritage today, and also because there is not much available literature about the last period.[4]

We need to review the Monanist movement. It was a second-century apocalyptic movement that believed that the outpouring of the Spirit was on the horizon. It was characterized by rigorous ethical demands, notably in advocating stricter fasting practices.[5] In his Montanist period, Tertullian exhibited a stress on the Holy Spirit, which is very interesting since he wrote so little about the Spirit throughout most of his career.

He insisted that ministers do not have absolute authority, asserting that Christians must practice rigorous life-style standards. Spiritual men have true authority in the Church, he contended.[6]

Theological Method

Tertullian's overall agenda in his first periods was to combat heresy. He was especially preoccupied with Marcion (a Gnostic who had totally rejected the authority of the Old Testament and its God), Heraclitus (a pre-Socratic Greek philosopher) and a later contemporary Zeno. In his view these Christian leaders had been too dependent on Philosophy. The famed North African theologian is perhaps most well known for his comment in this connection that Jerusalem (the mother of the Gospel) and Athens (the home of philosophy) have nothing in common! Reliance on the world's wisdom leads to rash interpretations of the faith.[7] In regard to his stance against heresy, Tertullian may have been influenced by a famed older contemporary, Irenaeus.[8]

A core supposition of Tertullian's is that faith and reason are always in tension. Indeed, faith's claims are even more credible when they offend reason. For example, the Son of God's death is credible because it is absurd.[9] (Faith, then, is a kind of existential rebellion, a vision that closely parallels

---

4. Jer. *Vir. Illus.*, 53; Alexander Roberts and James Donaldson, "Introductory Note," in *ANF* 3:5, 10.
5. Eus. *H.e.*, V.XVI.7ff. (*ANF* 2:1:231–33); Tert. *Jejun.*, I (*ANF* 4:102).
6. Tert. *Pudic.*, XXI (*ANF* 4:99–100).
7. Tert. *Praescrip.*, VII (*ANF* 3:246).
8. S. L. Greenslade, "Appendix I," in Greenslade, *Early Latin Theology*, 65ff.
9. Tert. *Carn.*, V (*ANF* 3:525).

modern Existentialist thinkers like Søren Kierkegaard.[10]) God is hidden, the African father adds; yet He can be known through grace.[11]

In light of these suppositions, Tertullian adds that Truth and so the Gospel is simple. However, our pride leads us to alter it by adding to it.[12] This is what philosophizing leads us to do. For one who is seeking in this vein will never find.[13] Perhaps this is the reason why truth is so evasive for modern people, why we have come to disbelieve the reality of truth (preferring instead to speak of personal "values"). Maybe it is because we are ever seeking. Better to know nothing, he claims, if it leads us from the Rule of Faith.[14] Philosophy leads to heresy precisely because it is the introduction of something new on one's own authority.[15]

Constructively, Tertullian insists that Truth is only found in the true Church, for She alone has the authentic Tradition and the authority to interpret Scripture. As a result, in his interactions with the heretic Marcion, Tertullian found no need to defend the God of the Old Testament from the heretic's emasculation of Him. Rather than find the true God missing from the Hebrew tradition, Tertullian spoke of "two testaments" which are divine Scripture.[16]

Believing that the Truth had been given to the Apostles, for right doctrine in his view has its origins in the tradition of the Apostles, Tertullian was a man of tradition.[17] For him, the Creed or Rule of Faith (an ancient creedal statement said to be handed down to bishops from the Apostles) is the norm by which heresy is to be judged.[18] The content of the Rule of Faith is first and foremost Christological. Indeed, much of its content prefigures the later Nicene Creed.[19]

These convictions led Tertullian to assert the inerrancy of Tradition, a belief like the Western concept of the Ordinary Magisterium, that whatever is taught and practiced everywhere and throughout all time by

---

10. Kierkegaard, *Training in Christianity*, 83ff.
11. Tert. *Apol.*, XVII (*ANF* 3:31–32).
12. Ibid., XLVII (*ANF* 3:51–52).
13. Tert. *Praescrip.*, XI (*ANF* 3:248–49).
14. Ibid., XIV (*ANF* 3:249–50).
15. Ibid., XLII (*ANF* 3:264).
16. Tert. *Prax.*, XX (*ANF* 3:615); Tert. *Praescrip.*, X, XIX (*ANF* 3:248–49, 251–52).
17. Tert. *Praescrip.*, XX–XXI (*ANF* 3:252).
18. Ibid., I–III (*ANF* 3:243–44).
19. Ibid., XIII (*ANF* 3:249; cf. Tert. *Prax.*, II (*ANF* 3:598).

the consent of the bishops must be true. It is not likely the whole Church would have erred.[20]

When turning to Scripture, the African Father would have us read the Bible literally to affirm its miracles and the prophecies of the end time.[21] In sorting out how he understood Scripture and Tradition to relate, it is interesting to observe that though he saw a role for Tradition in a controversy over whether virgins must be veiled, his final appeal in that instance was to Christ and the Rule of Faith over Tradition. In a way suggestive of his later embrace of Montanism he refers to being carried on to perfection by the Holy Spirit.[22] Even here, it seems, though, that Scripture is never read apart from Tradition (expressed authentically in the Rule of Faith).

A similar point of view is evident elsewhere. Tertullian claims that heretics appeal to Scripture. But he then insists that they not be admitted to any discussion of Scripture. Why? Because from the African Father's point of view heretics do not own Scripture rightfully. He contends that only where true Christian teaching is evident will Scripture and its right interpretation be found.[23]

Making Sense of the Paradox of Faith

Tertullian was not blindly systematic in his commitment to the paradoxical character of faith (its tension with reason). Provided the essence of faith is not disturbed, he was open to seeking and discussing Truth. (But he does concede that it is better to remain ignorant for fear of coming to learn what you should not know.[24]) This sort of approach is a kind of ad-hoc apologetics not unlike the approach practiced in the modern era by Karl Barth.[25]

In the same spirit, Tertullian offered a kind of Ontological Argument for God's existence. He contends that the Name God has always existed, just as God has.[26] At one point he even asserted that nature suggests that God is its Creator. The existence of the natural, known to reason, was also affirmed

---

20. Tert. *Praescrip.*, XVI (*ANF* 3:255–56).
21. Ibid., XLIV (*ANF* 3:265; Tert. *Res.*, XXVI (*ANF* 3:563–64).
22. Tert. *Virg. vel.*, I (*ANF* 4:27).
23. Tert. *Praescrip.*, XV-XIX, XXXVII (*ANF* 3:250–52, 261).
24. Ibid., XIV (*ANF* 3:249–50).
25. Barth, *Church Dogmatics* III/2, 87–90, 198ff. See Boersma, "Logic of the Logos."
26. Tertullian, *Adversus Hemogenem* (ca. 200–206), III (*ANF* 3:478).

by Tertullian.[27] Another apologetic move made by the African Father was his appeal for toleration of Christianity by Roman citizens. They warrant such treatment inasmuch as Christians are not only no danger to the state, but can be useful citizens.[28]

Assessment of African Religious Practice

In his own way Tertullian was an early Historian of Religion. He does concede a resemblance between pagan cults and Christian rites, in the sense that Christians may participate in some ceremonies like marriage and family festivals, as long as the Christians present not participate in any sacrifices to the gods.[29] And idolatry, Tertullian adds, is the world's deepest guilt.[30]

God and Trinity

Unlike the Alexandrians, Tertullian contends that God is a body, has a substance. This is necessary for God to be Personal and in order to account for how God could create entities which exist and have a substance.[31] Like the Greek philosophers he also claims that God is impassable. In God is every place, yet He is not at a place.[32]

Tertullian's reflections on God lead him to affirm something like the Trinity before the doctrine was formalized. He was perhaps the first Latin writer to use the Latin term *trinitatis*.[33] He was critical of Praxeas, a Monarchian, who claimed that Father, Son, and Spirit are one and the same.[34]

Distinguishing the Father and the Son, Tertullian claims that the Word of God is a Second Person in God, with God even before being sent out, just as we think of words before uttering them.[35] The Father, he contends,

---

27. Tertullian, *De Spectaculis* (c. 198–200), II (*ANF*3: 80); Tertullian, *De Corona* (n.d.), VI (*ANF* 3:96).
28. Tert. *Apol.*, XXXff. (*ANF* 3:42ff.).
29. Ter. *Idol.*, XVI (*ANF* 3:71).
30. Ibid., I (*ANF* 3:61).
31. Tert. *Prax.*, VII (*ANF* 3:602).
32. Ibid., XXIX (*ANF* 3:626).
33. Ibid., III (*ANF* 3:599).
34. Ibid., I (*ANF* 3:598). For an elaboration on Praxeas's views, see *ANF* 3:598 n. 1.
35. Ibid., V (*ANF* 3:600–601).

acts by mind and thought, while the Son Who is in the Father's mind and thought gives effect and form to what the Father sees.[36]

The Son is said to emanate from the Father like the root puts forth the tree, the fountain the river, and the sun its rays.[37] The Father, then, is the entire substance, and the Son a derivation and portion of the whole. He also uses images of root and tree as well as fountain and river to distinguish Father and Son.[38]

In turning to the Holy Spirit's relation to Father and Son, Tertullian notes that as spirit comes from spirit, so the Holy Spirit is of God Who is Spirit.[39] Anticipating the Filioque he claims that the Spirit proceeds from the Father through the Son.[40] Also Tertullian refers to the Spirit as the apex of the sun and its rays, as the fruit of the tree and its roots, or as the stream of the river and its fountain.[41]

In a manner further anticipating the Trinity doctrine, Tertullian proceeds to distinguish Father and Son by virtue of "Personality," not of substance. Their distinction is between one who issues a command and one who executes it.[42] In this sense Father and Son are distinguished by their distinct Work.[43] They are distinguished in degree, not in condition, in form and not in substance, in aspect and not in power.[44] (It should be noted here that "substance" had legal, not metaphysical, connotation for Tertullian. "Substance," then, is the property and right that a person has to make use of it. The emperor may share his substance with a son. Likewise, God may share the divine substance with His Son.[45])

On the other hand, Tertullian taught that by their works we understand that Father and Son are One, presumably in the sense of sharing one Work.[46] Father and Son are always together, he claims. Only in the economy (dispensation) are they separated, with One on earth and the

36. Ibid., XV (*ANF* 3:611).
37. Ibid., VIII, XXII (*ANF* 3:603, 617).
38. Ibid.
39. Tert. *Apol.*, XXI (*ANF* 3:34).
40. Tert. *Prax.*, IV (*ANF* 3:599).
41. Ibid., VIII (*ANF* 3:603).
42. Ibid., IX (*ANF* 3:604).
43. Ibid., III (*ANF* 3:599).
44. Ibid., II (*ANF* 3:598).
45. Ibid., III (*ANF* 3:599).
46. Ibid., XXI (*ANF* 3:616).

other in heaven.[47] In a similar manner Tertullian referred to the Spirit as the substance of the Word and the Word as the operation of the Spirit, that that the Two are One.[48] He refers to their unity as a Monarchy executed though different persons.[49] The final form of the Trinity doctrine provides little not already endorsed by this great African father.

Christology and Atonement

Tertullian insisted a distinction between Jesus's Two Natures, including each with its own unique properties and operations.[50] He refers to Christ as having two "substances" (likely employing the term with the same legal connotations as his use of the term when he articulated his view of the Trinity). He claimed to believe this because it was absurd, that it must be true because it is impossible.[51]

Tertullian's own treatment of how the Two Natures relate is suggestive of the Antiochene rejection of *communicatio idiomatum*. For example, he contends that Christ alone, not Jesus, is the Son of God.[52] Another affirmation about Christ he makes is to proclaim His sinlessness.[53]

Regarding Christ's Work (the Atonement), Tertullian spoke of this Work as a satisfaction. Sometimes this satisfaction is made to God. But a role for the devil is recognized; he is the perverter of truth as manifested in the cults.[54] Other times the satisfaction is made to the devil.[55] This suggests either confusion or a Governmental Theory of Atonement (the concept of the created order as out of harmony due to sin and so in tension with God's Will, only set right by Jesus paying the penalty mandated by the created structures' need for justice).

---

47. Ibid., XXIII (*ANF* 3:619).
48. Ibid., XXVI (*ANF* 3:622).
49. Ibid., III (*ANF* 3:599).
50. Ibid., XXVII (*ANF* 3:623).
51. Ibid. (*ANF* 3:623–24).
52. Ibid., XIII (*ANF* 3:608).
53. Tert. *Marc.*, IX-X (*ANF* 3:329).
54. Tert. *Jud.*, XIII (*ANF* 3:171); cf. Tert. *Praescrip.*, XL (*ANF* 3:262–63).
55. Tert. *De Pudic.*, XXII (*ANF* 4:100).

Creation and Anthropology

The great African theologian was one of the first teachers of the concept of creation out of nothing, also teaching that it is a gradual work.[56] Given his ontology, angels are said to rank next to God.[57]

In his view of human nature, Tertullian did embrace the dualism of body and soul that characterized Greek philosophy. In fact he was willing to acknowledge parallels between biblical truth and philosophy, evident in their affirmation of the soul.[58] The soul is naturally Christian, he contended.[59]

Tertullian was also an advocate of Traducianism, the idea that the soul is sown in the womb. This understanding of the soul's origin entails that the soul is composed of a material substance.[60] It is a commitment that may reflect the influence of Stoicism on Tertullian's thought.[61] By contending that the soul is sown by its mother, Traducianism also opens the door to the development of the doctrine of Original Sin.

The African Father does relate human nature to Christology. He speaks of human beings created in the image of God in terms of Christ as the head of man. That is to say, Christ is the authority of human beings.[62]

Sin

Tertullian affirmed that Adam was the pioneer of our race and of our sin.[63] At this point his rhetoric is indeed most suggestive of the doctrine of Original Sin. He did have a strongly pessimistic view of human nature. He spoke

---

56. Tert. *Apol.*, XLVIII (*ANF* 3:53); Tert. *Hermog.*, XXI (*ANF* 3:489). For the continuing character of creation, see *Hermog.*, XXIX (*ANF* 3:493).

57. Tert. *Res.*, V (*ANF* 3:548).

58. Tert. *Anim.* (c. 210), I, II, IV (*ANF* 3:181, 182, 184).

59. Tert. *Apol.*, XVII (*ANF* 3:32).

60. Tert. *Anim.*, VII; XXXVIII (*ANF* 3:187, 217); also see ibid., III-IV, XXVII (*ANF* 3:183-84, 207-8).

61. For this suggestion, see Shortt, *The Influence of Philosophy on the Mind of Tertullian*; Seyr, "Die Seelen- und Erkenntnislehre Tertullians und die Stoa."

62. Tert. *Marc.*, V.VIII (*ANF* 3:445).

63. Tert. *Castit.*, II (*ANF* 4:51).

of an evil spirit marring human purity from birth.[64] As Augustine did later, Tertullian even refers to sin as concupiscence.[65]

On the other hand, the great Carthaginian theologian still taught that we have a free will.[66] He even distinguishes sins, between the real and the spiritual,[67] something like the Catholic distinction between mortal and venial sins.

Justification and Sanctification

Tertullian embodies the unsystematic mixture of grace and works we have observed in the other pre-Augustinian African church leaders. We have already noted that he taught free will, even in sin. And he viewed Christ as One Who comes to proclaim the Law.[68] It seems that the Gospel is a new Law.

Along the same lines, this African Father contends that the fear of God leads to religious obedience.[69] He also asserted that no one can be a Christian without persevering to the end, that we can lose our salvation.[70] You have to do something to be saved, it seems.

On the other hand, we find statements by Tertullian affirming that salvation is God's Work. Faith saves, he claims. But then he adds that the Rule of Faith is its Law.[71] The Lord is willing to pardon, he claims, but we must repent.[72] When he does speak of the Holy Spirit's role in repentance (and so of God's role in bringing us to repentance) it is only ambiguously affirmed.[73] In this context he does claim that God inaugurated repentance in Himself by rescinding His earlier threats prior to Jesus's redeeming work.[74] But except for references to grace, the priority of God's Work is

---

64. Tert. *Anim.*, XXXIX (*ANF* 3:219); Tert. *Marc.*, I.XXII (*ANF* 3:287). He teaches the transmission of Original Sin through intercourse in Tert. *Anim.*, III (*ANF* 3:177).

65. Tert. *Ad Uxor.*, I.IV (*ANF* 4:41); cf. Aug. *Civ.*, XIV.15-16, 13.3 (*NPNF*[1] 2:275-76, 246); Aug. *Perf. Just.*, XIII.31 (*NPNF*[1] 5:170).

66. Tert. *Marc.*, II.V (*ANF* 3:301); Tert. *Castit.*, II (*ANF* 4:51).

67. Tert. *Poenit.*, III.III (*ANF* 3:658-59).

68. Tert. *Praescrip.*, XIII (*ANF* 3:249).

69. Ibid., XLIII (*ANF* 3:264).

70. Ibid., III (*ANF* 3:243); Tert. *Idol.*, I (*ANF* 3:61).

71. Tert. *Praescrip.*, XIV (*ANF* 3:250).

72. Tert. *Poenit.*, VIII (*ANF* 3:663).

73. Ibid., II (*ANF* 3:657-58).

74. Ibid. (*ANF* 3:657).

not unambiguously affirmed. On at least one occasion he even claims that repentance is in man's power (though he does subordinate repentance to Baptism, which is sent by God).[75]

Yet Tertullian did affirm salvation by faith more unambiguously when he reminded us of the implications of our being taught by the Apostles. This Methodological conviction entails that we learn the faith with no effort on our own, as the Apostles themselves were taught by the Holy Spirit.[76] Indeed, prefiguring his move to Montanism, Tertullian expresses his belief in ecstatic experiences.[77]

This African Father stands out from many of his contemporaries in proclaiming grace in another way. Flying in the face of the earlier consensus he taught that even sin after Baptism may be forgiven.[78] But he also taught a very Law-oriented vision of the Christian life. He emphasized the Christian's separation from pagan society in order to escape contamination from its immorality and idolatry.[79] While doing apologetics Tertullian makes the case that Christians are enjoined to love enemies and not retaliate. As a result, he claims, Christians ought to receive milder treatment in the empire.[80]

Sacraments

Regarding the Sacraments, Tertullian seemed to affirm Christ's Presence in the rites. Baptism truly destroys death, he taught. It is a washing away of sins, admitting us to eternal life.[81] Yet Tertullian insisted that the Holy Spirit was not given in this Sacrament, but in the laying on of hands.[82]

Despite his grace orientation on forgiveness of sins after Baptism, Tertullian followed the consensus of his day in advocating the delay of the Baptism of children; in his view it is better we come to the Sacrament while growing up, lest their age lead them to fail to fulfill their promises.[83] We

---

75. Tert. *Bapt.*, X (*ANF* 3:674).
76. Tert. *Praescrip.*, VIII (*ANF* 3:247).
77. Tert. *Marc.*, IV.XXII (*ANF* 3:383).
78. Tert. *Poenit.*, VII (*ANF* 3:662–63).
79. Tert. *Idol.*, XXIV; IV (*ANF* 3:75–76, 62–63); on separation from society, see ibid., XVff. (*ANF* 3:70ff.).
80. Tert. *Apol.*, XXVII-XXVIII (*ANF* 3:45).
81. Tert. *Bapt.*, I (*ANF* 3:669); Tert. *Marc.*, I.XXVIII (*ANF* 3:293).
82. Tert. *Bapt.*, VIII (*ANF* 3:672–73).
83. Ibid., XVIII (*ANF* 3:678).

are baptized not to stop sinning, but in gladness for having forsaken it.[84] But the possibility of repeated repentance after Baptism for lapsing is not granted.[85] Baptism of heretics is also not recognized.[86]

Tertullian spoke of the Eucharistic bread as a "figure" of the Body of Christ.[87] But he also deemed the communicant to be feeding on the flesh and blood of Christ in the Meal.[88] In a policy most suggestive of Christ's Presence in the consecrated elements, he expressed distress if any of the Sacramental bread and wine fell to earth.[89]

Another interesting affirmation by the African Father is his openness to making eucharisitc offerings for the dead.[90] Tertullian was an advocate of the practice of Penance, which he contended contributes to satisfaction of sin.[91]

Church and Ministry

Tertullian calls the Church the Body of Christ.[92] It is a Mother, he asserted.[93] The Church is holy, he claimed, because Christ is Present in it.[94] He even went so far as to identify it with the Spirit, insisting it has the power of forgiving sin.[95] Yet even before joining the Montanists he insisted on the purity of the Church's members.[96]

---

84. Tert. *Poenit.*, VI (*ANF* 3:662).

85. Ibid., VII (*ANF* 3:662–63).

86. Tert. *Bapt.*, XV (*ANF* 3:676).

87. Tert. *Marc.*, III.XIX; IV.XL (*ANF* 3:337, 418–19). This language, especially in view of the affirmation of Christ's Real Presence in the sacrament (see below), may suggest affinities to the position of John Calvin regarding the Lord's Supper in his *Institutes of the Christian Religion*, IV.XVII.16–18, 31.

88. Tert. *Res.*, VIII (*ANF* 3:551); Tert. *Pudic.*, IX (*ANF* 4:83).

89. Tert. *Coron.*, III (*ANF* 3:94).

90. Ibid.

91. Tert. *Poenit.*, XII (*ANF* 3:665).

92. Tert. *Marc.*, V.XIX (*ANF* 3:471).

93. Tert. *Orat.*, II (*ANF* 3:682).

94. Tert. *Marc.*, V.XIX (*ANF* 3:471).

95. Tert. *Pudic.*, XXI (*ANF* 4:99).

96. Tert. *Idol.*, XI (*ANF* 3:67).

Regarding ministry, the African Father posits Apostolic Succession. No one is to be received as a preacher, he contended, unless authorized by churches of apostolic foundation.[97]

There are even hints of Roman primacy in Tertullian's thought (not surprising in view of the heavily Romanized Maghrib region in which he lived). Rome, he claimed, is an Apostolic church, which has had a bond of friendship with Africa.[98] Ultimately for Tertullian the authorities for faith are the Apostles, who are merely passive in passing down the teachings received from Christ.[99] Despite this high view of Ministry, Tertullian also affirmed something like the priesthood of all believers.[100] Later in his career when influenced by Montansim, he was even willing to allow laity to affirm priestly tasks when no priests were available.[101] In that context he undermined the Catholic Church's claim to forgive sin, claiming that the Church of the Spirit by means of the spiritual man forgives sin, not the Church consisting of bishops.[102]

Eschatology

Tertullian prefigures something like the concept of purgatory. Not all souls will go directly to heaven after death, he claims, but only martyrs. Everyone else goes to Hades to endure exile, expereinceng both suffering and comfort, depending on what they merit.[103]

Again prefiguring his Montanist pilgrimage, Tertullian taught that Christ's Second Coming was near.[104] But he prayed for its delay, that all might be saved.[105] The world will experience great cataclysms with the coming of Christ, he conteded.[106]

---

97. Tert. *Praescrip.*, XXVI; XX-XXI (*ANF* 3:260–61, 252).
98. Ibid., XXXVI (*ANF* 3:260).
99. Ibid., VI (*ANF* 3:246).
100. Tert. *Castit.*, VII (*ANF* 4:54).
101. Ibid.
102. Tert. *Pudic.*, XXII (*ANF* 4:100).
103. Tert. *Anim.*, LV, LVI, LVIII (*ANF* 3:231, 232–33, 234ff.).
104. Tert. *Apol.*, XXI (*ANF* 3:35).
105. Tert. *Scap.*, IV (*ANF* 3:106).
106. Tert. *Res.*, XXIV-XXV (*ANF* 3:563).

Social Ethics

We previously noted Tertullian's problems with Gnostic egalitarianism with regard to women's leadership.[107] Elsewhere he insisted that women should not be permitted to teach or baptize.[108] Interestingly, though, he did accept women prophesying in the Church, a practice that the Montanists permitted.[109] And he may well have edited the account of Perpetua's Martyrdom, indicating an openness to reserving the witness of women to the Gospel. He even referred to women in ecclesiastical orders.[110] Writing letters to his wife, he addressed her as his "best beloved fellow-servant in the Lord."[111]

Despite these trends in his thought and a high, almost sacramental view of marriage, Tertullian still regarded women as the devil's gateway, the cause of the fall.[112] He spoke of marriage as "legalized fornication."[113] In his lifetime marriage was not unequivocally identified with the Church, but was still seen largely as a Roman cultural rite.[114] Nevertheless he extolled Christian marriage, calling it "an honourable estate, for the increase of the human race."[115] He also championed monogamy on grounds that as there is one God there should be but one marriage.[116] He is one of the first early Christian writers to reject abortion.[117]

Tertullian rejected ostentatious attire by women.[118] He also advocated that women wear veils in public (and so in church, which by his lifetime was no longer a private sphere institution). Veils were a visible demonstration of concern for modesty and chastity. They were a way to manifest concern for shame. Tertullian was also offended by public honors bestowed on virgins. It was his view that femaleness was associated with submission

---

107. See chapter 2, note 1.

108. Tert. *Bapt.*, VII (*ANF* 3:677); Tert. *Mar.*, V.VIII (*ANF* 3:447); Tert. *Virg. Vel.*, IX (*ANF* 4:33).

109. Tert. *Anim.*, IX (*ANF* 3:188).

110. Tert. *Castit.*, XII (*ANF* 4:58).

111. Tert. *Ad Uxor.*, I.I; II.I (*ANF* 4:39, 44).

112. On women as the devil's gateway, see Tert. *Cult. Fem.*, I.I (*ANF* 4:14). He embraces a sacramental view of marriage in his *Ad Uxor.*, II.VIII (*ANF* 4:48).

113. Tert. *Castit.*, IX (*ANF* 4:55).

114. Tert. *Idol.*, XVI (*ANF* 3:71).

115. Tert. *Marc.*, I.XXIX (*ANF* 3:294).

116. Tert. *Monog.*, Iff (*ANF* 4:59ff.; Tert. *Castit.*, VIII (*ANF* 4:54–55).

117. Tert. *Castit.*, XII (*ANF* 4:57); Tert. *Apol.*, IX (*ANF* 3:25).

118. Tert. *Orat.* (n.d.), XX–XXII (*ANF* 3:687–88).

and passivity. In this connection he was concerned about ostentation in personal grooming of women, their use of makeup, jewelry, and hairstyle.

With these proposals he seemed to be aiming to restore Christian virtues distinct from expectations of the empire.[119] Tertullian did advocate the continued valuing of virgins, because he took the position that a woman stops being a virgin as soon as it becomes possible for her not to be one.[120]

These patriarchal sensibilities may not have been unrelated to Tertullian's view of the Trinity. For him, the Trinity was a monarchy, a single individual rule that can be administered by others without impairing the unity of that rule. He argues further that the Father exercises a single and sovereign rule which is administered by the Son and the Holy Spirit as His representative.[121] Such hierarchical thinking seems readily to lend itself to patriarchy.[122]

Tertullian taught the flock loyalty to the empire. God is said to have set the emperor on the throne.[123] If the empire suffers, Christians likewise suffer, Tertullian contended. Evil is delayed by the existence of the Roman Empire.[124] Nevertheless, the African Father opposed engaging in war.[125] However, he does note the participation of Christians in the Roman army. But in general Tertullian believed that no Christian should serve in the military, though he was willing to concede that one already in the military might remain in as long as they were not engaged in violent actions.[126]

The African Father took a similar stance on whether Christians might serve in government positions. Holding such offices was deemed possible as long as the low-level officer could avoid performing sacrifices to other deities and supporting their temples.[127] Despite his praise of the empire, Tertullian could not imagine a Christian state. He believed Christianity would never permeate society, as society and its institutions will always

---

119. Tert. *Virg. vel.*, XIV (*ANF* 4:35–36); Tert. *Cult. Fem.*, II.Vff. (*ANF* 4:21ff.). Also see Torjesen, *When Women Were Priests*, 165–72).

120. Tert. *Virg. vel.*, XI (*ANF* 4:34).

121. Tert. *Prax.*, III, XXIV (*ANF* 3:599).

122. We have already noted Tertullian's subordination of women to men with regard to church leadership. He seems to endorse Roman suppositions that women are not to appear in public. See his *Cult. Fem.*, II.XI (*ANF* 4:24). For this sort of argument, see Torjesen, *When Women Were Priests*, 162.

123. Tert. *Scor.*, XIV (*ANF* 3:647); Tert. *Apol.*, XXX, XXXII (*ANF* 3:42–43).

124. Tert. *Apol.*, XXXII, XXXIX (*ANF* 3:42–43, 46).

125. Tert. *Idol.*, XIX (*ANF* 3:73).

126. Tert. *Apol.*, XXXVII (*ANF* 3:45); Tert. *Coron.*, XI.1–7.

127. Tert. *Idol.*, XVII (*ANF* 3:71–72).

be riddled with idolatry.[128] In the same vein, he also repudiated Christian engagement in the theatre because of its corrupting influences regarding their idolatry, licentiousness, and evil customs or passions it excites.[129] Similarly, he renounces engagement in public events, including the circus and also Roman festivals.[130] Second marriages for him were akin to adultery.[131]

Tertullian opted for an economic vision that is most suggestive of both premodern (non-Roman) visions and also of today's more progressive economics. We should not seek wealth, he claims.[132] God is said to despise the rich and plead the cause of the poor.[133] The African Father rejects capitalism in the sense that he opposed usury (lending with interest).[134] Indeed, he advocated a return to the early Pentecost-era church polity with all things shared in common except wives.[135]

Significance for Today

Tertullian provides us with a model for modern theology in several significant ways. If we cannot totally embrace his soteriology with its stress on works, and ambiguity of grace, theologically conservative Christians are given a model for a venerable and intellectually credible model for doing theology today. And he also shows us that such a conservative theology can stimulate a progressive, but realistic social ethic too. We turn next to a very different style of ancient African theology.

---

128. Ibid., I, XV, XXIV (*ANF* 3:61, 70–71, 75–76).
129. Tert. *Spect.*, X, XV–XVI, XXIV–XXV (*ANF* 3:84, 86, 89).
130. Tert. *Apol.*, XXXVIII (*ANF* 3:45–46); Tert. *Idol.*, XV (*ANF* 3:70–71).
131. Tert. *Castit.*, IX, XI, XIII (*ANF* 4:55–57).
132. Tert. *Pat.*, VII (*ANF* 3:711–12).
133. Tert. *Marc.*, IV.XI (*ANF* 3:368–69).
134. Ibid., IV/XVII (*ANF* 3:372–73).
135. Tert. *Apol.*, XXXIX (*ANF* 3:46–47).

5

Origen

SURNAMED ADAMANTIUS (185–254), ORIGEN was reared by a Christian father who was martyred during the persecution of Septimus Severus. His father had apparently been a new convert, as Origen's name derived from the Egyptian god Horus. It seems that the son always had a burning desire for martyrdom, as he was only prevented from joining his father's faith in his youth when his mother hid his clothes so he could not leave the house on the day of the persecution.[1]

Because his father's property had been confiscated, Origen's family was in poverty, but he was taken in by a wealthy woman of Alexandria who effectively adopted him as a son. A brilliant student of Clement, he was subsequently appointed by Demetrius, the Bishop of Alexandria, to succeed Clement as master of the Catechetical School. Besides his brilliance, he was so fervent in his faith that he is reported to have fasted, walked barefoot, slept on the ground, and literally to have made himself a eunuch for the Kingdom of God.[2] His passion for martyrdom never cooled. He always spoke wistfully of the days of the Church's conflict with government, when being a Christian was no easy affair. Only the martyr has immediate knowledge of God, he contended.[3]

When trouble broke out in Alexandria in 215 Origen fled to Palestine. He was recalled due to irregularities in polity, for he preached in the Holy

---

1. Eus. *H.e.*, VI.II.2–6 (*NPNF²* 1:249–50).
2. Ibid., VI.II.7–VI.III. VI.VIII.2 (*NPNF²* 1:250–52, 254).
3. Or. *Mart.*, 3,33 (LCC 2:394–95, 414).

Land as a layman. In tension with Demetrius (his longtime friend, who had objected to his emaciating himself), presumably over whether the bishop should control the Catechetical School, in 230 he returned to Palestine, apparently deposed of his position at the school, and was ordained by the local bishops.[4] Origen proceeded to found a school in Caesarea in 231. He was imprisoned and tortured during the Decian persecution in 250 AD.

Origen's brilliance is unquestioned to this day, and well known during his lifetime. His impact on many of the desert monks and his students, like Theognostus of Alexandria and Pierius of Alexandria (as well as Gregory of Nyssa) was great. But his theological positions, as we shall observe, were also most controversial. Some of his positions were condemned posthumously by the Second Council of Constantinople in 553.[5]

Theological Method

Origen's creativity and brilliance were legend, but it also made (still makes) him most controversial. In the traditions of Clement and the Catechetical School of Alexandria, Origen worked with a Method of Correlation, interpreting the Bible allegorically, to seek its hidden meanings in different senses (moral or spiritual as well as literal meanings).[6] The biblical texts are not a representation of real things but they must be read spiritually and mystically. Even historical accounts may be written with allegorical purpose, Origen contends.[7]

The African Father suggests that the rich variety in Scripture is to be construed like a net, which gathers in many different fish in different segments of the net.[8] Philosophy then plays a role in articulating these hidden meanings. It provides sound insights for faith.[9] Origen claims that the Gospel

---

4. Eus. *H.e.*, VI.VIII.4ff.; VI.XXIII (*NPNF*² 1:254-55, 271). Also see David Brakke, "Origenism," in Harvey and Hunter, *Oxford Handbook of Early Christian Studies*, 349-50.

5. Second Council of Constantinople, *Anathemae adversus Origen* (553) (*NPNF*² 14:318-20).

6. Or. *Princ.*, Pref. 2-9; IV.1ff., 17-22 (*ANF* 4:239-41, 349ff., 366-72); Or. *Jos.*, VI.I, XXI.I. For his claim that all Scripture is inspired, see his *Ex.*, IV.II; *Jos.*, XX, II. Also consider Benedict XVI, *Church Fathers*, 39, 35-36.

7. Or. *Jos.*, 6:1; 21:1; Or. *Cels.*, IV.LI (*ANF* 4:520).

8. Or. *Matt.*, X.12 (*ANF* 9:420).

9. Or. *Cels.*, VII.XLII-XLIII (*ANF* 4:628); cf. ibid., Pref. 5 (*ANF* 4:396).

is beneath these hidden meanings. He construes it as the announcement of good things.[10]

Another way to make the point on Origen's grounds is to contend that yes, Scripture is inspired. But that precludes imputing unworthy meanings to the text, which is why we need allegorical interpretation.[11] In this vein Origen contends that not all the biblical accounts happened as reported.[12] This is an especially fertile insight for the theological community today, in view of what we know from the insights of historical criticism. Consequently, the Resurrection and references and other miracles are read as allegory by the African Father.[13]

This philosophical bent and inclination to interpret life with tools other than the biblical text's surface is not the whole story for Origen. Theology should not be based merely on reasoning and conjecture, he contended. Conclusions are more credibly upheld when based on Scripture. Thus he contended that both reason and Scriptural authority are the sources of theology.[14]

Further elaborating on these commitments, the great theologian contended that whatever is done in accord with the Will and Word of God cannot be contrary to nature. He also acknowledged that he shared the doctrine of the immortality of the soul with philosophers.[15] In addition, Origen contended that Plato learned his views from the Bible (This last comment, implying that God's Word both shapes philosophy while is itself shaped by philosophical insights, is suggestive of the modern Method of Critical Correlation.[16])

With regard to the question of possible dependence on the insights of his African homeland, we find one pejorative reference to Ethiopians in Origen's corpus, while citing the Septuagint's version of Ps 73:13, 17. In the end, he claims, the wicked will be clothed in Black bodies.[17] He was also

10. Or. *Joh.*, I.6, 7 (*ANF* 9:300).
11. Or. *Ex.*, IV.II.
12. Or. *Princ.*, IV.I.12 (*ANF* 4:360–61); Or. *Joh.*, X.4 (*ANF* 9:383).
13. Or. *Cels.*, V.23; VII.32 (*ANF* 4:553, 623–24).
14. Or. *Princ.*, I.V.4; I.VII.4 (*ANF* 4:258, 264).
15. Or. *Cels.*, V.23; III.LXXXXI (*ANF* 4:553, 496).
16. Ibid., VI.XIX (*ANF* 4:582). For the Method of Critical Correlation (the intiation of theological reflection with God's Word which both revises our philosophical conceptions but is itself shaped by philosophical analysis), see 33 n. 24.
17. Or. *Orat.*, 12 (*LCC* 2:301); Or. *Prin.*, II.X.8 (*ANF* 4:296).

critical of ancient Egyptian beliefs that some animals are gods. He rejects the idea that it does not matter what one calls the supreme God, that all worship Him.[18] But he does contend that there is a religious longing in human beings.[19] In fact, Origen even goes further, contending in a radical way that every rational creature receives a share of Wisdom (Christ), the Word of God, and the Holy Spirit.[20] Reason puts us in touch with God and the truths of Christian revelation! The African Father also posits the natural law.[21] But he adds that there is no clear knowledge of God without His help.[22]

There is an ecclesiastical strand to Origen's Methodological thinking. He implies that Tradition and the Magisterium are Scripture in action.[23] And he speaks of Church doctrine transmitted in orderly successions from the Apostles to the churches of the present.[24]

In addition, we should note Origen's Catechetical orientation. He endorses classical Christian affirmations. And then, again suggesting the modern Method of Critical Correlation, he adds that all knowledge calling men to good and the blessed life is derived from Christ.[25] That is only to be believed, he adds, when it in no way conflicts with the Tradition of the Church and the apostles. In fact, Origen even quotes a creed most suggestive of the contents of the Nicene Creed, which was to develop later.[26]

Of course, there is a strand of Origen's Theological Method that invited the sort of controversial commitments that led to much controversy and his posthumous condemnation. In his famous work *On First Principles*, he claimed that the Apostles delivered certain necessary doctrines in the plainest terms to all believers. But the grounds of their statements, he adds, they left to be investigated by those who should merit the higher gifts of the Spirit. There were other doctrines about which the Apostles kept silent, then, in order to provide others who came after them with an exercise.[27]

---

18. Or. *Cels.*, I.XX, LII (*ANF* 4:404, 419); Or. *Mart.*, 45–46 (*LCC* 2:425–26).
19. Or. *Mart.*, 47 (*LCC* 2:429).
20. Or. *Princ.*, II.VII.2 (*ANF* 4:285); Or. *Joh.*, II.6 (*ANF* 9:329).
21. Or. *Cels.*, I.IV (*ANF* 4:398).
22. Ibid., VII.XLII (*ANF* 4:628).
23. For such an assessment, see Benedict XVI, *Church Fathers*, 34.
24. Or. *Princ.*, Pref. 2 (*ANF* 4:239).
25. Ibid., Pref. 1 (*ANF* 4:239).
26. Ibid., Pref. 4 (*ANF* 4:240).
27. Ibid., Pref. 3 (*ANF* 4:239).

According to Origen, there is a kind of hierarchy of understanding among Christians. With these reflections the great African Apologist offers insight into how he would have us regard his controversial commitments. In his view they are not fixed doctrines, but opinions. But he does urge us to press on beyond the first Principles.[28]

God and Trinity

In keeping with the universal forms of Greek philosophy in which all expressions of a form (like Good, Truth, Beauty, etc.) are thought to be embedded, in Origen's thinking all things participate in God.[29] He is All in All.

God has no Body, Origen insists.[30] (This subsequently became a very controversial commitment among the monks of the desert.) He is not contained to any one place.[31] God is thus far and away better than our thoughts about Him. He cannot really be known, Origen adds, because our bodies weigh down our souls.[32] And yet the African Father taught that we can know something of the Father from our experience of creation.[33] This conviction seems related to Origen's contention that the Logos, the Reason of God, is immanent in creation. As the beginning of God's ways, in which every form of creation is implicit, it opens to all created realities the Wisdom of God. This Word, said to be an interpreter of the mind's secrets, is identified as female![34]

The African Father soon speaks of the Son and His eternity, but also of His (or Her) eternal generation by the Father. Then he goes on to refer to a difference in substance, claiming that the Father is the fountain and root of divinity.[35] He makes these points by claiming that the Son is eternally generated by Father, that Spirit and Son proceed from the Father, rather

---

28. Ibid., IV.I.8 (*ANF* 4:356–57).

29. Ibid., I.III.6 (*ANF* 4:253); Or. *Orat.*, XXIII.2 (*LCC* 2:283–84).

30. Or. *Princ.*, I.I.2,6; II.IV.3 (*ANF* 4:242, 243, 277); Or. *Cels.*, IV.XXXVII; VII.XXVII (*ANF* 4:513, 621).

31. Or. *Cels.*, VII.XXXIV (*ANF* 4:624).

32. Or. *Princ.*, I.I.5 (*ANF* 4:243); Or. *Orat.*, Int.I.1 (*LCC* 2:238).

33. Or. *Princ.*, I.III/1 (*ANF* 4:252).

34. Ibid., I.II.2 (*ANF* 4:246).

35. Or. *Princ.*, I.II.4, 6; I.III.5 (*ANF* 4:247, 248, 253) (see Greek text); Or. *Herac.* (n.d.), 124 (*LCC* 2:438–39).

like brightness is begotten from light.[36] In another way of making the point, original goodness is said to reside with the Father from Whom the Son and Spirit draw Its goodness into themselves.[37] In a Greek version of *On First Principles*, Origen is credited with writing that the Father is superior to the Son and the Spirit.[38] Elsewhere in Greek he even referred to the Logos as creature, though this is eradicated in the Latin version.[39] At another point he seems to have subordinated the Spirit to the Son.[40] But in yet another context he claims that the Spirit is Christ's Mother.[41]

In these cases, Origen seems to place more emphasis on the distinction between the Persons of the Trinity than on their unity.[42] However, he asserts that nothing in the Trinity can be called greater or less. As he adds in a way that seems to protect him from charges of Arianism, "Moreover, nothing in the Trinity can be called greater or less, since the fountain of divinity alone contains all things by His Word and reason, and by the Spirit His mouth sanctifies all things which are worthy of sanctification . . ."[43] In the same spirit in this treatise the great Apologist claims that "Wisdom was the beginning of the ways of God [presumably eternal] . . . forming beforehand and containing within Herself the species and beginnings of all creatures . . ."[44]

Creation, Sin, Providence, and Anthropology

Origen's treatment of Creation (positing two creations) has been most controversial. Of course, in his more Catechetical works he opted for God's creation out of nothing.[45] He even claimed that creation is eternal, in the sense

36. Or. *Princ.*, I.II.4, 11, 13 (*ANF* 4:247, 251).
37. Ibid., I.III.13 (*ANF* 4:251).
38. Ibid., I.III.5 (see Greek text in *On First Principles*).
39. Ibid., IV.I.28 (also see Greek text, the use of the Greek term κτίσμα).
40. Or. *Joh.*, II.6 (*ANF* 9:328).
41. Ibid. (*ANF* 9:329-30).
42. Or. *Herac.*, 124-26 (*LCC* 2:438-39).
43. Or. *Princ.*, I.III.7 (*ANF* 4:255): "Porro autem nihil in Trinitate majus minusve dicendum est, cum unius divinitatis fovis verbo ac ratione sua teneat universa, spiritu vero oris sui quae digna sun sanctifiane sanctificet . . ."
44. Ibid., I.II.3 (*ANF* 4:246): "Quali autem modo intelleximus sapientiam initium viarum Dei esse, et quomodo creata esse dicitur, species scilicet in se, et initia totius praeformans et continens ceraturae . . ."
45. Or. *Joh.*, I.18(3) (*ANF* 9:306-7).

that it has always been present in God's Wisdom.[46] The first creation, of the spiritual realm that then fell again, was followed by the material creation. The initial creation transpired as a result of the mind's departure from its original dignity, its place in the being of the God Who in eternity is All in All. Minds or souls are those dimensions of the Godhead "seized with weariness of the divine love."[47] In the second creation these fallen souls are placed in bodies. The soul, then, preexists receiving a Body.[48] This has been made necessary by the fact that those souls with excessive spiritual defects require grosser, more solid bodies.[49] Souls with the most inclination to evil become incarnate in humans. When truly evil they are clothed as animal bodies.[50] Great affinities to Eastern religions, notably to Hinduism, seem apparent here. Origen refers to the sun, moon, and stars as living beings, because they receive commands from God. They have souls.[51] The latter point is reminiscent of convictions of certain ancient African religions. Such affinities have obviously been most controversial in the history of Christian thought. But could they be timely today as Christian faith dialogues with modern String Theory and the supposition that the whole cosmos can be explained in a single, eternally valid formula in which all participate (the Theory of Everything)? But Origen makes clear that he does not believe that evil is caused by God.[52]

This understanding of Creation and human origins entails that an affinity exists between the human mind and the mind of God, of Whom the mind is an intellectual image. For this reason, if purified and separated from bodily matter, the soul would be able to perceive divine nature.[53]

Rooted in God as the spiritual creation is, for it is an emanation of God, it is not surprising that Providence (God's continuing rule) would be portrayed in this manner. Thus, Origen describes the plan of the universe as like rays emanating from the sun.[54] In this manner he tries to bring together divine providence and free will. Divine foreknowledge is not the cause of

---

46. Or. *Princ.*, I.IV.4 (only in Greek text, not in *ANF* 4).
47. Ibid., II.VIII.1, 3; II.X.6 (*ANF* 4:286, 288, 291–92).
48. Ibid., I.VII.4; I.VIII (only in Greek text, not in *ANF* 4).
49. Ibid., I.VIII; III.V.4 (*ANF* 4:266, 267, 342).
50. Ibid., (*ANF* 4:266–67).
51. Ibid., I.VII.3 (*ANF* 4:263).
52. Or. *Cels.*, VI.LV (*ANF* 4:598).
53. Or. *Princ.*, I.I.7 (*ANF* 4:245).
54. Ibid., I.I.6 (*ANF* 4:243).

human actions, he asserts.[55] Indeed, Origen even implies that in God's foreknowledge He hears those who will pray intelligently and arranges things accordingly for them.[56]

This entails that the activity of the Father and the Son is found in both saints and sinners from the fact that all rational beings are partakers of the Word. As was previously suggested, in that sense it may be said that all rational creatures have Christ.[57] Reason, it seems, reveals the first principles of Christian faith. Origen goes so far as to contend that every rational creature receives the Spirit.[58] Angels rule over human beings, he contended, with different angels functioning for different ethnic groups.[59] But this is not to say that there is only good in the world. Origen claims that the Lord tempts us from time to time with trials.[60]

Christology and Atonement

Long before the Church officially authorized the doctrine of Christ having Two Natures, Origen used such language.[61] In line with other proponents of the Method of Correlation of this era, the African Father described Christ as Logos, universal Reason.[62] She (the Logos) is called the Word, an interpreter of the mind's society.[63] (Note the female character of the Word posited here.) As universal Reason, Christ the Logos opens the meaning of the whole of creation.[64] He is identified as the true Power of God, that power in all things in which energy resides.[65] In another context Origen speaks of Christ as all Good Things, as the full manifestation of the Gospel.[66] He also posited a provocative way of making sense of the Incarnation. He compared

---

55. Or. *Orat.*, VI.3-4 (LCC 2:251-52).
56. Ibid., 4 (LCC 2:252-53).
57. Or. *Princ.*, I.III.6 (ANF 4:253-56).
58. Ibid., II.VII.2 (ANF 4:285).
59. Or. *Cels.*, V.XXVII (ANF 4:554).
60. Or. *Mart.* 6 (LCC 2:397).
61. Or. *Princ.*, I.II.1; Pref. 4 (ANF 4:245-46, 240).
62. Ibid, I.III.6 (ANF 4:253).
63. Ibid., I.II.2 (ANF 4:246).
64. Ibid., I.II.3 (ANF 4:246).
65. Or. *Joh.*, I.38 (ANF 9:317).
66. Ibid., I.11 (ANF 9:302-3).

it to a glowing iron, so that Jesus's human nature is fully assumed with the Word as heat penetrates an iron in a fire.[67]

Origen posited something like the *communicatio idiomatum*, the idea that whatever is said of Christ's humanity must be attributed to His divinity, and vice versa.[68] Thus in language most suggestive of his appropriation by Oriental Orthodox churches of Africa (called Monophysite churches), Origen contended that Christ's human nature became divine.[69]

The African Father seems to have taught a Classic View of the Atonement.[70] Jesus is said to have dissipated all the conspiracies of the demons. To this day invocation of His Name drives out demons.[71] He deceives the devil by His death.[72] The Body of Christ is said to have died, His soul gone to hell where He converted many, and His Spirit gone back to the Father.[73] Christ came as the Savior of all men, Origen asserts, an affirmation he develops fully in connection with his treatment of Justification and Eschatology.[74]

Justification and Sanctification: Deification

Origen was one of the first theologians to teach deification.[75] Souls become like God by sharing in His Logos.[76] In accord with the way in which this concept has been developed he also taught that we play a role in this process of being saved, affirming free will while conceding that we are influenced by spiritual power.[77]

The ambiguity about the relationship between grace and works that characterizes proponents of deification is evident in Origen's reflections.

---

67. Or. *Princ.*, II.VI.6 (*ANF* 4:283).

68. Ibid., II.VI.3 (*ANF* 4:282). But the African Father compromises this commitment in ibid., IV.I.31 (*ANF* 4:378), with regard to an unwillingness to attribute the Man Jesus's suffering to God and claim that He suffered too.

69. Or. *Cels.*, III.XXVIII (*ANF* 4:475).

70. Or. *Joh.*, VI.37 (*ANF* 9:378); Or. *Matt.*, XIII.8–9 (*ANF* 9:480–81).

71. Or. *Cels.*, III/XXIX, I.VI (*ANF* 4:475–76, 398–99).

72. Or. *Matt.*, XVI.8.

73. Or. *Cels.*, II.XLIII (*ANF* 4:448). Cf. Or. *Herac.* (n.d.), 138 (*LCC* 2:442).

74. Or. *Cels.*, IV.IV; II.XLIV (*ANF* 4:499, 448).

75. Ibid., III.XVIII (*ANF* 4:475).

76. Or. *Jer.* (n.d.), 14.10.

77. Or. *Princ.*, I.5; III.I.2 (*ANF* 4:250, 303); cf. Or. *Cels.*, I.IX (*ANF* 4:400); Or. *Orat.*, VI.2–4 (*LCC* 2:251–52).

He offers strong affirmations of grace at points, contending that everything given to human nature is given by God as grace, implying that nothing is purely natural.[78] The reception of the Holy Spirit makes us holy, Origen contends.[79] It is the Spirit Who makes all knowledge of the Father and walking in the way of Christ possible.[80] Only the saints are said to possess the Spirit in this way.[81] But then he claimed we have no forgiveness without forgiving our brother, that we are not granted righteousness until one believes, that we are not saved unless a confession of faith is made.[82] Or as he puts it elsewhere, we are saved by faith and conduct.[83] Origen speaks of a power we have been given to defeat temptation, but it depends on us to use it.[84] Christ is the true power of God which we share with Him as does anything in which energy resides.[85] While teaching an *apokatastasis*, as we shall note, Origen claimed that God judges and grants rewards based on merit concerning progress made in imitating and participating in God.[86]

Regarding sanctification and the practice of the Christian life, Origen claims that by partaking of the Holy Spirit one is made purer and holier; Origen refers to our making progress.[87] In the spirit of progress in the Christian life (again consistent with the teaching of deification) he refers to reaching perfection.[88] But he also claims that we need to endure to the end (exhibit perseverance), noting that the love of God and human weakness cannot dwell together in us.[89] The world is said to be a kind of trial, so by making use of freedom we might return to the rational being ever immersed in God.[90] Christ is said to overcome our weaknesses by overcoming the power of the

---

78. Or. *Rom.*, frag.
79. Or. *Princ.*, I/VIII.3 (*ANF* 4:266).
80. Ibid., I.III.4, 5–6 (*ANF* 4:253).
81. Ibid., I.III7 (*ANF* 4:254).
82. Or. *Orat.*, VIII.1 (*LCC* 2:255); Or. *Mart.*, 6 (*LCC* 2:396).
83. Or. *Herac.*, 140 (*LCC* 2:443).
84. Or. *Princ.*, III.II.3 (*ANF* 4:331).
85. Or. *Joh.*, 1.38 (*ANF* 9:317).
86. Or. *Princ.*, I.VI.2 (*ANF* 4:260–61).
87. Ibid., I.III.8 (*ANF* 4:255).
88. Ibid.; Or. *Matt.*, III.24 (*ANF* 9:464).
89. Or. *Mart.*, 39, 27 (*LCC* 2:421, 410).
90. Or. *Princ.*, II.VI.3; II.XI.5ff. (*ANF* 4:282, 298ff.).

devil and granting illumination.[91] We are to live lives of self-denial and cross-bearing, in every action denying ourselves to testify to Christ.[92]

Church

Origen termed the Church as the Body in which all the glory of God dwells. He did distinguish between the heavenly and earthly church, while insisting that on earth there was only the Sacramental, hierarchical institution.[93] As the soul vivifies and moves the body which of itself does not have the natural power of motion, so the Word of God arouses and moves the whole Body to actions befitting each individual member.[94] He also taught that outside the Church no salvation.[95] Apostolic Succession is likewise affirmed. But so is the priesthood of all believers.[96]

Sacraments

Origen taught infant baptism (a tradition supposedly derived from the apostles), but was ambiguous about Original Sin.[97] In harmony with developing ideas in the early Church, Baptism is construed as a washing of regeneration.[98] It is said to provide the gift of the Holy Spirit.[99] It is interesting, though (given his own autobiography), that Origen spoke of a baptism of martyrdom that can purify us of subsequent sins.[100]

In the Eucharist, the African Father distinguishes the earthly elements from the heavenly bread.[101] It is said to be a symbol of gratitude to

---

91. See note 72 above.
92. Or. *Matt.*, XII.24 (ANF 9:464).
93. Or. *Joh.*, 10.23 (ANF 9:403, 404); Or. *Orat.*, 31.5 (LCC 2:325).
94. Or. *Cels.*, VI.XLVIII (ANF 4:595).
95. Or. *Jos.* (n.d.), c.5.
96. Or. *Princ.*, IV.I.9 (ANF 4:357); he teaches the universal priesthood in his *Lev.* (n.d.), IX.
97. For his ambiguity about Original Sin, see Or. *Rom.* (n.d.), 5:1; regarding the affirmation of infant baptism, see Or., *Rom.*, 4:13; 5.9.
98. Or. *Cels.*, I.LXIV (ANF 4:425).
99. Or. *Princ.*, I.III.2 (ANF 4:252).
100. Or. *Mart.*, 30 (LCC 2:413).
101. Or. *Matt.*, III.898.

God.[102] He defends the faith from critics, associating the Eucharist with love-feasts.[103]

Eschatology: *Apokatastasis*

As already noted, universal salvation seems at least implied in Origen's thought by the fact that if any creature faded into oblivion God's goodness would be diminished. Or as he puts it, "it follows logically and of necessity that every existence which has a share in that eternal nature must itself remain for ever incorruptible and eternal, in order that the eternity of the divine goodness may be revealed."[104] Even demons are restored to their former rank.[105]

Origen also affirms the perfect restoration of the whole of creation, "the salvation of the conquered and the restoration of the lost . . ."[106] He refers to the Word prevailing over the entire rational creation and changing every soul into perfection.[107] Apparently even the devil is saved.[108] Yet Origen is not systematic about this commitment. He expressly rejects the salvation of all in his *Commentary On Romans* as well as in redressing attacks on this teaching in his *Letter to Friends in Alexandria*, and in *Against Celsus* speaks of the punishment of the wicked along with rewards to the good — a common principle of humanity.[109] Of course, there are other references to universal salvation.[110] And yet our subjection or conquering is not

---

102. Or. *Cels.*, VIII.LVII (*ANF* 4:661).

103. Ibid., I.I (*ANF* 4:397).

104. Or. *Princ.*, IV.I.36 (*ANF* 4:381): ". . . enjus solius intellectualis lucis universa creatura participium trahit, incorrupta est et aeterna, valde consequens et necessarium est etiam onmen substantiam quae aeternae illius natureae participium trahit, perdurare etiam semper, et incurruptibilem esse et aeternam. ut divinae bonitatis aeternitas etiam in ea intelligatur . . ."

105. Ibid., III.I.21 (*ANF* 4:327).

106. Ibid., III.V.7 (*ANF* 4:343-44): ". . . et sicut cum dicitur Filius Patri subjectus, perfecta universae creaturae restitutio declaratur, ita cum Filio Dei inimici dicuntur esse subjecti, subjetorum salus in eo intelligatur et reparatio peritorum."

107. Or. *Cels.*, VIII.LXXII (*ANF* 4:667).

108. Or. *Princ.*, III.VI.5 (*ANF* 4:346).

109. Or. *Rom.*, 8.9.4; Origen's fragments in Jer. *Rufin.*, II.18 (*NPNF*[2] 3:511-12); Or. *Cels.*, VIII.LII (*ANF* 4:659). For these insights I am indebted to Scott, "Guarding the Mysteries of Salvation," 353.

110. Or. *Princ.*, I.II.4 (*ANF* 4:247).

by force, but more by persuasion.[111] Thus, as we have noted, Origen taught that Christ descended to hell to win back some of the damned.[112] Given his endorsement of universal salvation, Origen must allegorize references to the fires of hell and punishment at the end of time. He regards them as antidotes purging the defects of the soul.[113]

Origen's speculations about the eschatological state led him to even more controversial reflections. He distinguished between God's kingdom (the blessed state of reason) from Christ's kingdom (pertaining to salvation and righteous works which follow).[114] This raised the question for the great Apologist of whether the body might pass away in God's kingdom, whether at that time the human soul might be swallowed up in the divine majesty.[115] At the consummation, he concludes, the souls and rational creatures will be released from their bodily prisons, but some will move more slowly than others, as angels may become demons and some demons who moved more rapidly to the blessed state may become angels or humans. And likewise some souls of men may make progress and become angels.[116] Nothing guarantees that the cycle might not repeat again.[117] And yet in one commentary he did reject the transmigration of souls to other bodies.[118] The ideal is that all become one. In the end God will be all in all.[119] When diversity first transpired though spiritual defects of minds and matter was created because it lent itself to fashioning diversity, God created such diversity that none would be lost so that the final aim of complete restoration of all might be achieved.[120] Salvation is nonexistent for Origen unless it includes every rational being.

---

111. Ibid., III.V.8 (*ANF* 4:344).

112. See note 73 above.

113. Or. *Princ.*, II.X.1,6–7 (*ANF* 4:293, 295–96); cf. Or. *Ex.*, 13.4, where he might regard the fires of hell as enlightening the soul and so able to function salvifically.

114. Or. *Orat.* XXV.1 (*LCC* 2:289).

115. Or. *Princ.*, I.VI.4 (*ANF* 4:262).

116. Ibid., I.VIII.4; I.VII (*ANF* 4:72, 65). This reference pertains only to the original Greek text.

117. Ibid., II.I.3; II.III.4 (*ANF* 4:269, 272–73); Or. *Cels.*,IV.LXVII (*ANF* 4:527).

118. Or. *Matt.*, XIII.1 (*ANF* 9:474–75).

119. Or. *Orat.*, 25.2 (*LCC* 2:290); Or. *Princ.*, III.VI.3 (*ANF* 4:345).

120. Or. *Princ.*, III.VI.5 (*ANF* 4:346).

Social Ethics

Despite his close relations with women in receiving the sponsorship of a wealthy Alexandrian woman, Origen argued that it was not proper for a woman to speak in a Christian assembly.[121] He taught the divine right of the emperor.[122] If Christianity grows, converting the barbarians, they would become law-abiding and civilized.[123] But Origen was willing to accept Christianity's counter-cultural elements, advocating for the validity of forming associations in opposition to existing laws for the sake of truth.[124]

The renowned Alexandrian Apologist was open to something like a just war, a war to protect the empire from external threats.[125] Life and activities of bees are a model here in his view.[126] Christians are good for the Roman Empire, Origen argues, for they help preserve order in the world. They also support the king with prayers.[127]

Origen allegorizes the service Christians are to display; Christian service to the empire must be a spiritual service. He himself opts for pacifism.[128] Origen concedes that such pacifism breaks with Jewish practice. The demise of the Jewish state brought an end to the need for physical force, he contends. The Old Testament references to these acts of violence are to be interpreted allegorically.[129]

What to Make of Origen's Controversial Commitments?

In a way, Origen himself answered this matter for us, in a manner that explains his continuing contribution to the life of the Church. He does not seem to demand that we (the Church as a whole) follow him in his speculations.

Essentially the African Father stayed in touch with the simple faith of the majority of the African faithful (the simple faith of many of the Martyrs he so admired). He claimed in his most speculative work that the Apostles

---

121. Or. *I Cor.*, 74.
122. Or. *Cels.*, VIII.LXVIII (*ANF* 4:665).
123. Ibid.
124. Ibid. I.1 (*ANF* 4:397).
125. Ibid., VIII.LXXIII (*ANF* 4:668).
126. Ibid., IV.LXXXII (*ANF* 4:533–34).
127. Ibid., VIII.LXX,LXXIII (*ANF* 4:666, 668).
128. Ibid., III/VIII; V.XXXIII (*ANF* 4:467–68, 558).
129. Ibid., VII.XXVI (*ANF* 4:621); Or. *Jos.*, XV.1.

delivered certain necessary doctrines in the plainest terms to all believers. The grounds of their statement they left to be investigated by such as should merit higher gifts of the Spirit. The silence they kept on other doctrines regarding details was done so in order to provide others who came after with an exercise.[130]

This is the status of the controversial commitments in Origen's thought. They are not fixed doctrines but opinions. He urges pressing beyond the first principles.[131] Should we join him, or remain with Tertullian and many of the Desert Fathers literally bound to the Rule of Faith?

---

130. Or. *Princ.*, I.I.3 (*ANF* 4:242–43).
131. Ibid., I.VIII.4 (*ANF* 4:266–67).

6

Commodianus

WE ARE NOT SURE about the dates (ca. 240/250) or of the personhood of this author of poems. But the tradition tends to regard him as a convert to Christianity who became a North African bishop.[1] In his poem *Instructions* he does indicate that he himself had been a wanderer in faith and that his parents had not been believers.[2]

Theological Method

The poem mocks the gods of the Roman pantheon and gods of other regions in the empire. These gods are said to be cruel and that genesis assigns fate to people.[3]

Creation and Sin

Commodianus refers to the origins of demons when angels sent to earth despised God's laws and were contaminated by interactions with beautiful women. As a result God would not allow them to be brought back from

---

1. Evidence for Commodianus being a convert to the faith is provided by Jer. *Vir. Ilus.*, XV (NPNF² 3:388).
2. Comm. *Instr.*, Pref. (ANF 4:203).
3. Ibid., III–XVI (ANF 4:203–6).

death. Consequently they now subvert many and are really the gods who are falsely worshipped in the empire.[4] But God still governs all.[5]

The people of the age who are addressed grieve Commodianus, for they have been blinded by things of the world. Human beings have been ruined by luxury and shortlived joys.[6] Commodianus refers to infants who may suffer, contending on the one hand they cannot be blamed. But suggesting the development of the doctrine of Original Sin, he notes that perhaps infants deserve the ills that befall them on account of the fault of their parents.[7] Sin is identified as lust, desire, which is concupiscent.[8] "The greedy survey of the eyes is never satisfied," Commodianus writes.[9] These reflections clearly set the stage for Augustine's subsequent development of Original Sin as concupiscence.[10]

Justification

The Law of God is said to teach the Resurrection and the hope of eternal life, as long as vain idols are not worshipped.[11] To one who lives well there is advantage in death. God is said to reward the innocent.[12] But the Cross is still perceived as foolishness for adulterous people.[13]

Commodianus speaks of a first Law that is the foundation of the second Law. It is needful only to believe in order to rise again.[14] There is a clear Pelagian-like construal of salvation as related to works in Commodianus's poem.

---

4. Ibid., III (*ANF* 4:203).
5. Ibid., XXXIV (*ANF* 4:209).
6. Ibid., XXII–XXIII (*ANF* 4:206–7).
7. Ibid., LI (*ANF* 4:213).
8. Ibid., LXIV (*ANF* 4:215–16).
9. Ibid., 216: "Occulorum acies numquam satiatur avara."
10. See above, 56 n. 65.
11. Comm. *Instr.*, II (*ANF* 4:203).
12. Ibid., XXIV, XXVII (*ANF* 4:207, 208).
13. Ibid., XXVI (*ANF* 4:210).
14. Ibid., XXV (*ANF* 4:207).

Sanctification

This African Father urges that we forsake all idols and be watchful for good things, rejecting luxury and the shortlived joys of the world.[15] Women are urged to be modest in dress and grooming.[16] We are directed to avoid strife and quarrels.[17] We are called to yearn for martyrdom, but not to desire the goods of others. Commodianus directs us in this way to how we can have martyrdoms without shedding blood. Conquering by good deeds is said to be a martyrdom.[18] We sense the impact or influence of monasticism on Commodianus's vision of the Christian life at this point. With implications for social ethics the faithful are instructed to share with the poor.[19] Lending for interest is also rejected.[20] Christian life is described as a daily war with lust and luxury.[21]

Ministry and Church

Commodianus understands the minister to be an example.[22] He speaks of the Church in the female gender, as Mother.[23]

Eschatology

The African Father describes a first resurrection of the faithful and a day of judgment. The righteous will be separated from those receiving a second death.[24] Again an emphasis on the contribution of works to salvation is implied. But there is also a cosmic dimension to his vision, a premillennialist perspective that teaches that Christ will come again after a time of great tribulation.[25]

---

15. Ibid., XLVI, XVI, LVII (*ANF* 4:212, 207, 214).
16. Ibid., LIX (*ANF* 4:214).
17. Ibid., LXVII (*ANF* 4:216).
18. Ibid., XLVIII, LXII (*ANF* 4:212, 215).
19. Ibid., LXI, LXII, LXXI, LXXVIII (*ANF* 4:215, 217, 219).
20. Ibid., LXV (*ANF* 4:216).
21. Ibid., LXIII (*ANF* 4:215).
22. Ibid., LXVIII (*ANF* 4:216).
23. Ibid., XLIX (*ANF* 4:212).
24. Ibid., XLIV–XLV (*ANF* 4:212).
25. Ibid., LXVI (*ANF* 4:216).

Little as we know of Commodianus the main reason for identifying him as an African bishop has been the significant similarities between his thought and that of the next African Father we consider, Cyprian of Carthage. But his life provides a significant model for ministry today. We find in him a faith-quester, a talented artist (his poem that we have been examining exhibits the best and worst elements of the diction of the North African Latin dialect), administrative gifts (serving as a bishop), and yet for all these talents a man with a traditional, earnest faith. He reminds us that talent need not estrange us from the flock.

7

Cyprian of Carthage

CAECILIUS CYRPIANUS, ALSO KNOWN as Thascius (d. 258), was originally a highly educated teacher of rhetoric or a lawyer, reportedly skilled in magic. He was a wealthy man who converted to Christianity in midlife, around 245 AD. It is said at that time he gave away all his wealth.[1]

Cyprian succeed Donatus as Bishop of Carthage in AD 249. But he soon needed to flee due to a persecution undertaken by Decius. He fled because he believed, as a consequence of a dream, that it was necessary for him to hold the flock together, which mandated his survival. This persecution had been a shock, as the African church had not experienced persecution since Tertullian's time.[2]

Upon Cyprian's return from the persecution after it eased, he opposed easy reconciliation with Christians who had lapsed. There was much support in the African church, though, for a laxer policy of restoration. Five presbyters who opposed Cyprian on personal grounds, led by Novatus, secured the support of numerous Confessors (those who had confessed the faith in face of the persecution) who were persuaded that their spiritual authority as Confessors enabled them to guarantee forgiveness of the lapsed. They began by giving the penitents letters of recommendation to the bishop and later demanded restoration. Cyprian needed to respond

---

1. Jer. *Vir. Illus.*, LXVII (*NPNF*² 3:376). Also see Isichei, *History of Christianity in Africa*, 35–36.

2. See Cypr. *Ep.* (n.d.), II (*ANF* 5:280).

with an assertion of Episcopal authority, which he did in his treatise *The Unity of the Catholic Church*.

Meanwhile in Rome, which had lost its bishop, Pope Fabian, to martyrdom during the persecution, elected Cornelius as his successor, much to the chagrin of Roman presbyter Novatianus. He objected to the decision and secured his own consecration as bishop objecting to any departure in church discipline from the older norm that excommunicated apostates for life. For him, Cornelius was not the true bishop of Rome. This was the beginning of the Novatian heresy.[3]

Cyprian recognized the authority of Cornelius. Eventually the Novatian Party spread to Africa where it made common cause with opponents of Cyprian advocating more laxity. These Novationists went so far as to appoint a rival bishop to Cyprian in Carthage.

As the Novatian controversy was developing in Rome a similar debate over the degree of rigorous guidelines for readmitting the lapsed in Africa found Cyprian taking a position which basically sided with the Roman movement, holding that reconciliation should occur only after a suitable period of penance. Rebaptism of schismatics was demanded, arguing that no one outside the Church could validly administer Sacraments.[4] Cyprian himself had been under fire with this group, though, for fleeing persecution.

In response to these dynamics, Cyprian called a Synod to resolve the controversy. It decreed that (1) those who had purchased certificates of exemption from the persecution without actually having offered a sacrifice could be immediately readmitted to the Church; (2) those who had sacrificed would only be readmitted on their deathbeds or when a persecution provided them with opportunity to prove sincerity of their repentance; and (3) those who had sacrificed and showed no repentance would never be readmitted. (See *The Unity of the Catholic Church*, which rejected Novatian, though not the Synod itself, which did not remain in session long enough to do so.[5])

---

3. For an ancient account of these developments, see Eus. *H.e.*, VI/XLIII (*NPNF*[2] 1:286–90). For Novatian correspondence, see Cypr. *Ep.* (250), XXVII/XXXIV-XXX (*ANF* 5:306–11).

4. Cypr. *Ep.* (256), LXXII/LXXIII.1–2 (*ANF* 5:379–80); ibid. (255), LXX/LXXI.1–2 (*ANF* 5:377); ibid. (n.d.) LXIX.8, 3 (LCC 5:155–56, 152); Cypr. *Unit. eccl.*, 11,6 (*ANF* 5:425–26, 423).

5. Cypr. *Ep.* (252), LV/LI.17, 20 (*ANF* 5:331, 332); ibid. (251), XLII/XXXIX.7 (*ANF* 5:318–19); Cypr. *Unit. eccl.* (*ANF* 5:421–29).

The next controversy Cyprian faced grew out of the Novatian schism. Many African Christians soon sought restoration with Cyprian's See. The question was what to with those who had been baptized by Novatians, whether that was a valid Baptism. Tensions developed between Cyprian and Stephen the new bishop of Rome on this issue. He had agreed that the Novationists were outside the Church. But he also believed that Baptism could be conferred outside the Church through the invocation of the Trinity and the use of water. Thus rebaptism was not necessary. By contrast, Cyprian refused to acknowledge the validity of Sacraments outside the Church.

The whole of the African episcopate supported Cyprian in this controversy, refusing to yield to the Bishop of Rome. Cyprian clearly respected Rome and recognized that its See possessed considerable authority. But he stopped short of allowing it to have jurisdiction over other bishops.[6] The controversy ended with the death of Stephen. But then Valerian undertook a new persecution, ordering that bishops, presbyters, and deacons should offer a sacrifice to the Roman gods. When Cyprian refused, he was martyred.[7]

Theological Method

Because of the occasional nature of his writings, it is difficult to identify Cyprian's Method and view of biblical authority. His rigorous standards for Christian living, even to the point of rejecting church membership for actors and distrust of secular literature, made him a spiritual heir of Terullian. He was generally critical of the social and moral decline in the Roman Empire of his day.[8] He seems to have been somewhat charismatic, guided by visions and other revelations.[9] On this basis, and given his lack of dialogue with the prevailing philosophical currents of his day, it seems valid to conclude that he operated with similar Orthodox Methodological assumptions.

---

6. Cypr. *Ep.* (252), LIX/LIV.14 (*ANF* 5:344).

7. Pon. *Sanct. Caecili.*, 16–17 (*ANF* 5:273–74). For more details, see S. L. Greenslade, "Cyprian: General Introduction," in Greenslade, *Early Latin Theology*, 116–17.

8. Cypr. *Ep.* (ca. 249), II/LX (*ANF* 5:356). For more details, see Greenslade, "Cyprian: General Introduction," 117; Cypr. *Donat.*, 6 (*ANF* 5:277); González, *Story of Christianity*, 1:88–89.

9. Cypr. *Ep.* (250), XI/VII.3–7 (*ANF* 5:286–87).

Church and Ministry

Given his confrontations with heresy, it is not surprising that many of Cyprian's writings would address these topics. Heresy is perceived as an attack on Christ's teaching, an attempt to steal people away from the Church and shatter its unity. Thus, heresy is the work of the devil.[10] It thus became crucial for the Bishop of Carthage to clarify what the Church is.

Cyprian stresses the unity of the Church. She (note the female gender attributed to the community) has a unity like Christ's seemless garment.[11] She is said to be "a single whole, though she spreads far and wide into a multitude of churches as her fertility increases."[12] The Bishop of Carthage further elaborates on this point, writing, "We may compare the sun, many rays but one light, or a tree, many branches but one firmly rooted trunk. When many streams flow from one spring, although the bountiful supply of water welling out has the appearance of plurality, unity is preserved in the source."[13]

Cyprian defines the Church as the Bride of Christ, who is undefiled and chaste.[14] We have already noted that She is also identified as our Mother.[15] Efforts must be made to retain this purity, that her good dispositions not be corrupted.[16] Consequently, Cyprian advocates separating from heretics.[17] But this is not in violation of his concern with the Church's unity, for in the bishop's view it is not the Catholics who have withdrawn from the heretics. It is the heretics who have withdrawn from the Church.[18]

Given this view of the Church and concern to refute heresy, it is not surprising that a concern for church order and clerical authority would be highlighted by Cyprian. It is the job of bishops to uphold the Church's unity.

---

10. Cypr. *Unit. eccl.*, 3 (*ANF* 5:422).

11. Ibid., 5–6 (*ANF* 5:423).

12. Ibid.

13. Ibid., 5 (*ANF* 5:423): "Quomodo solis multi radii, sed lamen unum; et rami arboris multi, sed robur unum tenaci radice fundatum; et cum de fonte uno rivi plurimi defluunt, numerositas licet diffusa, videatur exnndantis copiae largitate, unitas tamen servature in origine."

14. Ibid., 6 (*ANF* 5:423); Cypr. *Test. Ad. Jud.*, II.Test.19 (*ANF* 5:523).

15. Cypr. *Ep.* (256), LXXIII/LXXII.24 (*ANF* 5:385); Cypr. *Unit. eccl.*, 6, 23 (*ANF* 5:423, 429); Cypr. *Laps.*, 2, 9 (*ANF* 5:437, 439).

16. Cypr. *Ep.* (252), LIX/LIV.15 (*ANF* 5:345).

17. Cypr. *Unit. eccl.*, 9 (*ANF* 5:424).

18. Ibid., 12 (*ANF* 5:425).

Every act of the Church is controlled by them.[19] God has ordered the office of bishop through apostolic succession, he argues.[20]

In fact, Cyprian goes so far as to contend that there is no Church apart from bishops. The Church is in the bishops. It is one and united by the glue of priests who are in harmony with each other.[21] If you are not with the bishop, you are not with the church.[22] All this is rooted in the ancient unity of the Apostles, as all were as Peter, partners.[23] But Cyprian insisted that Peter's primacy is an affirmation of the unity of the Church, not of Roman supremacy. Rome is the chief church from whence priestly unity has its source.[24] The Seventh Council of Carthage, led by Cyprian, rejected the idea of a single bishop over the bishops[25]—hardly surprising given Cyril's confrontation by Bishop Stephen of Rome. Despite this high view of the ministry, Cyprian was open to the power of the people in choosing worthy priests.[26] And in that connection he lamented how bishops in his day were more concerned with their business interests than with the poor.[27] The stress on the unity of the Church is not just an idea for Cyprian, but must be actual and cannot be broken.[28] The Church is said to shed forth Her united rays over the whole earth.[29]

With no valid ministry outside the Church among the heretics, and so no valid Sacraments or Gospel, Cyprian asserts his famed phrase: No salvation outside the Church.[30] The result of this conviction manifested itself in his view of the heretics he encountered and also his view of the Sacraments.

---

19. Ibid., 5 (*ANF* 5:422-23); Cypr. *Ep.* (250), XXXIIII/XXVI.1 (*ANF* 5:305).

20. Cypr. *Ep.* (250), XXXIIII/XXVI.1 (*ANF* 5:305); ibid., LXIX.5 (LCC 5:153).

21. Ibid. (254), LXVI/LXVIII.8 (*ANF* 5:374-75); cf. ibid. (n.d.), XXXIII (LCC 5:145).

22. Ibid., LXVI/LXVIII.8 (*ANF* 5:374-75).

23. Cypr. *Unit. eccl.*, 4-5 (*ANF* 5:422-23); Cypr. *Ep.*, LXXIII/LXXII.7 (*ANF* 5:381).

24. Cypr. *Ep.*, LIX/LIV.14 (*ANF* 5:344); ibid. (256), LXXV/LXXIV.16 (*ANF* 5:394). See Mark Edwards, "Introduction," in Edwards, *Optatus: Against the Dontatists*, xxiv.

25. Seventh Council of Carthage/Cyrpian of Carthage, *Quod Bapt.* (*ANF* 5:565).

26. Cypr. *Ep.* (257), LXVII.3 (*ANF* 5:370).

27. Cypr. *Laps.*, 6 (*ANF* 5:438).

28. For this assessment, see Greenslade, "Cyprian: General Introduction," 120.

29. Cypr. *Unit. eccl.*, 5 (*ANF* 5:423).

30. Cypr. *Ep.* (378), LXX/LXXII.21 (*ANF* 5:384); Cypr. *Unit. eccl.*, 6 (*ANF* 5:423).

Sacraments

Given his insistence on the necessary role of the Church in salvation, Cyprian was led to argue against the acknowledgment of the baptisms of repentant Novatians.[31] To acknowledge such baptisms would undermine the Church's unity.[32] Elsewhere the argument was made that no heretic possesses the Spirit and so cannot give it in Baptism.[33] Cyprian's rejection of the validity of heretical baptism seems to have been a change in earlier practice.[34]

Cyprian claims that grace is given in Baptism.[35] He appears to teach here and elsewhere that the remission of sins is granted in Baptism, that we are actually regenerated in the Sacrament.[36] We must be baptized, Cyprian asserts, in order to be saved.[37] We draw from this Sacrament as the Spirit flows freely not restrained by limits. We are given the power to quench our poisons. Something like living your baptism seems taught in this letter to Donatus.[38]

Cyprian proceeded to teach infant baptism, implying an affirmation of infant sin, or even Original Sin. Reference is made to the infant being born after the flesh according the Adam, having contracted the contagion of the ancient death.[39] Elsewhere he claims that our glory shall be filth and worms.[40]

Cyprian also endorsed an openness to alternatives to the traditional practice of baptismal immersion. He contended that the manner of the Sacrament, whether by immersion or not, was indifferent.[41] He also referred to a laying of hands in the Sacrament as a means by which the Spirit is

---

31. Cypr. *Ep.*, LXX/LXXII.1–2 (*ANF* 5:379–84); ibid., XXXIII.8 (*LCC* 5:155–56); Cypr. *Unit. eccl.*, 11,6 (*ANF* 5:424–25, 423).

32. Cypr. *Ep.*, LXIX.3 (*LCC* 5:152).

33. Ibid., 10 (*LCC* 5:156–57).

34. Ibid., LXX/LXXII.23 (*ANF* 5:385).

35. Ibid., (n.d.), LXIV/LVIII.3 (*ANF* 5:354); Cypr. *Donat.* (n.d.) 5 (*ANF* 5:276).

36. Cypr. *Donat.*, 4 (*ANF* 5:276); Cypr. *Ep.*, LXXIV/LXXII.6 (*ANF* 5:388); Cypr. *Test. Ad. Jud.*, III.Test.25 (*ANF* 5:542); Cypr. *Op. et Eleem.*, 2 (*ANF* 5:476).

37. Cypr. *Test. Ad. Jud.*, II.TestII.25 (*ANF* 5:542).

38. Cypr. *Donat.*, 4 (*ANF* 5:276); cf. Cypr., *Op. et Eleem.*, 2 (*ANF* 5:476).

39. Cypr. *Ep.* (n.d.), LXIV/LVIII.3–4 (*ANF* 5:354).

40. Cypr. *Test. Ad. Jud.*, II.Test.II.3–4 (*ANF* 5:533); Cypr. *Ep.* Ix (250). 2 (*ANF* 5:290); Ibid. XI (250). 2 (*ANF* 5:292).

41. Cypr. *Ep.*, LXIX.11 (*LCC* 5:157).

received.[42] In worship there seems to have been a place for "holy kisses" in his view (especially for Confessors).[43]

The Lord's Supper

The Eucharist is portrayed by Cyprian as a Sacrifice.[44] In a manner much like John Calvin held in the sixteenth century, the Bishop of Carthage taught Jesus's Presence in the Sacrament, but not for unbelievers.[45] Yet elsewhere he seems to have affirmed the more characteristically African/Eastern position in contending that heretics are guilty of the Body and Blood of Christ, even partaking unworthily.[46] We partake unworthily apart from the expiation of sin in Confession.[47]

In Cyprian's view the Eucharist was a Sacrifice in the sense of commemorating the Good Friday sacrifice.[48] He also contended that the Sacrament bespeaks unity among Christians. For Christ's Body, the bread, is made from many granules, and the wine is pressed from many grapes.[49] This stress on unity seems to include infants, who were apparently communed in Cyprian's diocese.[50]

Confession

Cyprian also seems to have advocated use of the rite of Confession.[51] He urges its use, along with satisfaction and remission affected by the priest.[52] In view of the controversy caused by the Novatians, he especially urges that those who escaped persecution by purchasing certificates or who

---

42. Ibid., LXIII/LXII.9 (*ANF* 5:381).
43. Cypr. *Laps.*, 2 (*ANF* 5:437).
44. Cypr. *Ep.* (253), LXIII/LXII.4,14 (*ANF* 5:359, 362).
45. Cypr. *Domin. Orat.*, 17,18 (*ANF* 5:452); Cypr. *Ep.* (253), LXII.2 (*ANF* 5:359); Cypr. *Laps.*, 25 (*ANF* 5:444); cf. John Calvin, *Institutionis Christiane Religionis* (1559), IV.XVII.33, 40, 47–50.
46. Cypr. *Laps.*, 15 (*ANF* 5:441).
47. Ibid.
48. Cypr., *Ep.*, LXIII/LXII.14,17 (*ANF* 5:362, 363).
49. Ibid., LXIX.5 (*LCC* 5:153).
50. Cypr. *Laps.*, 26 (*ANF* 5:444).
51. Cypr. *Ep.* (250), XVI/IX.2 (*ANF* 5:290).
52. Cypr. *Laps.*, 29 (*ANF* 5:445).

lapsed confess their sin.⁵³ In a manner most consistent of his appreciation of something like Original Sin, Cyprian asserts that some sinning will not be lacking before God.⁵⁴ For we are born into a situation of committing frequent and continual offense, he contends.⁵⁵

God and Christ: Providence

It may be that there is no salvation outside the Church in Cyprian's view. But the Christ, not the Church, is the agent of salvation in Cyprian's view. In fact, the Church could not be upheld without God.⁵⁶ Who is Christ for Cyrpian? First we need to consider the Father's relation to the Son and His Providential actions.

The Father Who sent is to be known first, Cyprian contends, and then the Son Who was sent. There is no hope of salvation, he asserts, unless they are known together.⁵⁷

Regarding Providence, the Bishop of Carthage claimed that all the good that we have comes from God, and so we should not boast.⁵⁸ We must not boast of anything since what we have is a gift of God.

This apparent strong doctrine of Providence entails that heresies are regarded as permitted by God.⁵⁹ In proportion to His effect as a Father, God is always indulgent, but by reason of His Majesty as Judge He is to be feared.⁶⁰ Reference is made to God's great patience towards the guilty and innocent.⁶¹

Practical theologian that he was, Cyprian does not deliberate too much on the Nature of Christ. Christ is said to be the Wisdom of God.⁶² His divinity and humanity were also affirmed, along with the Virgin Birth.⁶³ The prioritization of Father over Son already noted leads Cyprian to assert that God is

---

53. Ibid., 28–29 (*ANF* 5:445).
54. Cypr. *Op. et Eleem.*, 18 (*ANF* 5:481).
55. Cypr. *Bono Pat.*, 4 (*ANF* 5:485).
56. Cypr. *Laps.*, 20 (*ANF* 5:443).
57. Cypr. *Ep.*, LXXIII/LXII.17 (*ANF* 5:383).
58. Cypr. *Test. Ad. Jud.*, II.Test.4 (*ANF* 5:533).
59. Cypr. *Unit. eccl.*, 10 (*ANF* 5:424).
60. Cypr. *Laps.*, 35 (*ANF* 5:446–47).
61. Cypr. *Bono Pat.*, 4–5 (*ANF* 5:485).
62. Cypr. *Unit. eccl.*, 1 (*ANF* 5:421); Cypr. *Test. Ad. Jud.*, II.Test.1 (*ANF* 5:515).
63. Cypr. *Test. Ad. Jud.*, II.Heads.10; I.Test.10 (*ANF* 5:515, 519–20).

Christ's Creator.[64] But he does not seem to intend to lapse into Arianism here, but to be referring to the Father as Creator of Christ's humanity. In referring to the Son as Word he equates Him with the *sermo Dei* (a Latin phrase giving the concept Logos a liturgical, not philosophical context).[65]

Speaking of that humanity, Cyprian notes its vulnerability. Christ is said to have felt hunger and starvation. By his habitual forebearance He preserved and exemplified His Father's patience.[66] This seems consistent with Alexandrian Christology, as it implies that the Father is made vulnerable by the Son's vulnerability (that whatever is said of one of Christ's Natures is attributable to the other). In the same vein, Cyprian also speaks of God suffering.[67]

Atonement

Cyprian tends to construe Christ's Atoning Work as a Sacrifice offered to the Father (Satisfaction Theory).[68] But language like the Classic View appears when he refers to Christ conquering death for us.[69] He goes so far as to claim that God alone can bestow pardon, for we are justified by faith.[70]

Justification and Sanctification

Although Cyprian contends that we are not saved outside the Church, Christ is our Savior in his view. Christ dwells in the faithful, the Bishop of Carthage writes.[71] But side by side his affirmation of justification by faith, the African bishop claims that merits and works are of avail with Christ.[72] Thus in a manner similar to virtually everyone we have considered, it is not Christ alone or grace alone which saves. To be saved we need to keep

---

64. Cypr. *Ep.*, LXXIII/LXII.18 (*ANF* 5:384).

65. Cypr. *Test. Ad. Jud.*, II.3 (*ANF* 5:516). For this understanding of "sermo," see Pelikan, *Emergence of the Catholic Tradition (100–600)*, 187.

66. Cypr. *Bono Pat.*, 6 (*ANF* 5:485).

67. Cypr. *Laps.*, 20 (*ANF* 5:443).

68. Cypr. *Ep.* (253), LXIII/LXII.14 (*ANF* 5:362); ibid. (250), LXIII.LXII.16 (*ANF* 5:363); Cypr. *Laps.*, 17 (*ANF* 5:442).

69. Cypr. *Ep.* (250), X/VIII (*ANF* 5:287–88).

70. Cypr. *Laps.*, 17 (*ANF* 5:442); Cypr. *Mort.* (252), 3 (*ANF* 5:470).

71. Cypr. *Domin. Orat.*, 3 (*ANF* 5:448).

72. Cypr. *Laps.*, 17 (*ANF* 5:442).

His Commandments, Cyprian argued.[73] Reference is made to the Law of the Gospel. Christ is identified as Teacher, as an example.[74] He is said to instruct for the future what we ought to do, but (with a testimony to grace) also to pardon for the past when we erred.[75] In Cyrpian's view nothing prevents the whole human race from equally enjoying God's generosity.[76]

We have already observed how a testimony of grace is evidenced in Cyprian's thought in his strong affirmation of Providence and his claim that we should boast of nothing since nothing is our own.[77] But a strong legalist bent surfaces elsewhere as the African bishop claims we can propitiate God by works, that we will receive a reward for such works.[78] Each individual earns merits.[79] In these passages, works clearly contribute to justification.

With regard to the practice of the Christian life, Cyprian turns to the Law and Commands of God for guidance, typical of everyone we have examined.[80] He urges letting our light shine in good works.[81]

We are directed by Christ through God's example to live in certain ways (overcoming jealousy and practicing patience as well as modesty).[82] We can be like Christ, we are told; we are to imitate Him.[83]

Cyprian also exhorted martyrdom.[84] For him it is related to his understanding of Christian life as hatred of the world.[85] Tied with this was his critique of the worship of idols.[86] Other expectations include practicing charity, caring for the poor and needy, not swearing or cursing, not taking

---

73. Cypr. *Unit. eccl.*, 2,15 (ANF 5:421, 426).
74. Cyrpr. *Op. et Eleem.*, 8–9 (ANF 5:478); Cypr. *Bono Pat.*, 16 (ANF 5:488).
75. Cypr. *Ep.*, LXIII/LXII.17–18 (ANF 5:363).
76. Cypr. *Op. et Eleem.*, 25 (ANF 5:483).
77. Cypr. *Test. Ad. Jud.*, III.Test.4 (ANF 5:533).
78. Cypr. *Op. et Eleem.*, 5,24 (ANF 5:477, 483); cf. Cypr. *Test. Ad. Jud.*, III.Test.1 (ANF 5:531).
79. Cypr. *Ep.* (252), LV/LI.27 (ANF 5:334-35).
80. Cypr. *Unit. eccl.*, 6 (ANF 5:423).
81. Ibid., 27 (ANF 5:429).
82. Cypr. *Zel. et Liv.*, 1, 3 (ANF 5:491, 492); Cypr. *Domin. Orat.*, 4 (ANF 5:448).
83. Cypr. *Idol. Van.*, 15 (ANF 5:469).
84. Cypr. *De Exhort. Martyr.* (ANF 5:496ff.).
85. Cypr. *Laud. Mart.*, 28 (ANF 5:586).
86. Cypr. *De Exhort. Martyr.* (ANF 5:497-500).

usury, but visiting the sick and not telling tales.[87] His strict lifestyle commitments included his conviction that acting is a disgraceful career.[88]

In this connection, Cyprian stresses perseverance in the faith, claiming that in completing grace we may attain the Crown.[89] He is said by contemporaries to have begun to be perfect, largely evidenced in his monastic-like practices of selling all possessions and giving to the poor.[90] Yet he claimed that Christians are engaged in a struggle between body and spirit (simultaneously saint and sinner).[91] In fact, his description of the sinful condition is most compatible with Augustine's later formulations: "The mind of man is besieged, and in every quarter invested with the onsets of the devil, scarcely at each point meets the attack and scarcely resists it. If avarice is prostrated, lust springs up. If lust is overcome, ambition takes its place. If ambition is despised, and exasperates, pride puffs up . . ."[92]

We have already noted that related to the practice of the Christian life is Cyprian's view of martyrdom. On one hand he seemed to claim that it was a ticket to salvation, as he contended that Martyrs not yet baptized are saved. For they have been baptized with a baptism of blood.[93] But on the other hand he also taught that martyrdom is to no avail outside the Church, as there is no salvation outside the Church.[94] Even Confessors might lapse into heresy.[95] And he also contended that martyrdom is not the only way to salvation.[96] God is said to prove us by temptation, even postponing martyrdom sometimes that we be tried. They free us from desire for the world.[97]

On the other hand, we find occasions when the stress on grace manifests in the way in which the Christian life is described. Our good works

---

87. Cypr. *Test. Ad. Jud.*, II.TestII.1, 3, 13–15, 48–49, 103–10 (*ANF* 5:531, 533, 536–37, 546, 555).

88. Cypr. *Ep.*, II/LX (*ANF* 5:356).

89. Ibid. (n.d.), XII/VI.2 (*ANF* 5:28 Cypr. *De Exhort. Martyr.*, 8 (*ANF* 5:500).

90. Pon. Sanct. *Caecili.*, 2 (*ANF* 5:268); Cypr. *Bono Pat.*, 5 (*ANF* 5:485); cf. Cypr. *Domin. Orat.*, 33 (*ANF* 5:456).

91. Cypr. *Domin. orat.*, 16 (*ANF* 5:451).

92. Cypr. *Mort.*, 4 (*ANF* 5:470): "Obsessa mens hominis et undique diaboli infestatione vallata vix occurrit singulis, vix resistit. Si avaritia prostrata est, exsurgit libido: si libido compressa est, succedit ambitio . . ."

93. Cypr, *Ep.*, LXXIII/LXXII.22 (*ANF* 5:385).

94. Cypr. *Unit. eccl.*, 13–14 (*ANF* 5:425–26).

95. Ibid., 20 (*ANF* 5:427).

96. Cypr. *Laud. Mart.*, 27 (*ANF* 5:586).

97. Ibid., 15 (*ANF* 5:582–83).

are said to happen because they are inspired by Christ or by divine mercy.[98] In our spiritual struggles we receive the help of God.[99] The spontaneity of good works is affirmed along with a commitment to exhorting works. In Cyprian we see again, characteristic of Easter and ancient African thinking, this rich tension and harmony between grace and works.

Social Ethics

Cyprian taught that the Church is to care for the poor and the sick, widows and orphans.[100] He also criticized the vanity of military life. Violence and Christian mysteries are in conflict, he claimed.[101] The Bishop of Carthage critiqued many of the temptations of urban life, including attendance at theaters and the gladiatorial games of the empire.[102] Yet he seems not to have viewed all military conflict as immoral, as he prayed for the success of imperial armies in warding off enemies.[103] He also clearly expected men to maintain beards.[104]

While praising virginity and celibacy, he contended that women ought not to be adored in a worldly fashion. They are directed to stay silent in church.[105] But this patriarchy is balanced with some liberation themes. Slavery is critiqued (for all have the same lot of life and death) as well as the poor treatment of slaves.[106] He would have Christians give alms to the poor and would have the Church care for the poor.[107] It is like giving to God, Cyprian claims.[108]

---

98. Cypr. *Op. et Eleem.*, 1 (*ANF* 5:476).

99. Cypr. *Domin. orat.*, 14 (*ANF* 5:451).

100. Cypr. *Ep.* (c. 251), VII/XXXV (*ANF* 5:314); Cypr. *Test. Ad. Jud.*, II. Test.II. 113 (*ANF* 5:556).

101. Cypr. *Donat.*, 11,14 (*ANF* 5:278–79).

102. Ibid., 6–8 (*ANF* 5:277).

103. Cypr. *Dem.*, 20 (*ANF* 5:463).

104. Cypr. *Laps.*, 6 (*ANF* 5:438).

105. Cypr. *Test. Ad. Jud.*, II.Test.II.32, 36, 46 (*ANF* 5:543, 544–45, 546).

106. Cypr. *Dem.*, 8 (*ANF* 5:460).

107. Cypr. *Op. et Eleem.*, 2, 7, 20 (*ANF* 5:476, 477, 489); Cypr. *Domin. orat.*, 20 (*ANF* 5:453); Cypr. *Laps.*, 11 (*ANF* 5:440); Cypr. *Ep.* (251), VII/XXXV (*ANF* 5:314).

108. Cypr. *Domin. orat.*, 20 (*ANF* 5:453).

Again, in Cyprian's case we observe a rich diversity in his thought. And so like many of the African Fathers we are again challenged with a familiar question. Is this unsystematic richness a strength for ministry today or an untenable confusion? The Church historically has affirmed Cyprian's insistence on the indispensable role of the Church in Christian life. This seems a necessary affirmation today to stem the tide of individualistic spirituality which so plagues the West.

8

Dionysius, Bishop of Alexandria

DIONYSIUS (D. CA. 264) seems to have been a native of Alexandria. He was definitely a student of Origen. Before becoming bishop in 232, he served as Origen's successor in Alexandria's Catechetical School.

A contemporary of Cyrpian of Carthage, he was compelled like his colleague to flee his episcopacy during the persecution of Decius. He claims to have fled not by his own choice but by divine Providence, and that while in exile he and those who fled with him did confess their faith.[1] Great turmoil in Alexandria resulted over what to do with those Christians who had lapsed, and upon return Dionysuis was faced with these challenges. His surviving corpus is very occasional, addressing various pastoral issues.

Theological Method

There is some lack of clarity on this point regarding Dionysius's thinking. The closest we seem to get to something like Origen's allegorical method comes when Dionysius contended that "before the Incarnation it was a time to keep the letter of the Law; but it was a time to cast it away when the truth came in its flower."[2] But then in a manner more characteristic of

---

1. Dion. *Ep.*, X.1.4 (*ANF* 6:103–4, 104–5).

2. Dion. *Ap. Ekk.*, I.III (*ANF* 6:114): "Ἠχαὶ, τὸ νομιχὸν τράμρα πρὸ τῆς Ἐπιδημίας, χαιρὸς ὑπῆρχε ψυλαπισθαι ἐχσληθῆναι δὲ, ἡνιχα ηνθησιν ἡ Ἀλήθεια."

the Orthodox approach he also claimed that the wisdom of this world is foolishness with God.[3]

God and Trinity

Dionysius claims that God is impassible, immutable, and energetic.[4] There was never a time when God was not the Father, and so the Son is eternal, like if the sun exists there must be day. God is light and Christ the brightness.[5]

Other analogies to illustrate consubstantial relation of Father and Son are employed: It is like the spring is not the river, and the seed is not the plant.[6] Dionysius also affirms the Holy Spirit, and so a Trinity, even speaking in the language of the Trinity doctrine of three hypostases.[7] Another analogy of the relation between Father and Son is to think of it in terms of the relation between a mind and a word to be uttered. They cannot be separated from each other. The mind is the father of the word and the word the mind's son.[8]

Creation and Providence

With remarks of intriguing contemporary significance, Dionysius addresses the claim that the atomic theory of Greek philosophy entails no need for a creator. He argues that a creator is mandated, just as a cloak cannot be made without a weaver and as a house does not spontaneously arrange its stones without a builder or architect.[9] There is no way to account for the movement of the heavenly bodies without some captain, he contends. Likewise he refuses to believe that atoms explain the soul and human intelligence.[10] Dionysius also rebuts those who claim matter was not created, but merely arranged and regulated by God, insisting that matter is generated (created) by God.[11]

---

3. Ibid., I (*ANF* 6:111).
4. Dion. *Ad. Sabell.* (*ANF* 6:91).
5. Dion. *Ad Dion.*, I.3.4 (*ANF* 6:92).
6. Ibid., I.6.7 (*ANF* 6:92, 93); Dion. *Ap. Ekk.*, VI (*ANF* 6:120).
7. Dion, *Ad Dion.*, 8 (*ANF* 6:93).
8. Ibid. (*ANF* 6:93–94).
9. Dion. *Lib. Et Nat.*, I, IIA, III (*ANF* 6:85, 87).
10. Ibid., III.IV (*ANF* 6:88, 89).
11. Dion. *Ad Sabell.* (*ANF* 6:91).

In the context of explaining persecutions, Dionysius speaks of a Providence that regulates all things.[12] But elsewhere he posits a weaker sense of divine sovereignty, maintaining that God does not lead us into temptations, but merely tries us.[13]

Sin

We have already observed Dionysius's claim that the wisdom of this world is foolishness with God. We have an inclination not to turn naturally up towards heaven, but towards the belly.[14]

Justification and Sanctification

About the Christian life, Dionysius contends that love is always said to be forever on the alert to do some good, even to those unwilling to receive it.[15] This seems to imply that good works are spontaneous. The aim of knowledge is to occupy oneself with what is not vain, but to find what is good.[16]

We cannot overcome evil unless we struggle against it and unless God protects us.[17] Such language, in typical fashion for the pre-Augustinian African church leaders, seems to entail the belief that we are saved by grace and works.

Church

Dionysius pleads for unity in the face of controversy over what to do about the lapsed.[18] He reports that in the persecution of Alexandria he had absolved a man who was dying, even though he had lapsed.[19] He urges that we gladly receive the penitent.[20] The Alexandrian bishop also invokes his

---

12. Dion. *Ep.*, XI.3 (*ANF* 6:107).
13. Dion. *Ap. Ekk.*, II.48 (*ANF* 6:117).
14. Ibid., I.II.14 (*ANF* 6:113). See note 3 above.
15. Dion. *Ep.*, XIV (*ANF* 6:110).
16. Dion. *Ap. Ekk.*, I.II.2 (*ANF* 6:112).
17. Ibid., IV (*ANF* 6:119).
18. Dion. *Ep.*, II (*ANF* 6:97).
19. Ibid., III.11 (*ANF* 6:101).
20. Dion. *Ap. Ekk.*, VII (*ANF* 6:120).

predecessor in the episcopacy, Heraclus, regarding readmission to the Church of heretics. Claiming it to be a practice throughout Africa and elsewhere, he espouses receiving them in the Church without rebaptism, since they had previously received the Spirit in Baptism.[21] These commitments logically entail the rejection of Novatian, who he says has portrayed Christ as without mercy.[22]

Sacraments

This famed African bishop teaches that the Holy Spirit is given in Baptism.[23] We actually partake of Christ in the Eucharist, he contends.[24]

Eschatology and Biblical Authority

Dionysius believed that there would be a period when Christ would reign before the Last Judgment.[25] In this connection he affirmed the authority of the Book of Revelation in response to its critics.[26] On critical grounds, though, he is not so willing to concede that the Apostle John is the author.[27]

Social Ethics

The bishop firmly rejects the idea that women may not enter the Lord's house in the midst of their menstrual periods.[28] But he was open to abstinence in marriage in order that the partners might be free for spiritual discipline.[29]

---

21. Dion. *Ep.*, VII (*ANF* 6:103).
22. Ibid., VIII (*ANF* 6:103).
23. Ibid., VII (*ANF* 6:103).
24. Ibid., IX (*ANF* 6:103).
25. Dion. *Promiss.*, I.1,3 (*ANF* 6:81, 82).
26. Ibid., I.3,4 (*ANF* 6:82, 83).
27. Ibid., I.4 (*ANF* 6:83).
28. Dion. *Ad Bas.*, Con.II (*ANF* 6:96).
29. Ibid., Con.III (*ANF* 6:96).

Summary

Because of the occasional nature of his thought, it is difficult to assess Dionysius's contemporary contribution overall. He is clearly not a mere clone of his mentor Origen, a fact that makes the thought of both men more attractive, for then we see in Dionysius a man who thought for himself with a teacher who allowed his students to think. In our present context, the younger Alexandrian bishop offers some provocative suggestions about how God governs the universe. An energetic God like he posits is an image that helps us relate God's Providential activity to what we know about Modern Physics, how the cosmos was formed and continues to operate. And some of the languge Dionysius uses to describe how love operates, forever on the alert to do good even among those unwilling to receive it, offers glimpses of Protestant/Augustinian commitments to prevenient grace. This ancient Eastern theologian, then, has some very profound insights for those living and doing ministry in our twenty-first-century Western setting.

9

Anatolius of Alexandria and Minor Writers

ANATOLIUS (230–C. 282) ALSO seems to have been a native of Alexandria.[1] He served as bishop of Laodicea in Syria. He was of great service to his hometown when it was besieged by Romans in 262, saving many lives. He was noted as a man of great learning in geometry and astronomy.

We have few examples of his writings. Two that remain exhibit the mathematical and scientific brilliance of this African bishop. One is a means for calculating when Easter falls based on the course of the moon and the equinox. It is important, he argues, that Easter be held after the equinox so that darkness is overcome by the light.[2] His other surviving work was devoted to Mathematics. He defines it as "a theoretic science of things apprehensible by perception and sensation for communication to others."[3] But it is interesting that this native Egyptian credits his people with the origination of arithmetic and geometry.[4] The brilliance of the African Christian Fathers was clearly not limited to theology.

---

1. Jer. *Vir. Illus.*, LXXXIII (*NPNF*² 3:377).
2. Ana. *Can.pas.*, esp.VI, VII (*ANF* 6:146–51, esp. 147, 148).
3. Ana. *Arith.* (*ANF* 6:152).
4. Ibid.

Theognostus of Alexandria

Another master of the Catechetical School of Alexandria (d. ca. 282), Theognostus was very much a student of Origen. He addressed the emerging Trinity doctrine in his writings.[5]

On one hand, the Origenist says that the of the relation of Father and Son with some of the ambiguities that critics accused his mentor of exhibiting on this topic. The Son is said to be of a substance born of the Father's substance.[6] Some might claim the language here is Arian. But other images employed for the relationship, like steam to water or the reflection of light, seem to make clear that the intention is to affirm the *homoousios* of Father and Son.[7] These are promising images for articulating the Father-Son relation.

We can even gain interesting insights about making plain the entire Trinity from Theognostus as he introduces the Spirit in relation to Father and Son. He insisted that the Spirit is the "seal of the perfected," but on that account the teaching of the Spirit is not superior to the teaching of the Son.[8] Justification by grace is also affirmed. Theognostus writes, "for the imperfect there is pardon." But he also teaches along with later monks like Macarius that Christians can experience perfection.[9]

Pierius of Alexandria

Another card-carrying proponent of Origen's theology, Pierius, who lived in the later part of the third century, also served as master of the Alexandrian Catechetical School. He lived an ascetic lifestyle.[10]

Like his mentor, Pierius taught the preexistence of souls.[11] And some of the same allegations made against his mentor's Trinitarian reflections

---

5. See Ath. *Decr.*, VI.25 (*NPNF*[2] 4:166–67). For the relation between Theognostus and Origen, see Phot. *Bib.*, cod. 106.

6. Theog. *Hyp.*, I (*ANF* 6:155).

7. Ibid.

8. Ibid., III (*ANF* 6:156).

9. Ibid.: ". . . ἀλλ' ὅτι ἐπὶ μὲν τοῖς ἀτελέσιν ἐστὶ συγγνώμη, ἐπὶ δὲ τοῖς γευσαμένοις τῆς οὐρανίου δωρεᾶς χαὶ τελειωθείσιν οὐδεμία περιλείπεται συγγνώμτς ἀπολογία χαὶ παραίτησις." Cf. Macarius the Great (see 153, below); Clement of Alexandria (42, nn. 132–34).

10. See Eus. *H. e.*, VII.32.26 (*NPNF*[2] 1:321); Jer. *Vir. Illus.*, LXXVI (*NPNF*[2] 3:377).

11. Phot. *Bib.*, cod. 119 (*ANF* 6:157).

seem relevant. On one hand, Pierius spoke of Father and Son as different substances, though he did not seem to intend an Arian position. He also spoke of the Spirit as inferior to the Father and the Son in glory.[12]

Theonas of Alexandria

We know little about the career of Theonas, who served as Bishop of Alexandria, probably from 282–300.[13] But the literature he left behind does provide solid insights into his vision of the Christian life (Sanctification), particularly when living in times with a hostile government.

Persecution, in Theonas's view, affords a great opportunity for witnessing. Christ, Whom he identifies as the sole remedy for our salvation, is said to shine brighter in persecution, like gold does in a furnace.[14]

Further attending to Sanctification, the Alexandrian bishop noted that Christ is dishonored if we fall to a base way of thinking.[15] Regular Bible study is urged.[16] In harmony with the African sense that God is Present in all dimensions of reality, he noted that every command of the emperor that does not offend God should be regarded as if it were from God.[17] The doctrine of vocation, that every station in life is holy and provides opportunity to serve God, is clearly endorsed in at this point.

Theonas offers detailed advice to local bureaucrats on how to serve the emperor. A premium is placed on care in diligence in handling the ruler's personal properties, along with promptness and humility.[18] He concludes by noting that as we desire that Christ forgive our sin, so we should forgive those who injure us. He calls readers to despise all transitory objects, for God's Promises surpass all human understanding.[19]

---

12. Ibid.
13. See Eus. *H.e.*, VII.32.30 (*NPNF*[2] 1:321).
14. Theonas. *Epistle to Lucianus* (n.d.), I (*ANF* 6:158).
15. Ibid., II (*ANF* 6:159).
16. Ibid., IX (*ANF* 6:161).
17. Ibid., II (*ANF* 6:159).
18. Ibid., III-VIII (*ANF* 6:159–61).
19. Ibid., IX (*ANF* 6:161).

Phileas

From a town of Lower Egypt Phileas served as a bishop in Thmuis in that region. He died a martyr for the faith in 307 AD. His reflections focus on Sanctification (lifestyle issues).[20] Given his own life story it is not surprising that he praised martyrdom, claiming it is "Christ-bearing."[21] He insisted that the conversation and life of those ordained should be examined with great care.[22] High lifestyle standards on clergy are clearly advocated. Bishops, he argued, need to exercise the Sacrament of Ordination only in their own diocese.[23]

These minor writers indicate how characteristic were the trends we have observed in the thought of the major African Mothers and Fathers. Their focus on Sanctification with a Law orientation, admiration for martyrdom and monasticism, and a Trinitarian perspective is once again evidenced in all parties. We also see illustrated the impact of Origen on many African church leaders.

---

20. See Eus. *H.e.*, VIII.10 (*NPNF*² 1:330–31); ibid., VIII.13.6–7 (*NPNF*² 1:334); Jer. *Vir. Illus.*, LXXVIII (*NPNF*² 3:378).

21. Ph. *Ad. Thm.*, I (*ANF* 6:162).

22. Ph. *Ad. Mil.* (*ANF* 6:163).

23. Ibid. (*ANF* 6:163–64).

10

Lactantius

Lucius Caecilius Firmianus Lactantius (ca. 240–320) was born in either North Africa or Italy. The apologetic bent in his theology is hardly surprising since he himself was a convert to Christianity. A famed rhetorician, some have suggested that the name Lactantius may have been a moniker referring to the softness of his style. He was a student of Arnobius. But some have maintained that he was of Italian descent, though with no verification of that claim.[1] After the establishment of Christianity by Constantine, the emperor entrusted the education of his son Crispus to this learned apologist.[2] A confidante of Constantine, Lactantius is one of the sources of the story of Constantine's vision of how a Christian symbol could give him victory in Rome over Maxentius.[3]

Theological Method

Given his apologetic bent, it is not surprising to find Lactantius operate with something like the Method of Correlation, albeit in a qualified sense. He was especially concerned to show that philosophers approach truth frequently, but that their precepts have no weight because they are human.[4] It

---

1. For a discussion of these matters, see A. Cleveland Coxe, "Introductory Notice to Lactantius," in *ANF* 7:5.
2. Ibid., 5–6.
3. Lact. *M.P.*, XLIV (*ANF* 7:318).
4. Lact. *Inst.*, III.XXVII (*ANF* 7:96).

is difficult to pin down whether he is correlating philosophy and the Word of God in the qualified sense of Clement of Alexandria, simply regarding Philosophy as a preparation for God's Word, as a conceptual tool for articulating the Word. (He is clearly not an enthusiastic proponent of a constructive role for philosophy in the theological task like Origen was.) Or perhaps he is an ancient forerunner of the Method of Critical Correlation, using the Word and philosophy to critique and clarify each other.[5]

Lactantius believed that philosophy should be taught to all men. But he lamented that in reality it is only taught to the learned, excluding women, slaves, barbarians. It should be taught to people of every language, sex, and age, he asserted.[6]

Nevertheless, the famed Apologist maintained that philosophy is the search for wisdom.[7] In his view Philosophy can reach the height of human wisdom insofar as it can ascertain what is not truth. But of itself this discipline cannot know what truth is. To know truth, it must be revealed by God.[8]

Truth, then, cannot be attained through our own ability, for it is the secret of God. If human thought could reach God there would be no difference between Him and humanity. God's gift of truth shows the nothingness of human wisdom.[9] It is foolish to inquire about what we cannot know, the great rhetorician contends. God only wished us to know what concerns man in the attainment of life. Perfect wisdom is to know that there is but one God and all that is has been made by Him.[10] In fact faith is defined as the knowledge of God.[11]

In a similar assessment about the nature of wisdom, Lactantius contends that only divine instruction gives wisdom. Wisdom has been given to all, he asserted.[12] Philosophers agree, he contends, that God has made the world.[13]

---

5. See 33 n. 24 above.
6. Lact. *Inst.*, III.XXV (*ANF* 7:95).
7. Ibid., III.II (*ANF* 7:70).
8. Ibid., II.III; II.VII (*ANF* 7:44, 50).
9. Ibid., I. Pref (*ANF* 7:9).
10. Ibid., II.IX (*ANF* 7:56).
11. Ibid., II.XVI (*ANF* 7:65).
12. Ibid., III.XXVI; IV.IV; II.VIII (*ANF* 7:96, 104, 51).
13. Ibid., II.IX (*ANF* 7:55).

Wisdom is knowing that we do not know all the things that God knows, but it does not entail that we are ignorant of the things a beast knows.[14] Wisdom, then, is foolishness to God.[15] But there is no religion without wisdom.[16] On the other hand, not all religion provides wisdom, because wisdom is only joined with religion where the one God is worshipped. And the chief good of man is to know God.[17] Consequently, "All the wisdom of man consists in this alone, the knowledge and worship of God." In the same spirit he even affirms something like the Cosmological Argument for the existence of God.[18]

Philosophers are ignorant of good and evil, for they do not know the chief good. It is God, the source of all good things. This affirmation seems to represent a denial of the validity of Philosophy and experience in Theology, the Orthodox Method of Tertullian.[19]

The famed rhetorician's reflections on the nature of Scripture seem to proceed along these lines. He contends that the sacred writings indicate that the thoughts of philosophers are foolish. Divine things are not related eloquently by Scripture, but in a concise and simple manner. It is not befitting, in Lactantius's view, that God should confirm His words with arguments.[20] Indeed, he argues that God has willed that virtue should be hidden under the character of folly, so that the mystery and truth of the Christian faith should be concealed.[21]

But despite apparent similarities at these points, Lactantius deliberately distances himself from the Methodological approaches of both Tertullian and Cyprian of Carthage. The former is critiqued for only refuting critics of faith and not instructing them in Christian beliefs, while the latter is said to fail to teach.[22] Clearly Lactantius wants to do more than merely exposit the faith; he wants to package the Word in a way that it is intelligible in its context.

---

14. Ibid., III.VI (*ANF* 7:73).

15. Ibid., V.XVI (*ANF* 7:151).

16. Ibid., I.I. (*ANF* 7:11).

17. Ibid., IV.III; III.X (*ANF* 7:102–3, 77–78).

18. Ibid., III.XXX (*ANF* 7:100): "Omnis sapientia hominis in bot uno est, ut Deum cognoscat et enlat: hoc nostrum dogma haec sentential est." Ibid., III.X (*ANF* 7:77); cf. ibid., VI.IX (*ANF* 7:172); ibid., I.II (*ANF* 7:11).

19. Ibid., VI.VI (*ANF* 7:168); for Tertullian, see p.49, n.7.

20. Lact. *Inst.*, III.I; V.XVI (*ANF* 7:69–70, 151).

21. Ibid., III.I; V.XIX (*ANF* 7:155).

22. Ibid., V.I; V.IV (*ANF* 7:136, 140).

A Correlationist-like dialogue is evident in the famed educator's dialogue with Epicureans and Stoics.[23] He also dialogued with ancient beliefs of the Egyptians. He credits them with being both the first astronomers and the inventors of idolatry. He expressly addressed their gods, their worship of animals and chaste women like Isis.[24] Elements of the word cannot be God, Lactantius insists.[25]

Lactantius also turned his criticisms on the Roman gods and their outlandish behavior.[26] He in turn critiqued the identification of God with nature or fortune.[27] The belief in false gods developed, he argued, because men came to despise themselves, felt they are not cared for by God, and so give themselves to passions.[28] The construction of idols was to make it possible to retain the memory of those who had died.[29]

In a comment again suggesting some apparent commitment to correlating the Word with philosophy, the famed rhetorician claimed that men of the highest genius touch on truth, failing only because custom turned them back.[30] Like Clement of Alexandria he was critical of appeals to ancestors to justify religious practices, for many of these contradict reason.[31] Lacatantius may not be systematic in a commitment to correlating Word of God and Philosophy, but he clearly correlates them at some points (perhaps we should say in critical ways).[32]

God and Trinity

Correlationist propensities are evident in Lactantius's reflections on God. Drawing on images most compatible with Greek philosophy, he speaks of the Lord as the Eternal Mind.[33] Consequently, God must be One. In accord

---

23. Ibid., XII; XXVIII (*ANF* 7:24, 31); Lact. *I.D.*, IV,V,XX,XXII (*ANF* 7:260, 261, 276, 277–78).

24. Lact. *Inst.*, I.Vi; I.XX; I.XXI; II.XIV; V.XXI (*ANF* 7:15, 34, 35, 49, 63).

25. Ibid., II.VI (*ANF* 7:48–49).

26. Ibid., I.XIVff. (*ANF* 7:26ff.).

27. Ibid., III.XXVIII–XXIX (*ANF* 7:97–99).

28. Ibid., II.I (*ANF* 7:40).

29. Ibid., II.II (*ANF* 7:41).

30. Ibid., I.V (*ANF* 7:15).

31. Ibid., II.VII (*ANF* 7:50–51).

32. For the Method of Critical Correlation, follow the leads in note 5.

33. Lact. *Inst.*, I.II–I.III (*ANF* 7:11); cf. references in Plato and Aristotle as cited by

with Greek philosophical suppositions, Lactantius asserts that God would not be perfect were He not One. Even the poets are said to have inadvertently testified to the unity of God.[34] Poets and philosophers, he claimed, have touched on the truth of God in their definitions.[35]

Indeed, Lactantius cites the descriptions of God by philosophers like Aristotle, Plato, and Pythagoras with favor.[36] This line of thought is most reminiscent of Clement of Alexandria's idea of philosophy as preparation for the Word of God.

On the other hand, the African Father claimed that no one can conceive of God. For He does not have a body or gender. Lactantius identifies other characteristics of God. To have power is said to be the property of God.[37] This God is incapable of suffering.[38]

Happiness and wisdom are from God. This includes despising human affairs. God is the chief good.[39] Such a God cannot be represented visually, since God is above what is creaturely and is not to be sought in the low regions of the earth.[40]

As heavenly and spiritual as this God is, He is not impassable; He is not immutable. Indeed, He is never at rest.[41] (Lactantius will not let Greek and Stoic philosophical suppositions about the impassable universal forms undermine biblical references to God's anger and kindness, for if that were the case, he argues, God would not be kind.)

God is also identified as a Parent.[42] But this feminist-friendly claim is offset by the great scholar's claim that there can be no female gods because males are the stronger sex.[43]

God is also said to be the Fountain of Goodness. This leads Lactantius towards Trinitarian affirmations. In order that goodness might spring as a stream from God the Fountain, Lactantius contends that the Spirit was

---

Lact. Ibid., I.V (*ANF* 7:14).

34. Ibid., I.III; I.V (*ANF* 7:12, 13); Lact. *I.D.*, XI (*ANF* 7:268).
35. Lact. *Inst.*, I.V (*ANF* 7:15).
36. Ibid. (*ANF* 7:14).
37. Ibid., I.VIII; II.IX (*ANF* 7:18, 54).
38. Ibid., I.III (*ANF* 7:13).
39. Ibid., III.XXX (*ANF* 7:100).
40. Ibid., II.XIX (*ANF* 7:68).
41. Lact. *I.D.*, IV; XVII (*ANF* 7:261, 273).
42. Lact. *Inst.*, III.XI (*ANF* 7:77); Lact. *I.D.*, I (*ANF* 7:259).
43. Lact. *Inst.*, I.XVI (*ANF* 7:29).

produced endowed with the Father's perfections.[44] Other Trinitarian affirmations include the assertion that Father and Son are not separated, that one cannot be without the other. (This accords with his previous assertion of God's unity.) The Son is said to be like a stream flowing from the bubbling Fountain Who is the Father. Another familiar image: The Father is said to be like the sun, and the Son of God the rays extending from it.[45] This Majestic God, as we shall see, is also All-Powerful.

Creation and Providence

The matter of the world was made by God, out of nothing.[46] God must have made the materials of the universe or He would not have Power.[47] Lactantius is open to conceding the truth of atomic theory, first developed by the ancient Greeks, but not if it excluedes a role for God in creation.[48]

Regarding Providence, Lactantius again self-consciously breaks with Greek philosophy (especially with Epicurus) in asserting that God is not withdrawn from our concerns. He cares for the world.[49] Thus he claimed that God does not just aid us.

Indeed, the Lord is said to manage and rule the courses of stars.[50] There are no limits to His power.[51] But this strong doctrine of Providence then seems compromised by his assertion that God is said to have great foresight in planning. Evil is permitted in order that virtue (the overcoming of vice) is possible.[52] Yet God delays judgment to the End, permitting evil. Demons have no power over those in faith.[53]

Lactantius even claims that belief in divine providence is self-evident from observation of the world.[54] With these comments we once again observe a kind of Correlationist perspective, certainly not a perspective clearly

---

44. Ibid., II.IX (*ANF* 7:52).
45. Ibid., IV.XXIX (*ANF* 7:132).
46. Ibid., II.IX (*ANF* 7:53).
47. Ibid. (*ANF* 7:54).
48. Lact. *I.D.*, X (*ANF* 7:265, 266-67).
49. Ibid., VIII-IX; XCI-XVII (*ANF* 7:263ff., 273).
50. Lact. *Inst.*, I.XI; II.XII (*ANF* 7:23, 60).
51. Ibid., II.IX (*ANF* 7:54).
52. Ibid. (*ANF* 7:52); ibid., Ep. XXIX (*ANF* 7:232).
53. Ibid., II.XVI; II.XVIII; Ep.XXIX (*ANF* 7:64-65, 66-67, 232-33).
54. Ibid., I.II (*ANF* 7:11).

in accord with his claim elsewhere that belief which is the true wisdom is only revealed by God.[55]

Anthropology

Lactantius affirms the central place of human beings in the universe. He insists that the world was made for humans, but that humans alone can admire the works of God.[56] According to Lactantius, we are unique in that we can know God. The universe itself reveals God.[57]

Humans are said to have been made as a "priest of a divine temple, a spectator of His [God] works and of heavenly objects." As intelligent creatures, humans alone can know God.[58]

Because of the common ancestor humans share and the fact that all are animated by the same God, kindness is to be maintained. We are "social animals," Lactantius contends.[59] Humans are composed of two elements, the great rhetorician proclaims. One is endowed with the light; the other with darkness and ignorance.[60] Such a vision seems to suggest a Manichean dualism. Even animals are said to have reason, and so have souls, but they still cannot know God.[61] Lactantius rejects Traducianism (which Tertullian had affirmed)—the idea that the soul is the direct creation of God alone, without a productive role of father and mother.[62] The physical dimensions of man are not man, but the receptacle of man. A body-soul dualism is most clearly posited.[63]

---

55. See note 8 above.
56. Lact. *Inst.*, VII.IV (*ANF* 7:198–99).
57. Ibid., II.X; VII.Vi (*ANF* 7:78, 203).
58. Lact. *I.D.*, XIV (*ANF* 7:271): "Sicut mundem propert hominem machinatus est, ita ipsum propter se, tamquam divini temple antistitem, spectatorem operum rerumque coelstium." Cf. ibid., IV (*ANF* 7:263).
59. Lact. *Inst.*, VI.X (*ANF* 7:172–73).
60. Ibid., III.VI (*ANF* 7:73).
61. Ibid., II.III; III.X (*ANF* 7:58, 78).
62. Lact. *O.D.*, XIX (*ANF* 7:298–99); cf. Lact. *Inst.*, II.III (*ANF* 7:43).
63. Lact. *Inst.*, II.XIII; III.XII; III.XXVII; VII.V (*ANF* 7:61, 79, 97, 202).

God created souls on whom to bestow immortality and govern the body.[64] Man is made with an upright body in order to look to heaven to discern God.[65]

Sin

Lactantius was not as inclined as Tertullian to talk about Sin as to suggest something like Original Sin. Human beings are said to have turned away from the chief good, ceased to raise their heads to heaven. Instead, our minds have become depressed downward, clinging to the goods of the earth. All sorts of wickedness then followed. In a comment most suggestive of the later Augustinian construal of Original Sin, Lactantius speaks of this wickedness "necessarily" being the case.[66] Human life is now "overspread with gloom and darkness," trapped in depravity. Wisdom being taken away, humans began to claim wisdom for themselves.[67]

Envy of the Son of God is also noted as a cause of sin. Set over the world as he has been, the creature whom we call the devil, poisoned with such envy, passed from good to evil.[68]

Christology and Atonement

Lactantius asserted that Christ must be God and human. If not God, He would not have had the authority to lead human beings to justice. But if not human He would not have offered an example of virtue to humanity. Both of these tasks refer to the vision of His Work that Lactantius sketches—to provide a living law in a world where justice on earth had vanished.[69] Given this agenda, the stage is set for understanding Christ's atoning Work in terms of the Moral Influence Theory. It clearly underlies a poem on Christ's Passion that Lactantius wrote. In the poem, we find Christ promising that His sufferings can move the faithful to deny earthly things in favor

---

64. Ibid., II.X (*ANF* 7:58); Lact. *I.D.*, X (*ANF* 7:267).

65. Lact. *Inst.*, III.XXVII (*ANF* 7:97); Lact. *I.D.*, XIV (*ANF* 7:271).

66. Lact. *Inst.*, IV.I (*ANF* 7:101).

67. Ibid.: "Sic humanam vitam prioribus saeculis in clarissima luce versatam caligo ac tenebrae comprehenderunt; et quod huic pravitai congruens erat, postquam sublata sapientia est, tum demum sibi hominess sapientum nomen vendicare coeperunt."

68. Ibid., II.IX (*ANF* 7:52, 53).

69. Ibid., IV.XXV (*ANF* 7:126).

of sacred habits.[70] Yet we do find hints of the characteristic early African endorsement of a Classic View of the Atonement, as the great rhetorician contends that the sign of the Cross also contributes to salvation as it functions as a terror to demons.[71]

Justification

In line with the Moral Influence Theory of Atonement, it is said by Lactantius that God will reward virtue.[72] Works play a necessary role in salvation, an interesting tension with the strong doctrine of Providence he posits.

God's wrath is said to be appeased not by a victim or offerings but "by a reformation of morals."[73] The Lord will recognize as His own those who strive toward mastering negative emotions.[74] Yet a role for grace seems affirmed by Lactantius when he claims that happiness and wisdom must be received from hearing the voice of God, which includes despising human affairs.[75] The ambiguity of relating grace and works which we have observed in many of the early pre-Augustinian African theologians is again in evidence.

Sanctification

Just as there is no real distinction between Justification and Sanctification, so there is a close relation between Lactantius's vision of the Christian life and what it takes to get saved. Thus he advises that we should be fixed on immortal things and heavenly pursuits. Virtue despises opulence, he contends. Christian virtues appear foolish to the world.[76]

There is a realism about the Christian life, about how it remains marred by sin. For example, he notes that the knowledge of good and virtue are not identical. Even just human beings may admit evil into their

---

70. Lact. *P.D.* (*ANF* 7:327–28); Lact. *Inst.*, IV.XXVI (*ANF* 7:128).
71. Lact. *Inst.*, IV.XXVII (*ANF* 7:129).
72. Ibid., V.XIX; VII.V; III.XI; I.XVIII (*ANF* 7:155, 203, 79, 31).
73. Lact. *I.D.*, XXI (*ANF* 7:277).
74. Lact. *Inst.*, VI.XXIII (*ANF* 7:189–90).
75. Ibid., III.XXX (*ANF* 7:100).
76. Ibid., VI.VI; III.XII; V.XIX (*ANF* 7:168, 80, 155).

thoughts or speak evil.[77] There seems to be a place for forgiveness, then, in Lactantius's thinking.

At the heart of the African Father's vision of the Christian life is kindness and mercy, behavior that emerges from our common humanity and the One God Who animates us all.[78] The great rhetorician offers a compelling, socially rich image for depicting the Christian life:

> Though, therefore, in lowliness of mind we are on an equality, the free with slaves, and the rich with the poor, nevertheless in the sight of God we are distinguished by virtue. . . . For if it is justice for a man to put himself on a level even with those of lower rank, although he excels in this very thing, that he made himself equal to his inferiors; yet if he has conducted himself not only as an equal, but even as an inferior, he will plainly obtain a much higher rank of dignity in the judgment of God.[79]

Eschatology

The judging God of Lactantius is evident in his vision of the End Time. He speaks of God as a divine fire which consumes the wicked. Those who have been imbued with full justice will not feel the fire, for they have something of God in them. (Note the affirmation of forgiving grace here, or is it even an affirmation of deification?) It is claimed that there is no immediate judgment of souls after death.[80] God, it seems, is portrayed as an indulgent Father to the godly, but a Judge of the ungodly.[81]

---

77. Ibid., VI.V (*ANF* 7:167); Ibid., VI.XIII (*ANF* 7:178–79).

78. Ibid., IX.X (*ANF* 7:172–73).

79. Ibid., V.XVI (*ANF* 7:151): "Cum igitur et liberi servis, et divites pauperibus humilitate animi paressimus, apud Deum tamen virtute discernimur. . . . Si enim justitia est, parem set etiam minoribus facere, quanquam hoc ipso praecellat, quod se inferiribus coaequavit; tamen si non tantum quasi parem, sed etiam quasi minorem se gesserit, utique multo altiorem dignitatis gradum, Deo judice, consequetur."

80. Ibid., CII.XXI (*ANF* 7:216–17); cf. ibid.,V.XXIV (*ANF* 7:161).

81. Ibid., I.I (*ANF* 7:10).

There will be no judgment of those who never heard of God, Lactantius insists.[82] A postmillennialist perspective regarding Christ's return is also taught.[83] Christ is said to be revealed at the end of time.[84]

Social Ethics

Lanctantius's social ethic seems very much in accord with Roman ways in his affirmation of private property over against Platonic communalism of all aspects of life.[85] Yet this is held in tandem with a concern for the poor, which we have already observed. Virtue despises opulence, he claimed.[86] He opposed charging interest on loans, lest one use the merit of assisting others.[87]

Along these lines, Lactantius teaches that wealth is only for the sake of the poor: "Riches also do not render men illustrious, except that they are able to make them more conspicuous by good works. For men are rich, not because they possess riches, but because they employ them on works of justice; and they who seem to be poor on this account are rich, because they are not in want, and desire nothing."[88]

The Christian, he asserts, is not really just if he or she is unwilling to seek nothing other than what is necessary to life, if unwilling to be subject to injustice. Justice involves patience, he adds (a sound piece of political advice).[89] There is a kind of nascent liberation ethic here. This is evidenced in his claim that among Christians we have no servants, for they are brothers and fellow-servants.[90]

Lactantius was also critical of gladiatorial combat.[91] He proclaimed that Christian men and women should adhere to the same sexual standards.

---

82. Ibid., VII.XX (*ANF* 7:216).

83. Ibid., VII.XXII; VII.XXIV (*ANF* 7:217-18, 219).

84. Ibid., IV.II (*ANF* 7:102).

85. Ibid., III.XXII (*ANF* 7:92-93).

86. Ibid., III.XII (*ANF* 7:80); cf. ibid., VI.X (*ANF* 7:173).

87. Ibid., VI.XVIII (*ANF* 7:183).

88. Ibid., V.XVI (*ANF* 7:151: "Divitae quoque non faciunt insignes, nisi quod possunt bonis operibus facere clariores. Divites sunt enim, non quia divitias habent, sed quia utuntur illis ad opera justitiae. Et pauperes videntur, eo tamen divites sunt, quia et non egent, et nihil concupiscent." Cf. ibid., VI.XII (*ANF* 7:176).

89. Ibid., V.XXIII (*ANF* 7:160).

90. Ibid., V.XVI (*ANF* 7:151).

91. Ibid., VI.XX (*ANF* 7:186).

Christian men should not have sexual partners other than their wives not even slaves.[92]

Likewise, Lactantius opposed military service and capital punishment.[93] In a manner typical of other pre-Augustinian African church leaders it seems that his social ethic was driven distinctly by Christian principles, as he claimed that if all worshipped the one God there would be no dissension and no war.[94] Even when he switches positions after Constantine's unambiguous conquest of the empire and expressed openness to military action for good ends like establishing peace and justice, the actions are undertaken in dialogue with faith in God (Christian principles).[95] Such a Gospel orientation fits Lactantius's strong doctrine of Providence—all our actions under God's auspcies.

Summary

Lacantius's views on war and peace, on the relation between grace and works, on Providence and freewill defy logic, much like we have observed in the thought of other African leaders of the early church who reflect the celebration of mystery still characteristic of Eastern Christian thought today. We have even observed this lack of crystal clarity in his Theological Method. Is such richness of thought a lack of precision we will not find helpful today in our ministries (especially in the West)? Or is this a catholicity and conceptual richness embodied today in modern ecumenism and the Method of Critical of Correlation (and its commitment to using God's Word and philosophy to critique and clarify earch other)?

---

92. Ibid., VI.XXIII (*ANF* 7:189ff.). For a more detailed analysis, see Glancy, *Slavery in Early Christianity*, 58.

93. Lact. *Inst.*, VI.XX (*ANF* 7:187).

94. Ibid., V.VIII (*ANF* 7:143).

95. Ibid., I.1 (*ANF* 7:10); Lact. *Ep.* LVI (*ANF* 7:245).

11

Alexander of Lycopolis

It is uncertain whether Alexander was born in the city of Lycopolis in upper Egypt (present-day Asyut) or Lycopolis in Lower Egypt. Either way he seems to have been a native Egyptian who served in the African episcopacy early in the fourth century.

Little else is known of Alexander save his critique of the Manichees. Based on some passages in the one existing work by the bishop, some commentators have concluded that Alexander must have been a Manichee adherent at some point, later becoming Christian.[1]

Theological Method

Alexander was critical of the Manichees for their speculative tendencies. Suggestive of an Orthodox approach to Theology (reminiscent of Tertullian) he claimed that the philosophy of Christians may be termed simple. It makes possible for common people to endorse its attention to moral formation.[2] Heresies are said to emerge among those skilled in philosophical subtleties.[3] At one point the Bishop of Lycopolis even critiques Manichee use of allegorical interpretation.[4]

---

1. For this background, see Alexander Roberts and James Donaldson, "Introductory Notice," in *ANF* 6:239–40.
2. Alex. *Tract. Man.*, I (*ANF* 6:241).
3. Ibid., II (*ANF* 6:241).
4. Ibid., XXV (*ANF* 6:252).

God and Providence

Of course, the dualism of the Manichees has no place in Christian thinking. Noting that they view matter as evil, Alexander critiques Manichean propensities to avoid this evil by abstaining from marriage and procreation.[5] Alexander continues his critique of the Manichean dualism for its idea of claiming that God has injected virtue into matter.[6] As will become obvious, the primary concern Alexander has with this set of commitments is that it involves the neglect of contingency and makes virtue a consequence of matter, not something acquired through discipline.[7]

In offering these reflections we gain insight into Hellenized perceptions of Egyptian culture in the fourth century. The Bishop of Lycopolis observes cynically that Manichean dualism correctly verifies Egyptian practice of worshipping the crocodile, lion, and wolf, because these animals devour their weaker rivals.[8] To this absurdity Alexander adds that we need not destroy matter to be liberated from the troubles of the flesh, for lust and injustice can be subdued by discipline and law.[9]

Christology and Atonement

Alexander critiqued Manichean thinking about Christ. They had portrayed Him as Mind, which Alexander happily points out is in line with the traditional teachings of the Church. But this would be to identify matter with that which is not produced.[10]

More problems are apparent with the Manichean treatment of the Atonement. They are condemned for denying that Christ suffered. It is a mere display in their view.[11] In endorsing the language of "Sacrifice to God" in these instances, Alexander seems to endorse the Satisfaction Theory of Atonement.

---

5. Ibid., III; XXV (*ANF* 6:242, 251).
6. Ibid., XI; XVII (*ANF* 6:245–46, 248).
7. Ibid., XIV (*ANF* 6:247).
8. Ibid. (*ANF* 6:246–47).
9. Ibid., XIV; XVII (*ANF* 6:247).
10. Ibid., XXIV (*ANF* 6:251).
11. Ibid.

Justification and Sanctification

There is a definite tone of legalism in Alexander's comments, little place for grace. As we have noted, he praises Christian faith for its moral teachings and insists that virtue is acquired through discipline.[12] These commitments are no doubt related to Alexander's commitment to rejecting the necessitarianism of the Manichean idea that some portions of matter have virtue but not others.[13] The whole Manichean project in Alexander's view is absurd, as in positing that God transcends evil matter, but exists, it makes it difficult to portray this God as anything other than as evil (like matter) or as less than matter.[14]

Lessons Learned

Alexander's critique of the Manichean dualism is impeccable for modern Christians encountering the dualism of many New Age modes of spirituality. And his stress on free will and Christian responsibility clearly foreshadowed the critique of the Manichees issued by a famed later African Bishop of Hippo, Augustine.[15] But can we meaningfully articulate the faith apart from clearer references to grace? If we need to be critical of Alexander on this account, we may need to be just as critical of another famed African enemy of heresy, Tertullian, and perhaps of many of the pre-Augustinian theologians of the early church.

---

12. Ibid., XVI (*ANF* 6:247).
13. Ibid., XXI (*ANF* 6:249).
14. Ibid., XXVII (*ANF* 6:252).
15. Augustine, *Vera relig.*, xiv.27 (LCC 6:238); Augustine, *Grat. et lib. arb.*, II.3-6 (*NPNF*[1] 5:444-45).

12

Peter of Alexandria

PETER (CA. 260–311) SERVED as Bishop of Alexandria from 300 until his death. He survived a persecution by Diocletian and was responsible for drawing up rules of readmission of the lapsed. These policies led to a controversy with Meletius, the bishop of Lycopolis in Egypt, which eventually culminated in the formation of a schismatic church led by Miletius. Peter himself died in the persecution of Maximin. Eusebius of Caesarea offered high praise for this Alexandrian bishop's eminence and holy life.[1]

Christology

Against Arius, Peter spoke of the majesty of Christ.[2] He even uses the language of Christ having Two Natures.[3]

Creation

The Alexandrian bishop rejected the preexistence of the soul.[4]

---

1. Eus. *H.e.*, IX.VI.2; VII.XXIII.32; VIII.13 (*NPNF*² 1:360, 322, 334). Also see Alexander Roberts and James Donaldson, "Introductory Notice," in *ANF* 6:257–59.
2. Petr. *Act. Sinc.* (*ANF* 6:264, 263).
3. Petr. *Frag.*, III; VI (*ANF* 6:280, 283).
4. Ibid., VI (*ANF* 6:283).

Justification

Peter claimed that he himself was a sinner and not worthy of what he has received.[5] He refers to God's mercy even though he had been smitten with sin.[6] We are saved by grace, not by works, he claims.[7]

Sanctification

Faith is a powerful witness in Peter's view. "For we know that on account of the faith of others some have obtained the goodness of God," he asserts.[8]

Church

Peter urged that those who had lapsed during the persecutions be seen as not willing this, but as having been betrayed by the flesh. Consequently, they are to be readmitted upon a three-year period of submission and then a forty-day period of remembering Jesus's forty days of fasting.[9] An additional one year to the above disciplinary punishments is recommended to be added for those who lapsed and were not tormented in prison.[10] Three years exclusion for those who deserted faith only for reasons of fear, during which time repentance must be shown for readmission, was also prescribed.[11] Those who are unrepentant (like the Ethiopian's unchanging skin) are not to be readmitted.[12] Only six months penance for those who feigned a sacrifice was mandated.[13] He also describes punishments for other circumstances, such as what sort of penance is expected for punishing slaves instructed by their masters to perform sacrifices to the Roman gods and what to make of those who confessed the faith, but then fell.[14]

---

5. Petr. *Act. Sinc.* (*ANF* 6:266).
6. Petr. *Frag.*, VII (*ANF* 6:283).
7. Ibid., II (*ANF* 6:280).
8. Petr. *Ep. Can.*, Can. XI (*ANF* 6:276).
9. Ibid., Can. I (*ANF* 6:269).
10. Ibid., Can. II (*ANF* 6:269–70).
11. Ibid., Can. III (*ANF* 6:270).
12. Ibid., Can. IV (*ANF* 6:270).
13. Ibid., Can. V (*ANF* 6:271).
14. Ibid., Can. VI (*ANF* 6:271–72).

Clergy who lapsed should not remain in office, Peter asserts.[15] But this is with the stipulation that if the faithful were physically compelled to eat food sacrificed to idols they should be deemed as confessors.[16]

With Peter of Alexandria we seem to see a break with the pre-Augustinian African and Eastern) mixing of salvation by grace and works. He clearly seems to teach salvation by grace without works. But in actually implementing the grace-directed core of his thought in the realm of church discipline he insists that the lapsed need to do something in order to be redeemed. Many modern American Christians along with those in the Eastern Church believe that too.

---

15. Ibid., Can. X (*ANF* 6:274).
16. Ibid., Can. XIV (*ANF* 6:278).

13

Alexander of Alexandria

ALEXANDER (D. 328) WAS a friend and patron of Athanasius, just in the period when the persecutions of Christians were coming to an end thanks to Constantine. A leading participant in the Council of Nicea and its steps in formulating the Trinity doctrine, he knew all the major players in the dispute—both his protégé Athanasius, who became the primary spokesman for the Nicene Party; and Arius, whose teachings rendering Christ a mere creature, occasioned the controversy, and who was a priest in the region of Alexandria. Alexander tried to win Arius away from his views and actually excommunicated him in 321, four years before the Council of Nicea.[1]

Anthropology

Alexander affirms free will.[2] He also endorses a body-soul dualism. In sin, the soul that had governed the body has been carried to the lower regions, bound by material fetters.[3]

---

1. See Alexander Roberts and James Donaldson, "Introductory Notice," in *ANF* 6:289–90. For Athanasius's account of Alexander's efforts to refute Arianism, see his *Apol. Ar.*, II.23; III.46 (*NPNF*[2] 4: 112, 125).
2. Alex. Alex. *Ep. Ar.*, IV (*ANF* 6:299).
3. Ibid., V.3 (*ANF* 6:300).

Christology

The Savior has an immutable nature, Alexander and his Nicene allies contended.[4] The Father and Son are Two, but inseparable.[5] Jesus says that He and the Father are One. But the Son is begotten and the Father unbegotten.[6] Like Origen, Alexander teaches the eternal generation of the Son.[7]

Mary is referred to as "Mother of God."[8] Jesus's humanity is affirmed.[9] But the bishop of Alexandria only speaks of Jesus's humanity suffering.[10] Such an affirmation seems to be a break with the characteristic Alexandrian way of describing Christology in favor of the more Antiochene view and its emphasis on distinguishing Christ's Two Natures.

Atonement

Christ is said to release us from bondage by uniting that which death had separated (body and soul).[11] The Classic View of Atonement is implied at this point and elsewhere in the bishop's remarks. Alexander notes that the Lord conquers hell and death.[12] But then in a manner more suggestive of the Satisfaction Theory of Atonement, Alexander speaks of Christ discharging the debt of death.[13] Perhaps this is a contradiction endorsing different, not necessarily compatible Atonement models. But it is also possible to interpret Alexander's remarks as an endorsement of the Governmental Theory of Atonement, teaching that sin has made the world and the Law by which it has been structured out of whack with God's original aims, that good would be rewarded and sin punished. Since we are no longer able to do good due to our sin, the world and the divine Commandments no longer function as God intended (as a context in which good would be rewarded), for now they only function to condemn us. In a sense the world is no longer

---

4. Ibid., I.2 (*ANF* 6:292).
5. Ibid., 4 (*ANF* 6:292).
6. Ibid., 8, 4, 11 (*ANF* 6:294, 292, 295).
7. Ibid., 7 (*ANF* 6:293).
8. Ibid., 12 (*ANF* 6:296).
9. Ibid., V.5 (*ANF* 6:300).
10. Ibid., VI (*ANF* 6:302).
11. Ibid., V.5 (*ANF* 6:300).
12. Ibid., 6 (*ANF* 6:301).
13. Ibid., VI (*ANF* 6:302).

under God's governance. And so in order to restore it to its original purpose, He needs to pay the Law and the cosmos the debt (through Christ's Sacrifice). But unlike with the Satisfaction Theory this sacrifice is not paid to the Father. It is a sacrifice aimed at restoring the creation to its original aim, returning it to God's governance.

Alexander is a most important contributor to the Trinity doctrine and the condemnation of Arius. His impact on Athanasius is obvious, even in the glimpses of his theological convictions that the remnants of his corpus provide.

14

Arnobius

THIS AFRICAN APOLOGIST FOR the faith (d. c. 330) is often regarded as operating in the best traditions of the Alexandrian School, though, as we shall see, he operated with a different Theological Method than typified the venerable Egyptian institution. Converted late in life, he was the teacher of Lactantius, though not necessarily his student's elder. Writing in Latin, his and his student's works doubtless set the stage for the further development of theology written in Latin, culminating with Augustine.[1]

Arnobius's extant work is a defense of Christianity largely pointing out the absurdities associated with the gods of the Roman Empire (in its various regions). Responding to charges of atheism, leveled against Christians, he claims that some of the tales of the gods actually undermine morality.[2]

The African Apologist begins his defense of the faith by refuting critics of Christianity who claim that the wars and famines in the world since the dawn of this religion have been sent by the gods as punishment, pointing out the absurdity of such thinking. Arnobius claims that the gentle, peaceful spirit of the faith has relieved the world of many conflicts.[3] He notes that the empire has enjoyed many blessings since the advent of Christianity.[4] It seems that Christians were being criticized in Arnobius's lifetime for

---

1. See Jer. *Vir. Illus.*, LXXIX, LXXX (*NPNF*[2] 3:378).
2. Arnob. *Ad. Gen.*, V.29, 31 (*ANF* 6:501).
3. Ibid., I.1–6 (*ANF* 6:413–15).
4. Ibid., 13–14 (*ANF* 6:417).

not building temples and not offering sacrifices to the gods.[5] In response, the great Apologist rejects prayer to idols and sacrifices.[6] In his dialogue with these gods, Arnobius's view of a number of the classical doctrines becomes apparent.

Theological Method

Arnobius was critical of Stoic and other philosophical efforts at allegory.[7] In the fashion of Tertullian, he argues for the truth of the biblical accounts.[8] Also like his famed predecessor, Arnobius also contended that most divine things are couched in obscurity.[9] Thus learning does not necessarily equip one to know truth.[10] Nothing can be revealed in human language about God, Arnobius asserted.[11] This was also a basis for his critique of the gods of the Roman Empire.[12]

God and Providence

Despite his use of an Orthodox Method, Arnobius posited something like a natural knowledge of God, contending that all human beings have an idea of the great God.[13] This is a God of the inner powers, he asserts.[14] In a fascinating apologetic move, this later Apologist contended that if other gods exist they must derive their divinity from the supreme God of Christians.[15]

---

5. Ibid., VI.1ff. (*ANF* 6:506ff.).
6. Ibid., 10, 17, 19; VII.1ff. (*ANF* 6:510, 514, 518ff.).
7. Ibid., V.33 (*ANF* 6:502ff.
8. Ibid., I.54–59 (*ANF* 6:428–30).
9. Ibid., II.7 (*ANF* 6:436).
10. Ibid., 5–6 (*ANF* 6:435).
11. Ibid., III.9 (*ANF* 6:469).
12. Ibid., 1ff. (*ANF* 6:464ff.).
13. Ibid., I.33 (*ANF* 6:421).
14. Ibid., 42 (*ANF* 6:424).
15. Ibid., III.3 (*ANF* 6:464).

God's incomprehensibility leads Arnobius to note that though God may be described in a masculine word, sex or gender is not appropriate to Him.[16] The divine nature is devoid of bodily features, he insists.[17]

Our African Apologist did speak of the Lord's compassion and kindness for souls bound to the body. This gift is offered to all, and no one is hindered from accepting it.[18] He gives assistance in equal measure to both good and evil.[19] God's goodness and love is asserted in another way. He is not the source of of evil, Arnobius insists. Indeed, he contends, we do not know its source.[20]

Anthropology

Not surprisingly, Arnobius conceives of human nature in terms of a body-soul dualism akin to Greek philosophy.[21] But he rejects the idea that we can claim as our own a divine and immortal nature.[22] Indeed, he contends, such a viewpoint might readily lead to slothful living without fear of punishment.[23] We are only immortal by the goodness and grace of God, Arnobius reports.[24]

In a manner we have observed in the case of a number of the pre-Augustinian Fathers and Mothers, Arnobius is clearly cognizant of our sinfulness. He speaks of humanity's habitual arrogance, and in a manner suggestive of Augustine on our pride and inborn depravity.[25] Indeed, he contends we must struggle against this depravity, as it shows we are not perfect.[26] But unlike Augustine, and in view of his obvious openness to asserting our free will to accept or reject God's goodness, Arnobius teaches that there may be good people, not sunk in sin.[27]

16. Ibid., 8 (*ANF* 6:466).
17. Ibid., 12 (*ANF* 6:467).
18. Ibid., II.63–64 (*ANF* 6:458).
19. Ibid., I.49 (*ANF* 6:427).
20. Ibid., II.55 (*ANF* 6:454–55).
21. Ibid., 37, 63 (*ANF* 6:448, 458).
22. Ibid., 19 (*ANF* 6:441).
23. Ibid., 33 (*ANF* 6:446).
24. Ibid., 33, 34, 36 (*ANF* 6:447, 448).
25. Ibid., I.16; I.38; II.50 (*ANF* 6:440, 423, 453).
26. Ibid., II.50 (*ANF* 6:453).
27. Ibid., 48,49 (*ANF* 6:452).

Christology and Atonement

Christ is said to be the sole way of salvation.[28] Arnobius affirms the divinity and humanity of Christ long before the Council of Chalcedon. He is to be regarded as God, the African apologist asserts. Though like us, He has shown us what God is.[29] Christ is also very much a human being in the estimation of Arnobius. God needed to appear in human shape, for no mortal could have seen Him had He come to earth as He is.[30] But this humanity does not authenticate charges of some critics that Jesus merely stole the secrets of his Power from Egyptian shrines.[31]

Sometimes Arnobius spoke of Christ's Work in line with the Classic View of the Atonement, as a struggle with the fates and afflictions, like demons.[32] Christ's acceptance of the violence done to Him destroys the arrogance of the proud and fires of lust. Afflicted with troubles, He is said to bring us back to soundness.[33]

Other times, language used to describe Christ's Work is more suggestive of the Moral Influence Theory of Atonement in asserting that Christ's Work sets an example that can save us. Thus Arnobius in these instances contends that Christ points out what is profitable and salutary for the human race, that by His great kindness He has made known the One Who is the Creator of the world. At this point he refers to Christ getting us to acknowledge our weakness, raising our thoughts to heaven. He also attributed to Christ the experience of speaking in tongues.[34]

Justification and Sanctification

We have already noted that Arnobius teaches that God's gift is offered to all, and that no one is hindered from accepting it. No one is forced to accept the gift, he asserts.[35] This teaching of free will is indicative of how little Arnobius refers or appeals to the grace of God and its role in saving us.

---

28. Ibid., 65 (ANF 6:459).
29. Ibid., I.39 (ANF 6:423–24).
30. Ibid., 61 (ANF 6:430).
31. Ibid., 43 (ANF 6:425).
32. Ibid., 47, 50; I.76 (ANF 6:426, 427, 463).
33. Ibid., I.63 (ANF 6:431–32).
34. Ibid., 38 (ANF 6:423); on Jesus's speaking in tongues, see ibid., 46 (ANF 6:425).
35. Ibid., II.64, 65 (ANF 6:458, 459).

There is an interesting twist to the Apologist's treatment of the Christian life (especially in view of his Orthodox Theological Method and critique of reason as a vehicle for truth). Christian teaching often overlaps with Philosophy, he contends. He cites as examples the Christian expectations that we exhort souls to flee the earth, be engaged in meditation, and believe in the resurrection of the dead.[36]

Social Ethics

Arnobius was critical of the god of war of some pagans.[37] He seems to take a passivist position in claiming that we ought not pollute our hands and conscience with the blood of another. He clearly opposes Roman military actions.[38] Christianity has not been bad for the empire, he contends. During its existence Rome has enjoyed countless victories and expansion.[39]

Significance for Today

Arnobius's main agenda was to refute the validity of faith in the other gods of the Roman Empire, to defend Christian faith and demonstrate its comprehensibility in face of critiques. As a result, he does not offer us as much in the way of insights regarding the classical doctrines. Articulating these was not his agenda. But in a time and place like ours, when Christian faith needs to encounter the false gods of our era, Arnobius's insights and arguments may be yet applicable today.

---

36. Ibid., 13 (*ANF* 6:439).
37. Ibid., III.26 (*ANF* 6:471).
38. Ibid., II.1 (*ANF* 6:433–34).
39. See note 4 above.

15

Athanasius

BORN NEAR ALEXANDRIA, ATHANASIUS (296–373), was ordained a deacon in AD 319. He soon became the young protégé of Alexander the Bishop of Alexandria and later functioned as the bishop's successor and prime spokesman for the Nicene cause.

Since he may have been born outside the city, it is likely he was born in a town in the Nile Delta that had a majority Coptic population. Although currently under scholarly dispute about the claim of some historians that his Arian critics mocked him as a "Black dwarf," indicating that he was a Black man, it is clear that Emperor Julian the Apostate deemed him no better than a common man, called him "not even a man, but only a common little fellow/puppet."[1] And even Athanasius called himself a "poor common man" in a dispute with the Arian Eusebius of Nicomedia.[2] If so, this could

1. Julian, *Epistol.* (362), 47: "ὃν γὰρ ἂν ἕλησθε τοῦ πλήθους, ὅσα γε εἰς τὴν τῶν γραφῶν διδασκαλίαν ἥκει, χείρων οὐδὲν ἔσται τοῦ παρ᾽ὑμῶν ποθουμένου. εἰ δὲ τῆς ἄλλης ἐντρεχείας ἐρῶντες Ἀθανασίου. πανοῦργον γὰρ εἶναι τὸν ἄνδρα τυνθάνομαι. ταυ᾽τάς ἐποιήσασθε τὰς δεήσεις ἴστε δι᾽αὐτὸ τοῦτο αὐτὸν ἀπεληλαμένον τῆς πόλεως ἀνεπιτήδειος γὰρ φύσει προστατεύειν δήμου πολυπραγμων ἀνήρ. εἰ δὲ μηδὲ ἀνήρ ἀλλ᾽ἀνθρωπίσκος εὐτελής, καθάπερ οὗτος ὁ μέγας οἰόμενος περὶ τῆς κεφαλῆς κινδυνεύειν, τοῦτο δὲ δίδωσιν ἀταξίας ἀρχήν."

For a testimony to the fact that the majority of the Egyptian population in this era was Coptic and was polarized from the Roman and Greek settlers, see Henry Green, "The Socio-Economic Background of Christianity in Egypt," in Pearson and Goehring, *Roots of Egyptian Christianity*, 108–10. A critical voice against the conclusion that Athanasius was Black has been R. A. Baker, "Was Saint Athanasius of Alexandria a Black Man, the 'Black Dwarf'?"

2. Ath. *Apol. Ar.*, Int.9 (NPNF[2] 4:105): "Εἶτα τοῦ Ἀθανασίου ὀδυρομένου ἐπὶ

entail his Coptic background, since Copts were the majority of the population in Roman-era Egypt. Also relevant is that thirteenth-century Coptic icons portray him and Cyril of Alexandria as Black.

On the other hand, Athanasius's education was clearly Greek. He was not a man with a great interest in Egyptian antiquities and its religion.[3] But he does express a thrill over Jesus's sojourns into Egypt. He reports that the idols of Egypt fell when he entered the land.[4] A further argument for his being Coptic is that he probably spoke Copt, evidenced in the fact that many of his writings appear in ancient Coptic manuscripts.[5]

This Alexandrian bishop was influenced by monasticism as it developed in Africa. He was very devoted to St. Anthony, as evidenced in his authorship of *Life of St. Anthony*.

Athanasius's fame is closely related to his fidelity to and promotion of the Council of Nicea. He accompanied his beloved patron Alexander to the Council as his Secretary and three years later succeeded him to the episcopacy. From that point on he became a staunch defender of this nascent creed. It cost him the enmity of both the Arians who had been condemned by the Council and also the emperor's family beginning in the final years of Constantine's life, as he and his family gradually came under Arian influence. As the key spokesman of the Nicene Party, Athanasius endured exile on a number of occasions. But he continued bravely and stubbornly to propagate the teachings of the Council, functioning often as its prime PR man. The eventual success of the Trinitarian formula owes much to his persistence, skill, and influence.[6]

Not only has Athanasius impacted the Church's reception of the Trinity doctrine. He is credited with writing in 367 the old list of books of the Bible corresponding to the canon as we have it today.[7] This list refers positively to books of the Apochrypha, but does not refer to them as having the same value as the Old and New Testaments. It is noteworthy in this con-

---

τῇ διαξολῇ, χαὶ διασεξαιουμένου, μὴ εἶναι ταύτην ἀληθῆ. πῶς γὰρ ἂν ἰδώτης ἄνθρωπος χαὶ πένης πηλιχαῦτα δύναιτο..."

3. For this assessment, see Archibald Robertson, "Prolegomena," in *NPNF*[2] 4:xiv.

4. Ath. *Log. Eoan.*, 36, 37 (*ANF* 2:4:54, 55).

5. For this assessment, which is gaining increasing credence, see Barnes, *Athanasius and Constantius*, 13. Given his travels while in exile and communication with Coptic monks, the African father's mastery of Copt seems hard to dispute.

6. For this assessment, see Livingstone, *Concise Oxford Dictionary of the Christian Church*, 38–39.

7. Ath. *Ep.* (367), XXXIX. esp. 4, 5 (*NPNF*[2] 4:552).

nection that Councils of the African church (Hippo in 393 and Carthage in 397) finalized this apparent consensus about the books of the Bible.

Theological Method

Generally speaking, Athanasius, despite his Alexandrian training, employed an Orthodox Method of Theology. Scripture in his view was written by God.[8] The inspired Scriptures are sufficient for the proclamation of the truth.[9] As such, he contends that the Bible does not contradict itself.[10]

These commitments did not lead the Alexandrian bishop to opt for a naïve literalism. While claiming Scriptures are sufficient, he opted for a Christocentric understanding of Scripture.[11] That is, Athanasius claimed that there is nothing else found in Scripture but Christ.[12] He also contended that without a pure mind and an honorable life Scripture is not properly understood.[13]

This focus on the biblical text in a critical way led Athanasius occasionally, but not typically, to allegorize the Bible.[14] Also after the manner of the Alexandrian tradition, Athanasius did point to a kind of natural knowledge of God. As he put it, all people have a portion of the Word as rational human beings.[15] In another context, he spoke of God ordering creation in such a way that He might be known by it.[16] Yet he was at the same time critical of Greek philosophy, calling for use of biblical phrases to guide theology.[17]

Athanasius was not a proponent of the authority of Scripture alone. He also appealed to the authority of Tradition, in the sense of the consensus of bishops (what is now termed the *consensus fidelium*).[18] Echoing the Coun-

---

8. Ath. *Log. Eoan.*, 56 (NPNF² 4:66).

9. Ath. *Log. Hellen.*, I.1 (NPNF² 4:4); see Ath. *Ep.* (367), IIIXI.1 (NPNF² 4:551), on the inspiration of Scripture.

10. Ath. *Ep.* (347), XIX.3 (NPNF² 4:546).

11. Ath. *Log. Hellen.* I.1 (NPNF² 4:4); cf. Ath. *Log. Eoan.*, 31 (NPNF² 4:53).

12. Ath. *Log. Eoan.*, 37 (NPNF² 4:56); Ath. *Log. Hellen.*, I.I (NPNF² 4:4).

13. Ath. *Log. Eoan.*, 57 (NPNF² 4:67).

14. See Ath. *Log. Hellen.*, I.3 (NPNF² 4:5). But see note 17.

15. Ath. *Log. Eoan.*, 3,11 (NPNF² 4:37, 42).

16. Ath. *Log. Hellen.*, III.35 (NPNF² 4:22).

17. Ath. *Log. Eoan.*, 46 (NPNF² 4:61–62); Ath. *Decr.*, 18–19 (NPNF² 4:162).

18. Ath. *Apol. Ar.*, 30 (NPNF² 4:115–16).

cil of Arminum and Seleucia, he writes, "for what we do not understand in the sacred oracles, instead of rejecting, we seek from persons to whom the Lord revealed it, and from them we ask for instructon."[19]

The African Father speaks of faith coming to us from the Apostolic Tradition. We are to hold such opinions as these saints have handed them down.[20]

An apologetic sensitivity surfaced in other ways. While attacking the absurdity of paganism, Athanasius defended the rationality of the principle that the universe is work of one Creator Who rules with the Logos.[21] The fact that the cosmos is one, that it is characterized by harmony among opposites, proves that there is one Creator, he argued.[22]

Another argument used on behalf of the truth of Christianity emerged from Athanasius's observation that since Christianity had been adopted in many regions, Greeks and barbarians who used to war against each other and were actually cruel to their own kin have now laid aside their savagery. And likewise since receiving Christ, barbarians who had sacrificed to idols and practiced savagery with each other and others began to practice careful guardianship of their economic interests.[23] The Alexandrian bishop claims the Savior's doctrine is everywhere increasing while idolatry is dwindling.[24]

An additional point made by Athanasius is noteworthy: He contends that while the wise among the Greeks were unable to persuade even a few concerning immortality and virtuous life, Christ by ordinary language has persuaded whole churches to think of nothing but divine glory.[25]

Perhaps relevant to Athanasius's African roots is his assessment of indigenous African cultures. We have already noted comments suggesting a pejorative view of these cultures (references to barbarians). But he expressly singled out Egyptians, Ethiopians, Persians, and Scythains for criticisms. He claims that they are men that mind magic, are superstitious and

---

19. Ath. *Synod.*, 40 (*NPNF*² 4:471): "τοῦτο δὲ εἰ ἀληθῶς Ἐλεγον, οὐχ ἔδει λέγειν αὐτοὺς, Ἐχσάλλομεν ταύτας ἀλλ'ἤξιουν μαθεῖν παρὰ τῶν ἐπισταμένων, ἐπεὶ οψείλουσί γε, χαὶ ἅπερ ἂν ἐν ταις θειαις Γραψάις μὴ νοήσωσιν ἐχσάλλειν, χαὶ χατηγορεῖν τοὺς γράψαντας αυτα."

20. Ath. *Ep.* (330), II.5 (*NPNF*² 4:511); cf. ibid., LX.6 (*NPNF*² 4:576–77).

21. Ath. *Log. Eoan.*, 4ff. (*NPNF*² 4:38ff.).

22. Ath. *Log. Hellen.*, III.35–39 (*NPNF*² 4:22–25).

23. Ath. *Log. Eoan.*, 51–52 (*NPNF*² 4:64).

24. Ibid., 55 (*NPNF*² 4:66).

25. Ibid., 47 (*NPNF*² 4:62).

savage in their ways.[26] Though we might wonder about his motives for this comment, with Athanasius we find a sophisticated Orthodox approach.

God and Trinity

Though it is not clear that the Athanasian Creed is Athanasius's own work, it does seem to offer insights about how his tradition viewed God and His triune Nature. However, given disputes about its authenticity we will concentrate more on the indisputably authentic Athanasian reflections on God and Christology.

Champion of the Nicene formula that he was, it is hardly surprising to find Athanasius speaking of God as Father, Son, and Holy Spirit, their unity, while not collapsing their distinctions. He did draw on philosophy self-consciously to claim that God is beyond all substance and human discovery.[27] In fact, He is self-sufficient and filled with Himself.[28] This is one reason to stress God's unity and the unity of the divine Persons.

In view of his links to the Nicene formula, it is hardly surprising to find Athanasius insisting that the Son is of the same substance as the Father.[29] The brightness of the Father is said to exist eternally, and that this is His Word. Thus the Father is in the Son like the sun is in its brightness, like the light and its radiance.[30] Speaking of the Son being begotten of the Father, elsewhere, Athanasius provides another compelling analogy to make this point. He construes their relation to be akin to a river produced from a well, distinct realities and yet the two are not the same.[31] He also employs the terms *hypostases* and *ousia*.[32]

In like manner, the African Father refuses to collapse distinctions among Father, Son, and Holy Spirit. They are said to be One and yet distinct, as a river is generated from its source yet is not separated from it. The source is not the river, and the river is not its source, yet each is water. So the Godhead flows from the Father to the Son.[33] Likewise, since

---

26. Ibid., 51 (*NPNF*² 4:64).
27. Ath. *Log. Hellen.*, I.2 (*NPNF*² 4:5).
28. Ibid., I.28 (*NPNF*² 4:18).
29. Ath. *Ag. Ar.*, I.III.9; II.XXIII.2 (*NPNF*² 4:311, 394).
30. Ibid., III.XXIII.3–4; II.XVIII.33; I.VII.24–25 (*NPNF*² 4:394–95, 366, 320–21).
31. Ath. *Ek. Pis.*, 2 (*NPNF*² 4:84).
32. Ath. *Ag. Ar.*, III.XXX.66 (*NPNF*² 4:430; Ath. *Ep. Af.*, 4 (*NPNF*² 4:490–91).
33. Ath. *Ep. Pis.*, 2 (*NPNF*² 4:84).

the Holy Spirit can only be sent by God, and since the Son conferred the Spirit, Athanasius is enabled to make his core Nicene affirmation, that the Son must be God.[34]

Creation and Providence

The divinity of the Word also enables Athanasius to assert the sovereignty of God. He ties Christ's deity to His universal providence. For through Christ the Father is said to order all things.[35] Indeed, Christ is Present in all creation as the One through Whom it had come into being.[36] Creation is said to partake of the Word.[37] And the creation, he insists, was made out of nothing.[38] We have already noted that in a manner characteristic of Alexandrian thinking he contended that everyone has at least a portion of the power of the Word of God because we are all rational.[39] In making these affirmations he of course operates with the Greek philosophical body-soul dualism.[40]

Athanasius's view of Providence is not one of monolithic divine domination. With images most suggestive of efforts today by theologians to relate religion and science, Athanasius writes in *Against the Heathens* that God rules the cosmos like a conductor governs a chorus or like a royal founder supervises the public and private life of a town.[41]

Christology

Athanasius offers a neat apology for the Incarnation. Since Greek philosophers contended that the Word of God is in the universe (which they regarded as a body), Athanasius could contend that it is hardly surprising to say that the Word is united with a Man.[42] The African Father proceeds to offer an intriguing reflection that resonates with much theology today.

---

34. Ath. *Ag. Ar.*, II.XV.18–XVI.18 (*NPNF*² 4:357); cf. Ath. *Ep. Serap.*, 2.10.
35. Ath. *Log. Eoan.*, 1 (*NPNF*² 4:36).
36. Ibid., 17 (*NPNF*² 4:45).
37. Ath. *Log. Hellen.*, III.42 (*NPNF*² 4:26).
38. Ath. *Log. Eoan.*, 2–3, 4 (*NPNF*² 4:36–37, 38).
39. See note 15 above.
40. Ath. *Log. Hellen.*, II.30ff. (*NPNF*² 4:20ff.).
41. Ibid., III.43 (*NPNF*² 4:27).
42. Ath. *Log. Eoan.*, 41 (*NPNF*² 4:58).

He contended that the Word did not appear in the nobler parts of creation, since He did not come to make a display, but to heal suffering.[43]

Athanasius proceeded to cite four reasons for the Word of God to appear in bodily form: (1) To turn corruption into incorruption; (2) None other than God could create the *imago Dei* anew; (3) None other than God could render the mortal immortal; and (4) Only God's Word could teach of the Father.[44] Elsewhere the famed Alexandrian bishop added that the Incarnation was necessary because it unites us to Christ's Body, which is a better state than the original creation.[45] In another correspondence he insisted that Christ must be God, for a creature could not save other creatures.[46]

Elaborating further on the rationale for the Incarnation, Athanasius also notes that our idolatry and godlessness hide the knowledge of God. Only He Who was teaching human beings concerning the Father by His own Providence and ordering of all things [Providence] could renew these teachings. In our idolatry we have turned our eyes downward, no longer looking upward. Consequently, God must sojourn down here as a Man (where we are looking) in order to teach by the works of His Body those who would not know Him from His Providence (looking upward).[47] Who fails to see Christ with his rational understanding may now apprehend Him by the works of His Body.[48]

Athanasius proceeds to argue that it is not inconsistent for the Father to have brought about salvation by the means He made it, at least not if we begin with the nature of creation.[49] The African Father posits a creation-redemption continuity, which is tied to his endorsement of the concept of creation out of nothing.[50]

Regarding the relation between the Word and Jesus's Body, Athanasius further contends that Christ took on flesh without changing, as Aaron was still Aaron when clothed as a high priest.[51] Relying on the image of Christ's reign over the universe as akin to the king who had founded a city's

---

43. Ibid., 43 (*NPNF*[2] 4:59).

44. Ibid., 20 (*NPNF*[2] 4:46–47).

45. Ath. *Ep.* (371), LXI.3 (*NPNF*[2] 4:579); Ath. *Ag. Ar.*, II.XXII.74–76 (*NPNF*[2] 4:388–89).

46. Ath. *Ep.* (n.d.), LX.8 (*NPNF*[2] 4:577).

47. Ath. *Log. Eoan.*, 14 (*NPNF*[2] 4:44).

48. Ibid., 54 (*NPNF*[2] 4:65).

49. Ibid., 1 (*NPNF*[2] 4:37).

50. Ibid., 3 (*NPNF*[2] 4:37).

51. Ath. *Ag. Ar.*, II.XIV.7 (*NPNF*[2] 4:351–52).

ongoing supervision of it, Athanasius notes that in sin the world-city has rebelled. Therefore, it takes a visit from the true prince to bring it back to its original allegiance.[52]

Typical of the Alexandrian tradition, Athanasius emphasized the unity of the Person of Christ, affirming the *communicatio idiomatum*.[53] Whatever is said of one of Jesus's Natures may be attributed to the other. Consequently he spoke of Mary as Mother of God.[54]

But then in another sense, this African Father seemed it take it back. He claimed that it is impossible for the Word to suffer. But he argues that Jesus did need to take a body capable of death in order to die in our place.[55] It is fitting for Christ to die publically he contends, because it would have been unfitting for Him to die in weakness.[56] Athanasius seems to unite the historically distinct Christological strands by contending that some things may be attributed to one of Christ's Natures which are not attributed to the other.[57]

Sin

The need for Christ to die of course relates to the doctrine of sin. Athanasius describes Sin as man's turning back to his natural state, an absorption in natural things.[58] This leads to a state of nothingness.[59] Sin has rendered humans mortal and corruptible.[60] As such it is a fall into nothingness.[61] This is language that anticipates Augustine's later treatment of sin.

In the same line of thought, the Alexandrian bishop referred to sin as a falling back into selfish desires, preferring one's own good to contemplation of the divine. Those desires lead to terror, fear of death, and not satisfying these desires leads to more evil. The soul abuses the term "good," equating

---

52. Ath. *Log. Eoan.*, 10, 55 (*NPNF*² 4:41, 66).
53. Ibid., 17 (*NPNF*² 4:45); Ath. *Ep.* (n.d.), LIX.9 (*NPNF*² 4:573–74).
54. Ath. *Ag. Ar.*, III.XXVI.33 (*NPNF*² 4:411).
55. Ath. *Log. Eoan.*, 9 (*NPNF*² 4:40–41).
56. Ibid., 21–22 (*NPNF*² 4:47–48).
57. Ath. *Ag. Ar.*, III.XXVI.34–35; III.XXVIII.53 (*NPNF*² 4:412–13, 422).
58. Ath. *Log. Hellen.*, I.3 (*NPNF*² 4:5).
59. Ath. *Log. Eoan.*, 4 (*NPNF*² 4:38).
60. Ath. *Ag. Ar.*, IIIXXVI.33 (*NPNF*² 4:412).
61. Ath. *Log. Eoan.*, 4 (*NPNF*² 4:38); Ath. *Log. Hellen.*, 7 (*NPNF*² 4:7); cf. Aug. *Civ.*, XIV.13 (*NPNF*¹ 2:273).

it with pleasure.⁶² Much like Augustine's later conception of sin as concupiscence Athanasius spoke of an insatiable desire to sin.⁶³

On the other hand, though, Athanasius was no Augustinian ahead of his time. In a manner consistent with the construal of Justification as demanding works he contended that we have a free will, that some can maintain holiness their entire lives.⁶⁴ Repentance from sin alone does not guard the just claims of God, Athanasius claims. For repentance does call men back from what is their nature.⁶⁵

Atonement

Athanasius seems to teach a Governmental Theology of Atonement.⁶⁶ In accord with this model, he speaks of Christ bringing to nought the power of death and the devil, but also refers to a sacrifice putting an end to the Law.⁶⁷ The sacrifice paid to the Father, he claims at one point, is only to reclaim us from the forces of evil, as a king reclaims his properties from such forces. A cure is required, not a mere decree like creation was.⁶⁸

Athanasius also refers to many proofs of Christ's Resurrection. One provocative point he makes is that the fact that the Savior continues to act and exercise power to this day belongs only to the living, which indicates that He cannot be dead.⁶⁹

Justification and Sanctification: Deification

We find the same ambiguity about our own role and the role of God's Work in saving us that we have observed in other pre-Augustinian leaders of the African church. On one hand, he was concerned about the decision of the believer, that it be a rational choice for the Gospel that can be defended on

---

62. Ath. *Log. Hellen.*, I.3–4 (*NPNF*² 4:5–6).

63. Ath. *Log. Eoan.*, 5 (*NPNF*² 4:38); Ath. *Log. Hellen.*, I.2 (*NPNF*² 4:4–5); cf. Aug. *Civ.*, XIV.15016 (*NPNF*¹ 2:275–76).

64. Ath. *Ag. Ar.*, IIIXXVI.33 (*NPNF*² 4:411–12).

65. Ath. *Log. Eoan.*, 7 (*NPNF*² 4:39–40).

66. Ibid., 9, 10, 21 (*NPNF*² 4:41, 47–48); cf. ibid., 15–16 (*NPNF*² 4:44–45).

67. Ibid., 9–10 (*NPNF*² 4:41).

68. Ibid., 44 (*NPNF*² 4:60).

69. Ibid., 30 (*NPNF*² 4:52). For other, related proofs, see ibid., 31ff. (*NPNF*² 4:52ff.).

rational grounds.[70] We have already observed other examples of his apologetic bent. But he also regarded faith as a gift of God, a work of the Holy Spirit.[71] This intertwining of faith/grace and our own actions in coming to faith is typical of Athanasius's writings. We see this heritage in the Athanasian Creed, as it is not really clear from that document whether it teaches salvation by faith or makes faith a new law.[72]

Such an intertwining is characteristic of the doctrine of deification. And Athanasius clearly embraced this manner of construing salvation. "For He [the Son of God] was made Man so that we might be made God."[73] Athanasius writes, concerning Christ, "He Himself made us sons of the Father, and deified men by becoming Himself man."[74]

Athanasius makes this affirmation in other ways at points. He contends that by the sharing of Christ's Body we are quickened from death.[75] His human nature is exalted, being raised form the dead and ascended into heaven so that we might be exalted.[76] And it is the Spirit, he writes, Who knits us into the Godhead.[77] There is certainly in any case a clear role for grace in deification, on Athanasius's grounds.[78]

---

70. See Ath. *V. Ant.*, 1-3 (*NPNF*² 4:195-96) for a good example of how Athanasius portrayed Anthony's life as providing a rational, compelling witness of Christ to the pagans.

71. Ibid., 93 (*NPNF*² 4:221); Ath. *Ep. Serap.*, 1.22, 24.

72. See for example Ath. *Ep.* (331), III.2. Regarding the Athanasian Creed (*ANF* 7:366-67), it was probably not written by the African Father, but it represents his thinking, even regarding its references to the need to believe the Creed and do good in order to be saved.

73. Ath. *Log. Epan.*, 54.3 (*NPNF*² 4:65): "Αυτὸ γὰρ ενηορωπησεν, ἵνα ἡμεις θεωποιηθωμεν."

74. Ath. *Ag. Ar.*, I.XI.38 (*NPNF*² 4:329): ". . . ἀλλὰ μᾶλλον ἐξελτίωσεν αὐτὸς τὰ δεόμενα Βελζιώσεως. χαὶ ἐι Βελτιῶσαι χάριν χαταξεξηχεν οὐχ ἄρα μισθὸν ἔσχε τὸ λέγεσθαι γιὸς χαὶ Θεὸς, ἀλλὰ μᾶλλον αὐτὸς υἱοποίησεν ἡμᾶς τῷ Πατρὶ χαὶ ἐθεοποίησε τοὺς ἀνθρώπους γενόμενος αὐτὸς ἄνθρωπος." Cf. ibid., I.XI.39; II.XIX.47; III.XXVI.33 (*NPNF*² 4:329, 374, 411); Ath. *Log. Eoan.*, 54 (*NPNF*² 4:65); Ath. *Ep. Serap.*, I.24, in *Catechism of the Catholic Church*, 1988.

75. Ath. *Log. Eoan.*, 8 (*NPNF*² 4: 4:40).

76. Ath. *Ag. Ar.*, I.XI.41 (*NPNF*² 4: 4:330).

77. Ibid., III.XXV.24 (*NPNF*² 4: 4:407).

78. Ibid., III.XXV.25 (*NPNF*² 4: 4:407).

Ministry

Athanasius endorsed a high view of ministry. Without bishops there would be no Church, he claims. But their authority is rooted in Scripture, as their task is identified as nothing more than bringing "instruction from the Scriptures."[79]

Sacraments

Generally speaking, Athanasius does not offer much that is unique in his reflections on this issue. He claimed that Baptism makes us sons of God or united to the Son.[80] The Spirit is also conferred in this (apparently born-again) experience. It is God Who is credited with doing the Baptism.[81]

The Alexandrian bishop speaks of the flesh in the Eucharist as spiritual, suggesting a Calvinist model of the Sacrament.[82] But elsewhere, he claims, along with the dominant witness of the early Church, that in the sacraments we put on Christ, that presumably He is present in the sacramental elements.[83] He even speaks of the elements becoming Christ's Body.[84]

Social Ethics

Given tensions with the empire over the Arian controversy it is not surprising that Athanasius claimed that the judgment of the Church had not received its validity from the empire.[85] He called for a distinction of Church and Empire.[86] He was open to military service by Christians and even countenanced killing the enemy in battle.[87] But he urged the faithful to remember the poor with kindness.[88]

---

79. Ath. *Ep.* (354–55), XLIX.2, 4 (*NPNF*² 4:558).
80. Ath. *Ag. Ar.*, II.XVIII.41 (*NPNF*² 4:370); Ath. *Ep.*, XLIX.4 (*NPNF*² 4:558).
81. Ath. *Exp. Ps.*, LXXV.13; Ath. *Ag. Ar.*, II.XVIII.41 (*NPNF*² 4:370).
82. Ath. *Ep. Serap.*, 4.19 (*NPNF*² 4:lxxix). For references to Calvin, see p.88, n.45.
83. Ath. *Ep.* (332), IV.3 (*NPNF*² 4:516).
84. Ath. *Frag. Al.*; see Volz, *Faith and Practice in the Early Church*, 108, 219.
85. Ath. *Hist. Ar.*, V.39 (*NPNF*² 4:283–84).
86. Ibid., VI.44 (*NPNF*² 4:286).
87. Ath. *Ep.* (354), XLVIII (*NPNF*² 4:557).
88. Ibid. (329), I.11 (*NPNF*² 4:510); ibid. (332), IV.3 (*NPNF*² 4:516); ibid. (373), XLV (*NPNF*² 4:553); Ath. *Hist. Ar.*, VII.61 (*NPNF*² 4:292–93).

Eschatology

Given the Alexandrain heritage's dialogue with Greek philosophy, it is not surpising that Athansius would endorse this tradition's body-soul dualism and affirmation of the immortality of the soul.[89] But in the case of Athansius this immortality is not a function of human nature, but of Christ, since we are made of nothing.[90] However, because as we have noted Christ is intertwined with all creation, there are hints (in the Alexandrian traditions of Origen) that in Athanasius's view no human beings are totally annihilated, that there is a continued existence for all.[91]

Summary

Athanasius's contribution to the Church in facilitating its reception of the Nicene and Trinitarian formulas is indisputable. His role in emphasizing the importance and contribution of monasticism is also quite significant. His reflections on Sin doubtless paved the way for Augustine's insights on this doctrine. But this Black man also offers us a model for doing theology in a sophisticated Orthodox way, not systematically dependent on philosophy and our context in reading Scripture, but also not in the world-denying, apparently anti-intellectualist mode of Tertullian and the monks. Athanasius's theology is also a reminder that when justification is portrayed as deification, the Work of God is not beclouded (or at least his language is still useful in making that witness).

---

89. See note 40 above.

90. Ath. *Log. Eoan.*, 3, 11, 13 (*NPNF*² 4:37, 42, 43).

91. Ibid., 4 (*NPNF*² 4:38). See the discussion in Archibald Robertson, "Editor's Introduction to the Treatise," in *NPNF*² 4:32.

16

Macarius the Egyptian

WE CANNOT BE CERTAIN that the literature we have that has been attributed to this Egyptian monk is really his own writings. This literature may have been the work of Syrian monks of the fifth century that they credited to Macarius (300–390). What we know of the historical Macarius comes largely from oral traditions of the Egyptian desert. We know him as a famous monk who lived as a hermit for sixty years, founding a large colony of monks.

We need to examine data in support of the arguments for the Syrian origins of the Macarian sermons, in order to assess their validity and because such reflections lead us to the conclusion that this literature still reflects the theology of the early North African church. The champion for the Syrian origins has been Werner Jaeger. He contended that the actual author of these sermons was either a fifth-century Syrian monk whose conception of spirituality derived from Gregory of Nyssa or a Syrian heretical movement, the Messalians.[1]

The case for an indebtedness to Gregory of Nyssa can be made on the basis of a comparison between Macarius's *Great Letter* and one of Gregory's works, *De instituto Christiano*. Jaeger thinks they developed from a common source, if not a Macarian document dependent on Nyssa. In addition, given the fact that Gregory of Nyssa knew of the Messalians and was impressed by Mesopotamian monks, he might have been interested in preparing a document that expressed the themes of this community. Also the early church historian Socrates Scholasticus noted that a disciple of the two early monks

---

1. Jaeger, *Two Rediscovered Works of Ancient Christian Literature*.

named Macarius (the one from Alexandria, not the Egyptian) had close interaction with Gregory's family friend Gregory of Nazianzus.[2]

The viability of this thesis, then, is related at least in part to the question of a possible relation between the Macarian sermons and the Messalian movement. Messalians were ascetics whose whole discipline consisted in prayer, even to the exclusion of fasting, labor, or other practices. They emphasized the outpouring of the Holy Spirit, minimizing the efficacy of the Sacraments. They were also critical of the clerical hierarchy. They sought to uproot the passions, achieve a state of passionlessness, so that even moral failings would become innocent since they were perpetrated without passion.[3] But here we see that the authentic statements of Macarius himself as reported in the *Sayings of the Desert Fathers* were concerned to still his passions, both when reproving others and when receiving praise.[4]

Under the leadership of Dadoes, Sabbas, Adelphios, Hermas, and Symeon, Messalianism spread especially in Mesopotamia, but had a gradual impact in Egypt. The ecclesiastical hierarchy condemned the movement in 390 and later at various Synods. Its final condemnation came in 431 at the Council of Ephesus.

Links suggesting the Syrian origin of the Macarian sermons include the latter's de-emphasis on the Sacraments. Also references in these sermons to the Spirit employ the feminine gender, a characteristic of Syrian Christianity.[5] The personal manner of numbering months is also employed (April as the first month of the year).[6] And of course, like the Messalians, the Eucharist was not frequently celebrated among the Anchorites.

Are These African Documents After All?

Still to be explained in Jaeger's thesis about the Syrian origins of the Macarian corpus is how they came to be identified with the great Egyptian monk. One argument might be that after the condemnation of Messalianism the texts of

---

2. See George A. Maloney, "Introduction," in *PM* 9–11. Aslo see Gregory of Nyssa, *Treatise on Virginity* (*Virginitate*) (ca. 370), 23:3–6.
3. Socr. *H.e.*, IV.XXIII (*NPNF*[2] 2:107). See also Maloney, "Introduction," 8.
4. Macarius, 20, 23, 41, in *AP* 131, 132, 138.
5. Maloney, "Introduction," 7, 19.
6. Mac. *Hom. IInum.*, 5.9 (*PM* 73, 275).

its leaders, purged of any glaring Messalian errors by editors, might come to achieve orthodox status if they were attributed to the venerable Macarius.[7]

Several rebuttals to this thesis can be offered. The first refers to the purely hypothetical suggestion of why these texts came to be identified with Macarius. What can be stated with documentation is the overlap between the core themes of the Macarian corpus and themes rooted in ancient African theology (especially themes we identified in the sayings ascribed to Macarius the Egyptian). We will see this when we examine overlaps on Theological Method, Classic View of the Atonement, Justification/Deification, as well as Sanctification as struggle with the devil and as striving for perfection. In addition, the Macarian sermons' emphasis on gifts of healing and teaching of a sovereign God are themes that appear in sayings of Macarius and/or other monks or else (in the case of a sovereign God) suggest links with the piety of traditional African religions.[8]

Given the data, then, it seems that who wrote the Macarian literature is as much an open question as who wrote certain New Testament Books, as akin to the question of whether Paul actually had a role in writing the Deutero-Pauline Books. Even if the author was a monk of a later period, working in a setting outside Africa, it does not seem irresponsible to suggest that the tradition's subscription of these documents to Macarius might suggest that the author accurately represented the monk's views, as the monk was the actual author's mentor. And if the author of the Macarian corpus was an African, the fact that he was a monk, living and writing about the disciplines and teachings rooted in Africa, suggests that this is literature clearly reflecting African Christian commitments.

At least in that sense, if in no other, the Macarian literature we now consider seems legitimately identified as a work of African Christian spirituality.

Theological Method

The Macarian author compares the Bible to a letter of a king to those upon which he wants to bestow special privileges.[9] Reflecting something that seems like an allegorical model of interpretation, in one sermon it is

---

7. Maloney, "Introduction," 9.
8. Mac. *Hom. IInum.*, 48.3-4; 45.6 (*PM* 240, 229). See 15–17, above.
9. Mac. *Hom. IInum.*, 3.9.1 (*PM* 213).

claimed that the Word of God is only a shadow of the truth of Christ.[10] Thus we should not only trust in Scripture. Grace, it is said, writes the laws of the Spirit in the heart.[11]

The only other time we see something like traces of apologetics and a Method of Correlation in Macarian thought is when he posits a kind of cosmological relation between human being and divine being. One who knows the dignity of the soul, he contends, knows the mysteries of God.[12]

Nevertheless, unlike Gregory of Nyssa, the Macarian author is not a Correlationist, not seeking links between reason and the Word of God.[13] Much more like the Orthodox approach of the Desert Fathers, figural interpretation, having believers identify with the biblical characters, is employed.[14] Also much like the early African monks we can identify the use of proverbs or short stories to make points.[15]

God and Providence

There is little attention given to the Nature of God and none given to the Trinity. In typical African fashion, Macarius celebrates the mystery of God, His incomprehensibility.[16] When He wishes He becomes fire, "burning up every coarse passion that has taken root in the soul."[17] But this is a God of love and compassion: "When He wishes, He becomes an inexpressible and mysterious rest so that the soul may find rest in God's rest. When He wishes, He becomes joy and peace, cherishing and protecting the soul."[18]

---

10. Ibid., 30.1 (*PM* 190).

11. Ibid., 15.20 (*PM* 116).

12. Ibid., 27/1 (*PM* 174).

13. Ibid., 42.1; 45.2 (*PM* 218, 227). Cf. Gregory of Nyssa, Λογος Κατεχετικος (n.d.), 2.

14. Ibid., 47.1-6; 50.1-2 (*PM* 232-34, 244).

15. Ibid., 15.20; 16.12; 18.4-5 (*PM* 115, 134, 142-43).

16. Ibid., 16.5; 26.17; 29.1 (*PM* 131, 170, 186-87).

17. Ibid., 4.11 (*PM* 55): "Ὅτε βούλεται πῦρ γίνεται, πᾶν ψαῦλον καὶ ἐπείσαχ-τον πάθος τῆς ψυχῆς χατακαιοῶ."

18. Ibid. (Latin version only): ". . . quandu vult fit ineffabilis et arcona requies, ut requiescat anima in requie divinas quando vult, fit gadium et pax, fovens et protengens animam."

Such an affirmation is made at a number of points.[19] We can approach God with confidence, not with despair over past sins.[20]

God is said to be omnipotent.[21] A strong doctrine of Providence is affirmed at one point. "All things that exist come about by divine providence . . ."[22] Yet paradoxically free will is affirmed at points.[23] This loving God is said to rule by testing us, permitting afflictions.[24] God is said to guide us providentially according to reason.[25] But Macarius adds, some will be rejected by God, as a fisherman rejects the least useful fish in the net.[26]

Anthropology and Sin

Generally speaking the Macarian literature reflects a positive view of the physical. The body is said to be worthy of the indwelling of God.[27] Of course, typical of Easter thinking and pre-Augustinian African thought, human nature is not complete unless united with the heavenly nature.[28] Full manhood is achieved through the discipline of grace.[29]

Like most monks, Macarius took sin seriously. Though as we noted he affirms free will at points, he also speaks of our bondage to sin. Sin is born in man, he claims.[30] With language most suggestive of the developing doctrine of Original Sin, it is claimed that in Adam's fall a leaven of evil passions infecting the whole earth was released.[31]

---

19. Ibid., 2.5; 4.16; 15.44; 16.3 (*PM* 47, 57, 125, 231); Mac. *Ep.* (*PM* 271).

20. Mac. *Hom. IInum.*, 4.24 (*PM* 61).

21. Ibid., 15.23 (*PM* 117).

22. Ibid., 15.7 (*PM* 111): ". . . καὶ πάντα τὰ δημιουργήματα, διὰ τὴν Βασιλείαν, ἣν μέλλουσι κληρονομεῖν οἱ ἐχλεχτοί, γεγόνασι, διὰ τὸ τὴν εἰρηνιχὴν χαὶ χαθ᾽ὁμόνοιαν συστῆναι Βασιλείαν."

23. Ibid., 24.6; 26.6; 27.9.10, 22 (*PM* 159, 166, 177, 178, 183); Mac. *Ep.* (*PM* 253–54).

24. Mac. *Hom. IInum.*, 15.29; 26.3; 27.8; 32.7; 47.13; 48.1 (*PM* 119, 165, 177, 199, 237, 239).

25. Ibid., 40.3 (*PM* 215).

26. Ibid., 15.52 (*PM* 128).

27. Ibid., 1.3; 5.11; 11.1 (*PM* 38–39, 74, 90).

28. Ibid., 32.6 (*PM* 199).

29. Ibid., 32.10 (*PM* 200–201).

30. Ibid., 2.1; 15.34–36, 21; 30.8 (*PM* 44–45, 121; 116, 193); Mac. *Ep.* (*PM* 255).

31. Mac. *Hom. IInum.*, 24.2 (*PM* 157).

Although as we shall observe Macarius believed in growth in grace, there are times when he spoke as if sin ever plagues the Christian. Sin is said to remain after Baptism, in the depth of the soul.[32] Employing a term crucial for the doctrine of Original Sin, the corpus refers to the sin that remains in the faithful as *concupiscence*.[33]

Christology and Atonement

Although we find little discussion of the nature of Christ, Macarius did speak of the necessity of the Incarnation. It is necessary so that God might be seen.[34] About the Person of Christ the corpus does speak of Him as One Substance, who inhabits the soul by the Word.[35]

About the Atonement, the Macarian corpus most characteristically refers to it as a sacrifice (suggesting the Satisfaction Theory).[36] But we also find indications of the characteristic monastic reliance on the language of the Classic View of the Atonement. Christ is said to have bought our ransom from slavery.[37] There is one reference to Christ's descent into hell, freeing souls from hell.[38] Could this entail a second chance for those who did not die in faith, in the tradition of Origen and the belief that many or all will be saved?

Justification and Sanctification: Deification

In the tradition of many of the African Fathers, Macarius taught salvation as deification, as participation of the believer in the divine life. For example, he writes, "For the person that truly believes in Christ must be transported and changed from his present state of evil to another state, one that is

---

32. Ibid., 15.13–14; 41.1 (*PM* 113, 216–17).
33. Ibid., 16.4; 17.6; 26.2 (*PM* 130, 137, 164).
34. Ibid., 4.11 (*PM* 55).
35. Mac. *Ep.* (*PM* 257).
36. Mac. *Hom. IInum.*, 24.3; 47.8 (*PM* 157–58, 235).
37. Ibid., 20.6; 30.9 (*PM* 152, 193).
38. Ibid., 11.10–11 (*PM* 94–95).

good, and from his present lowly nature into another, divine nature."[39] "For man is divinized."[40]

Our humanity is brought to divinity.[41] Grace is mingled in our nature, Macarius claims.[42] The soul becomes the Lord's Throne, in which we bear Christ in our souls.[43] God forms His heavenly image in man.[44] We need the Spirit to clothe us with divine energies. The Spirit makes us one with the Lord.[45]

We are intoxicated with (drunk on) God.[46] In another work that attributes teachings to Macarius (albeit perhaps not authentic), he is reported to have compared prayer to Jesus to good chewing gum, which sweatens the salvia and cleanses bad breath.[47]

It is interesting to note in these texts the emphasis on God's action, on grace, in bringing about this saving reality. Also of interest is the fact, as we have noted, that the historical Macarius himself seems to have taught deification, is said to have become a god on earth.[48]

In a similar vein a marriage analogy is employed by Macarius. Christians are brides of Christ, sharing all in common with Him.[49] We become like Christ. He burns in believers like a lamp.[50] We are made one with the Lord by the indwelling Spirit.[51] We come to be dominated by the Holy

---

39. Ibid., 44.5 (*PM* 224): "Δεῖ γὰρ τὴν Ψιχὴν τὴν ἐν αληθεία πιστεύουσαν Χριστῶ, μετασεθῆναι χαὶ αλλαγῆναι ἀπὸ τῆς νῦν πινηρᾶς χαταστάσεως, εἰς ἑτέπαν χατάστασιν αγαθήν, χαὶ ἀπὸ τῆς νυν ψύσεως ταπεινῆς, εἰς ἑτέρὰν Θείαν ψύσιν, χὰι χαινὴν αυτὴν απεργασθῆναι . . ." Cf. ibid., 4.10; 10.4; 24.1; 25.3, 5; 34.3; 44.1 (*PM* 54, 90, 157, 160, 161, 204, 223).

40. Ibid., 26.2 (*PM* 164): "Αποθηεουται γαρ ο ανθρωποσ."

41. Ibid., 11.9; 34.2 (*PM* 93, 204).

42. Ibid., 8.2 (*PM* 81).

43. Ibid., 1.2; 32.2 (*PM* 37-38, 197).

44. Ibid., 11.6 (*PM* 92).

45. Ibid., 20.2 (*PM* 150; Mac. *Ep.* (*PM* 269-70).

46. Mac. *Hom. IInum.*, 15.40; 27.16 (*PM* 123, 178).

47. Mac. *Virt*. See Harmless, *Desert Christians*, 220.

48. Macarius, 32, in *AP* 134.

49. Mac. *Hom. IInum.*, 4.14; 15.2; 17.13; 16.13; 18.7; 32.9; 45.7; 46.6; 47.17 (*PM* 56, 108-9, 140, 135, 144, 200, 229, 232, 238); Mac. *Ep.* (*PM* 256-57).

50. Mac. *Hom. IInum.*, 15.38; 43.1-2 (*PM* 123, 219).

51. Mac. *Ep.* (*PM* 269-70).

Spirit, intoxicated with God.[52] In a manner most suggestive of the Forensic View of Justification, it is said that God covers us with grace.[53]

The Macarian literature goes so far as to claim that we are captives of grace. Salvation is said to be a gift.[54] Anyone who stands on his own righteousness labors in vain. It is not our work but God Who saves.[55] God gives grace even to those not meriting it.[56] Predestination is even affirmed.[57] This produces a sense of our total dependence on God. Though chosen by Him Christians still feel themselves as worthless.[58]

Of course, this is only part of the story when it comes to salvation. As we have noted there is a component of works involved in saving us when we are teaching deification. We see this in the Macarian literature. One way in which this is manifested is in the teaching that there are degrees of grace in the believer.[59] Only part of the soul is touched by grace.[60] One rich in grace is said to have humility.[61]

We are still said to have to free will. Though intoxicated with God and dominated by the Holy Spirit, we still have free will.[62] Grace, it is said, works on our free will. Indeed, in Macarius's view, the believer would deserve no reward if free choice were not involved.[63] Grace is given for the testing of free will.[64] We can lose the Spirit if not cooperating.[65]

Typical of pre-Augustinian theology and for a proponent of deification, the Macarian corpus does not make clear the priority of grace in our collaboration with grace. Comments are made regarding the need to make oneself worthy of God and the heavenly kingdom.[66] Christians are said to be

52. Mac. Hom. IInum., 9.1; 27.9 (PM 83–84, 177–78).
53. Ibid., 16.11 (PM 133).
54. Ibid., 26.16; 4.27 (PM 170, 62).
55. Ibid., 20.3; 37.10 (PM 151, 210).
56. Ibid., 6.2 (PM 76).
57. Ibid., 9.2–4 (PM 84).
58. Ibid., 27.4 (PM 176).
59. Ibid., 29.6; 41.2 (PM 189, 217).
60. Ibid., 50.4 (PM 246).
61. Ibid., 41.3 (PM 217).
62. Ibid., 15.40; 27.10–11 (PM 123, 178).
63. Ibid., 9.1–2; 27.21, 8–9 (PM 83–84, 183, 177).
64. Ibid., 29.1 (PM 186–87).
65. Ibid., 27.9,13 (PM 177, 179–80).
66. Ibid., 1.2; 4.1,6; 29.5–6; 30.3, 4 (PM 37, 50, 52–53, 188–89, 191); cf. Mac. Ep. (PM 260).

recompensed for their love. If we wish to be born again, Macarius contends, we ought to act differently.[67] We need to prepare ourselves for grace.[68] If one is not prepared, Macarius notes, he loses grace. He would have us beg the Lord that we be worthy to receive the Spirit.[69] We become worthy and filled with Spirit and perform the Commandments by renouncing all things. We must be worthy in order to receive the heavenly birth.[70]

The language of cooperation of grace and works is expressly affirmed at a number of points.[71] We are told that we must work out the Justification accomplished in us.[72] God needs the working of man; yet of himself man cannot produce worthy fruits.[73] God is said to give grace to all who believe or desire it, but in a very Augustinian manner (ahead of its time) Macarius asserts all must be ascribed to grace in this case.[74] He claims that we are like helpless babes who cry and then mother (God) responds.[75] In fact, something like the Pauline/Augustinian/Reformation-like distinction between Law and Gospel is posited at one point. When the soul gives up all opinion of itself, God is said to give grace.[76]

Despite this emphasis on grace in saving us, the Macarian insistence stands: works and grace are necessary to grow in the spiritual life.[77] This has implications for a different construal of the Law (the divine Commandments). The Law, it seems, is not just the agent of condemning our sin. Fulfilling the Commandments with the help of grace is said to be a light matter.[78] Its fullness consists in forgiveness. Keeping the Law contributes to our deification, the completeness of justice in us.[79]

---

67. Mac. *Hom. IInum.*, 15.22; 14.5 (*PM* 116,106–7).
68. Ibid., 4.4.; 9.13; 19.2; 37.9–10; 47.8 (*PM* 51, 87, 147, 210, 235).
69. Ibid., 19.6; 18.3; 20.7 (*PM* 148, 142, 152).
70. Ibid., 19.1,7–8; 48.1–2; 49.3, 5 (*PM* 146, 149, 239, 242, 244).
71. Ibid., 17.8; 27.18 (*PM* 138, 181).
72. Ibid., 38.5 (*PM* 213).
73. Ibid., 26.28–29 (*PM* 171).
74. Ibid., 5.4–5; 16.12; 37.10 (*PM* 64–65, 134, 210).
75. Ibid., 46.3; 31.4 (*PM* 230–31, 195).
76. Ibid., 47.13 (*PM* 237).
77. Ibid., 26.10 (*PM* 167).
78. Mac. *Ep.* (*PM* 265–66).
79. Mac. *Hom. IInum.*, 37.304 (*PM* 207–8); cf. Mac. *Ep.* (*PM* 266).

Sanctification

Although Sanctification is part of Justification when teaching deification, it is still useful to examine the Macarian vision of the Christian life. With a further stress on grace Macarius speaks of Christ directing the soul. Love of the Spirit sanctifies.[80] All spiritual works, Macarius asserts, are works of grace, for which we can take no credit.[81] The heavenly image calls us out of captivity to conduct ourselves by serving holiness. We ought to pursue holiness.[82]

When grace abounds in the believer, the sin that remains has no power to control him.[83] We have already noted a reference to the believer being intoxicated by God, implying the spontaneity of good works.[84] But to that Macarius adds that grace is given for the testing of free will.[85]

Typical of the early monks, Christian life is interpreted as a struggle with evil, a struggle with Satan.[86] Indeed, Macarius writes of the Christian, "Such a one regards himself as the greatest of all sinners.... And the more he progresses in knowledge of God, the more simple and unlearned he considers himself.... This grace acts as a guiding force, almost second nature to him."[87]

Christians who know themselves as great sinners, feel they have accomplished nothing, no matter how much they have done.[88] We can fight sin, he writes, but God alone can uproot it.[89] This is the sense in which the Christian life is characterized by humility. We need great prudence in

---

80. Mac. *Hom. IInum.*, 1.9; 4.8 (*PM* 42, 53–54).

81. Ibid., 10.3–4 (*PM* 89; Mac. *Ep.* (*PM* 269).

82. Mac. *Ep.* (*PM* 255–56); Mac. *Hom. IInum.*, 5.12 (*PM* 74–75).

83. Mac. *Hom. IInum.*, 26.22 (*PM* 172).

84. Ibid., 15.40; 27.9 (*PM* 123, 178).

85. Ibid., 29.1 (*PM* 186–87).

86. Ibid., 5.6; 11.14; 21.1–3; 23.2; 26.18; 40.7; 42.3; 43.3 (*PM* 66, 96, 153–54, 156, 170–71, 216, 219, 220); Mac. *Ep.* (*PM* 264); cf. Mac. *Hom. IInum.*, 16.2; 17.3 (*PM* 129–30, 136).

87. Mac. *Hom. IInum.*, 16.12 (*PM* 134): "Ἔχει δὲ ὁ τοιοῦτος ἐξουδενούμενον ἑαυτὸν παρὰ πάντας ἁμαρτωλοὺς, χαὶ ἔχει ἐν ἑαυτω τὸν τοιοῦτον λογισμὸν ἐμψτευθέντα ὡς ψυσιχὸν, χαὶ ὅσον ἐισίργεται εἰς γνῶσιν Θεοῦ τοσοῦτον ἔχει αὐτὸν ἰδιώτην, χαὶ ὅσον μανθάνει, εἰς μηδὲν εἰδώς ἐστι. Ταῦτα δὲ ἡ χάρις διαχονοῦσα, ὡς ψυσιχὰ ἐν τῇ ψυχῇ ἀπεργάζεται."

88. Ibid., 26.11 (*PM* 167).

89. Ibid., 3.4, 5; 21.4; 27.22 (*PM* 48, 49, 154, 183).

living the Christian life, for the believer is to be like a servant using the master's property.[90]

In this sense the monastic disposition of Macarius to view Christian life as a life of renunciation of the self and worldly things makes sense. But Macarius's monastic influences lead him to take the next logical step, claiming that such a life should be lived without passion. He claims that this is a consequence of being united to a passionless Lord.[91] Such a life of renunciation, it is claimed, is fully realized in asceticism, the possessing of nothing.[92]

Sometimes Macarius speaks of these actions of the Christian life as purely spontaneous. He writes, "By means of this heavenly treasure they [Christians] work to acquire every virtue, relying on the fullness of the spiritual richness within them. They easily observe all righteousness and every commandment of the Lord by means of the invisible richness of grace within them."[93]

When it comes to doing good works, Christians are filled with joy and happiness, like spouses enjoying sex with a partner, like drunks with a strong drink.[94]

Most of the time, though, living the Christian life is not portrayed in terms of such spontaneity, but as a task that is commanded. The Law gives us instruction in how to live.[95] Imitation of Christ is urged.[96] Christians are to live differently from unbelievers.[97]

We are to persevere in the face of all the temptations.[98] And we can and must make progress in Christian life (as progress towards becoming

---

90. Ibid., 15.5 (*PM* 110).

91. Mac. *Ep.* (*PM* 253, 258); Mac. *Hom. IInum.*, 18.7; 24.2; 31.3; 45.1 (*PM* 144, 157, 195, 226–27).

92. Mac. *Ep.* (*PM* 260).

93. Mac. *Hom. IInum.*, 18.1 (*PM* 141–142): "Διὰ γὰρ τοῦ ἐπουρανίου Θησαυροῦ πᾶσαν ἀρετὴν δικαιοσύνης χατεργάζονται, πεποιθότες ἐπὶ τῷ πλήθει τοῦ ἐν αὐτοῖς πλούτου πνευματιχοῦ, καὶ εὐχόλως πᾶσαν διχαιοσύνην χαὶ ἐντολὴν τοῦ Κυρίου διὰ τοῦ ἀοράτου τῆς χάριτος ἐν αὐτοῖς πλούτου ἐργάζονται." Cf. Mac. *Ep.* (*PM* 265).

94. Mac. *Hom. IInum.*, 18.7 (*PM* 144).

95. Ibid., 37.1–5 (*PM* 206–8).

96. Ibid., 12.5 (*PM* 99).

97. Ibid., 4.27 (*PM* 62).

98. Ibid., 1.4; 4.8; 5.6; 21.4; 26.4,8; 29.2; 49.4 (*PM* 39, 53–54, 66, 72, 87, 155, 165, 166–67, 187, 242–43).

Godlike is mandated by the idea of deification).[99] We are to progress like an infant in the womb progresses.[100]

The Christian on the way to being deified is on the way to perfection, since God is perfect. We are ever striving, Macarius asserts.[101]

Perfection, like becoming deified, is a process, and so growth in perfection is possible.[102] Perfection is being drowned in sweet contemplation of divine and heavenly things. Perfection is not merely refraining from evil, but purging all uncleanness.[103] Perhaps as a way of linking with his earlier admission of the ongoing sinfulness of Christians, Macarius continues to regard perfection as a process, the perfect in Christ must still struggle.[104] Indeed Macarius claims that he has never seen a perfect Christian.[105] It is a work of grace. We cannot affect a perfect work without the help of the Spirit.[106]

Regarding Eschatology, Macarius simply noted that in the resurrection our bodies will be glorified.[107] This affords us another example of his break with dualism in favor of an affirmation of the goodness of the physical creation. An additional aspect of Eschatology is the Macarian claim that there are different levels in hell and in heaven, even different degrees of punishment in hell. The historical Macarius also believed there were degrees of punishment in hell.[108]

Monastic Life

The Macarian copus provides instruction on monastic life. It calls for lives of simplicity in organization and concord, for humility, humble service, and detachment.[109] Could this indicate the authentic, African monastic

---

99. Ibid., 4.27; 12.3; 50.4 (*PM* 62, 98, 139, 245).
100. Ibid., 15.41 (*PM* 123–24).
101. Mac. Ep. (*PM* 259, 256).
102. Mac. Hom. IInum., 15.37; 17.11 (*PM* 122, 139).
103. Ibid., 8.1; 17.5 (*PM* 81, 140–41).
104. Macarius, *Great Letter* (*PM* 258).
105. Mac. Hom. IInum., 8 (*PM* 81–83).
106. Ibid., 17.1; 24.4; 25.3 (*PM* 135, 158, 160).
107. Ibid., 34.2 (*PM* 203).
108. Ibid., 40.3,6; 17.5–6 (*PM* 214, 215, 137); cf. Macarius, 38, in *AP* 137.
109. Mac. Ep. (*PM* 261–62, 260, 261).

roots of the corpus? But unceasing prayer after the fashion of Messalianism is also exhorted.[110]

As we would expect given this monastic ethos, Macarius says nothing about social ethics. We do find some patriarchy when it is claimed that a woman needs a strong husband to protect her.[111] But it is interesting to note that strictures in 1 Cor 11:5 against women praying without head coverings are interpreted as teaching about the need for the whole Church to be clothed with the Spirit.[112]

The monastic ethos of the literature would also lead us to expect a de-emphasis on the Sacraments. And that topic is neglected, save several references to baptisms of the Holy Spirit, and a reference to merely receiving Christ in The Lord' Supper.[113]

Conclusions

Do we have an African theology here? We have clearly identified a number of themes in the Macarian corpus that accord with the sayings of the historical Macarius the Egyptian, which we previously analyzed in an earlier chapter. Both sets of sayings espouse the monastic life, teach deification, posit levels of Christian growth, the struggle with the devil, and a lifestyle of humility. Even if these documents were not written by Macarius himself, the fact that we have documents clearly shaped by early African monasticism seems to indicate that early African spirituality is the mother of these documents.

The daughter of Africa has clearly enriched the Church catholic. One major Protestant denomination, the Methodist church, was inspired by a number of the ideas we have been considering. Note John Wesley's comment in his June 30, 1736, diary entry: "I read Macarius and sang."[114] Should the ideas we have been considering in the Macarian corpus, its embodiment of a spirituality striving for perfection, make the Church sing too?

---

110. Ibid., (*PM* 267–68); Mac. *Hom. IInum.*, 33.1–2, 4 (*PM* 201–2).

111. Mac. *Hom. IInum.*, 45.5 (*PM* 228).

112. Ibid., 12.15 (*PM* 103).

113. Ibid., 26.23; 32.4; 43.3; 47.1 (*PM* 172, 198, 220, 222–23); cf. ibid., 27.17 (*PM* 181).

114. For more details, also see Albert C. Outler, "Introduction," in Outler, *John Wesley*, 9–10.

17

Caius Marius Victorinus

CAIUS (ALSO KNOWN AS Gaius, and more widely as Caius Marius and Marius Victorinus Afri) was a fourth-century Roman grammarian, rhetorican, and Neo-Platonic philosopher born in Africa (according to Jerome).[1] Living during the reign of Constantius II, an era in which The Nicene Party (supporters of the formulations of the Council of Nicea) was being harassed by Arian policies. He taught rhetoric in Rome. (One of his pupils was the famed early Christian scholar Jerome.) In old age, he converted to Christianity, an event that influenced Augustine's own conversion.[2] The works we have by him were directed against the Arians on behalf of the Nicene formula.

Victorinus is the first Latin writer to offer a systematic treatment of the Trinity. Two dimensions of his approach are noteworthy. He mounted his defense not just with theological treatises, but also with hymns. Also of interest in view of the vitriolics involved in the Arian Controversy, he referred to his Arian opponent in his writings as a friend.[3]

The largest bulk of Victorinus's extant writings pertain to the nascent Trinity doctrine. But they do reveal some insights about his views on the other classical doctrines.

Regarding Theological Method, in a manner most suggestive of the Orthodox Method of Tertulllian, Victorinus claims that discourse about God is too great for man. It is impossible to know God from Reason alone,

---

1. Jer. *Vir. Illus.*, CI (*NPNF*[2] 3:381).
2. Aug. *Conf.*, VII.II.3 (*NPNF*[1] 1:117).
3. Mar. Vict. *Can. Ar.*, IV.6.(30) (FC 69:8).

he claims. He does contend, though, that a sense of God's paternity is innate in our souls. Yet though the soul wishes to see inevitable things, it is too difficult to understand such things.[4] In the same spirit of paradox he employs a kind of negative theology in his exposition of the Trinity, contending what does not exist (in the sense of having infinite potentiality and power, which is true of the triune God) is above the Existent. Such potentiality entails plentitutde, and so in that sense, as we shall note, the Trinity makes sense.[5] And in making sense of the doctrine he regularly relies on Neo-Platonic philosophy, interpreting Scripture in light of its categories in such a way as to suggest reliance on the Method of Correlation, like Clement and the other Alexandrians.[6]

God and Trinity

Albeit in a critical way at points, Victorinus clearly relies on some of the insights of the Neo-Platonic philosopher Plotinus. Especially useful to him was the philosopher's insights regarding the supposition that the being of existing things is derived from the first Being.[7] God is said to be above everything—the existent and the nonexistent.[8] But the Word is the voice of the unknowable God, and this voice reaches hearts through the Spirit.[9] The Son is the form in which God is seen.[10]

Drawing on Neo-Platonic thinking, Victorinus speaks of God as pre-existent, not an actuality, and yet existent because He is the potentiality of the power of existence.[11] The Father is said to be pre-existence.[12] This first "to be" is beyond simplicity, is the universal of universals, is prior to

4. Ibid., I (FC 69:59–60).

5. Ibid., III.A.1–IV.5 (FC 69:61–81).

6. See notes 37 and 38 below for examples of this hermeneutic. For its use by Clement of Alexandria, see 31–32, nn.7–9.

7. Mar. Vict. *Can. Ar.*, III.A.1(2) (FC 69:61–62); Mar. Vict. *Ar.*, IV.B.(22) (FC 69:285). See Mary T. Clark, "Introduction," in FC 69:3–4; see ibid., 7, 38–40, for examples of his critical appropriation of the philosopher.

8. Mar. Vict. *Can. Ar.*, III.A.1,(2) (FC 69:61–62).

9. Ibid., III.B.1–4.(17–20) (FC 69:73–75); Mar. Vict. *Ar.*, IA.II.C.(13) (FC 69:106); ibid., III.C.2.b. (14) (FC 69:242). See also Clark, "Introduction," 14.

10. Mar. Vict. *Ar.*, IB.II.3.(e).(53) (FC 69:178).

11. Ibid., IA,VI.2.(a).(33) (FC 69:144); Mar. Vict. *Can. Ar.*, III.A.2. (d).(13–14) (FC 69:70).

12. Mar. Vict. *Ar.*, IB.II.2.A.(50) (FC 69:172).

the One.[13] Since He is not One, He is all things in all.[14] Consequently, the Son must be construed as the act of the Father's potentiality.[15] Just as to be includes act and the act includes "to be," so the Logos is in God, is God Himself.[16] "To be" is the Father; to act is the Son.[17] Or as Victorinus puts it elsewhere, "movement is identical with substance," so Father and Son are One.[18] Another way of putting it is to note that as life is begotten of being, so the Son is begotten of the Father.[19] The Spirit is also a term signifying with God "to be."[20] Thus God is Spirit substantially.[21]

Victorinus was obligated to address the Arian critique that the Son is a creature, and so he insisted that there is no inferiority or superiority on the Son's procession from the Father. The Son also causes His own begetting.[22] This self-begetting is not a begetting involving change, and in this sense is consistent with God.[23] In this regard he seems to rely on something like the Neo-Platonic concept of emanation.[24] Thus the African Neo-Platonist insists on these grounds that the Arian alternative makes no sense. For if Christ is begotten before creation, as the Arians also contend, then there was no other substance before all things, except the Father.[25]

The Logos is said to be the paternal power of God, disposing itself in all.[26] Where there is power (as in the case of God) there is action, Victorinus observes.[27] And God is said to act through the Logos.[28] In this sense Logos

13. Ibid., VI/II.2.B.(a)(19) (FC 69:280).

14. Ibid., IVI.II.3.B.(b).(22) (FC 69:285).

15. Mar. Vict. Can. Ar., III.A.3.(14) (FC 69:71); Mar. Vict. Ar., IA.II.3.C.a.(18) (FC 69: 116).

16. Mar. Vict. Can. Ar., III.B.4.(22) (FC 69:76); Mar. Vict. Ar., IA.IV.2..(33) (FC 69: 144–45).

17. Mar. Vict. Can. Ar., II.B3.(19); II.B.4.(20) (FC 69:75).

18. Mar. Vict. Ar., III.II.1.(2) (FC 69:223).

19. Ibid., IB.II.3.b-c.(52); IB.II.3.e.(53) (FC 69:176–77, 178).

20. Ibid., IB.III.2A.(55) (FC 69:180).

21. Ibid., III.III.2.C.2.b.(14) (FC 69:243).

22. Ibid., IB.II.3.c-d.(52) (FC 69:177); see Clark, "Introduction," 15.

23. Mar. Vict. Homo. Recip., III.A.(3) (FC 69:309).

24. For this assessment, see Clark, "Introduction," 16. See Plotin. En., V.6-7, for the concept of emanation.

25. Mar.Vict. Ar., II.I.E.(2) (FC 69:199).

26. Mar.Vict. Can. Ar., III.B.1.(17) (FC 69:73–74).

27. Mar. Vict. Ar., III.I.2.(1) (FC 69:221).

28. Mar. Vict. Can. Ar., III.B.1.(17) (FC 69:74).

and Father are One. God, we might say, is the unbegotten Logos, but the Logos in repose.[29] But to move and to act are from that which is to be.[30] The Father as "to be" is tranquil or immobile, while the property of the Logos is to move and act.[31] And so as substance by its power is prior to act, so the Father Who is Substance begets the Son Who is act.[32]

Several other points made by Victorinus speak directly or indirectly to the Arian critique of *homoousios* of the Son and the Father (of the Son's divinity). He claims that existence and substance are synonymous.[33] Likewise, he adds, there is no difference between substance and quality.[34] These affirmations help further assert the single substance that the Father as preexisting substance (potentiality) and Son as act, existence, and quality share. God is termed the Pre-Existent, not actuality. And yet He exists in a sense, because as we have noted, He is the "potentiality-power" of Existence.[35] The Existent is a self-manifestation, self-actualized. In this sense we may say that the Father is the Son in potentiality and that the Son is the Father in act.[36] An argument is mounted for the biblical roots of the concept of substance (responding to critics), finding derivatives of "substance" in Matt 6:11, John 6:51, Heb 1:3, Titus 2:14, and Jer 23:22.[37] Substance is implied, Victorinus asserts, by God being all in all (1 Cor 15:28). Likewise, he adds, to call God Light and Spirit as the Bible does is to speak of Him as substance.[38]

In another context, Victorinus makes his points in a different, related way. The *Esse* of the Father conceived as Act is said to be best expressed as "to Live."[39] And, he adds, there is no difference between substance and action, that "to be" and life are identical with understanding.[40] Likewise "to

---

29. Ibid., III.B.2.(17) (FC 69:74).

30. Ibid., III.B.3.(19) (FC 69:74-75).

31. Mar. Vict. Ar., IA.II.3.F.4.(27); IA.III.5.(42); IB.II.B.(9).(51) (FC 69:132, 159, 173-74).

32. Ibid., III.II.2.(3) (FC 69:224).

33. Ibid., IA.III.3.(b).(30) (FC 69:137).

34. See Ibid., IV.II.1.(30) (FC 69:296-97).

35. See notes 11 and 15 above.

36. See notes 27 and 29 above for relevant documentation.

37. Mar. Vict. Ar., IA.III.2.b.(30); II.II.2.B.2.(3); II.IIi.3.B.(8) (FC 69:138-39, 202-3, 208-9); Mar. Vict. Homo. Recip., II.1.B (FC 69:306-7).

38. Mar. Vict. Ar., II.II.2.A.(3); II.II.3.C.(10); II.II.3.D.(12) (FC 69:201, 213, 216).

39. Ibid., IV.II.1.(18) (FC 69:279).

40. Ibid., IB.III.1.(a).(54); IB.III.2.(b).(58); IB.VI.1.(60); IV.I.1.b.(2)ff.; IV.I.3.(a).(16) (FC 69:179, 184, 187-88, 254ff., 274).

live" and "life" are also said to be identical with understanding. The Son is identified as God's Begotten Life. This is the case, Victorinus states, because God is Spirit.[41] The Son, then, is the form of the Father, like Life is the form of to live.[42] The Spirit is "to live" and also life in Spirit. He brings "to live" and Life together.[43]

At this point it is relevant to note that God transcends time, in Victorinus's thinking. The "to live" of God is an ever-present act, and by the act of living life is produced that which is always present. And so "to live" has all the aspects of living life always present in it.[44] Eternity (to live), it seems, contains all the present moments ever to exist.

On these grounds, through the Work of the Spirit bringing "to live" and Life together, the Father and Son become One.[45] And Christ and the Spirit are then themselves distinguished, but only by their distinct economic and salvific functions.[46] They are one as movement, but one and yet distinct as life and knowledge.[47] Because memory is obscured for human beings, there is need for the Spirit to give testimony, teach, and strengthen love.[48]

Another analogy Victorinus used is to speak of the relation between Son and Father as analogous to vision being externalized when the power of vision is in action.[49] Likewise, the Son is in the Father and the Father is in the Son. Thus all things may be attributed indifferently to both.[50] The Son is an "exterior" knowing, understanding the interior knowledge which is God, and so they are identical.[51]

Speaking of the distinction of the Persons, Victorinus next proceeds to distinguish Father and Son. As we distinguish between Being and Act, so

---

41. Ibid., IV.I.1.B.(4); IV.I.2.B.2.(9); IV.I.3.a.(16) (FC 69:34, 257–58, 265–66, 274).
42. Ibid., IV.I.2.B.2.(c).(13) (FC 69:271). See also Clark, "Introduction," 34.
43. Mar. Vict. Ar., IV.I.2.B.2.(10) (FC 69:266).
44. Ibid., VI.I.B.2.e.(15) (FC 69:273).
45. Ibid., IV.2.B.2.(a).(10) (FC 69:266–67).
46. Ibid., IV2.B.3.(d).(18) (FC 69:277–78).
47. Ibid., III.III.1.C.2.(b).(14) (FC 69:242–44).
48. Ibid., IV.I.2.B.3.(c).(17) (FC 69:276).
49. Ibid., IA.IV.4.(40) (FC 69:154–55).
50. Ibid., IA.IV.3.(b).(39); VI.I.B.2.(c).(13) (FC 69:153, 271).
51. Ibid., IV.II.3.C.(c).(28–29) (FC 69:293–94).

the Logos activates the creative power of God.[52] The Logos is the power of creating something.[53]

Of course, the Son cannot come from nothingness. He cannot have been perfect coming from nothing. He must have come from the nonexistent (preexistent) superior to the existent (God).[54] For only by the Power of God can what exists come from nonexistent, and so what is potential "to be" is already in existence.[55]

In a sense Victorinus, while insisting on equality of Father and Son, concedes that the Father is greater. He is said to be the cause of the Son's Being and mode of being. Also, the Father is said to be greater "because He is inactive action; such act has more happiness because it is without effort . . ."[56] And yet just as form is substance, and so *homoousios*, so Father and Son are One.[57]

The African Neo-Platonist also addressed the attempted compromise with Arianism intended by those who claimed that the Son is *homoiousion* with the Father (of a similar substance). Victorianus contends that this affirmation entails either placing the Logos before God (making God begotten) or implicitly affirming that the Son is another god—both absurdities.[58] The heresy implies, then, that there is a double truth. This viewpoint is a secret sort of Arianism, he asserts.[59]

Victorinus likewise provides other concrete images for depicting the Trinity. He speaks of a community of substance of Father, Son, and Spirit, for all Three are Spirit, though engaged in distinct actions.[60] Elsewhere, in one of his hymns, the Holy Spirit is said to be the bond of the Father and the

---

52. Mar. Vict. *Can. Ar.*, III.A.4–III.B.3 (FC 69:72–75); cf. Mar. Vict. *Ar.*, IB.II.2.(a-b).(50) (FC 69:173).

53. Mar. Vict. *Ar.*, IA.3.(c).(31) (FC 69:140).

54. Mar. Vict. *Can. Ar.*, III.A.2.(a).(3); III.A.4.(14–15) (FC 69:63, 71–72).

55. Ibid.,IV.1.(25) (FC 69:77–78).

56. Mar. Vict. *Ar.*, IA.II.1.C.(13) (FC 69:105): "Ad hoc autem major, quod actio inactuosa: beatior enim quo sine molestia et impassibilis, et fons omnium quae sunt, requiescens, a se perfecta; et nullius egens: filius autem ut esset, accepit . . ."

57. Ibid., IA.II.1.3.E.(d).(22) (FC 69:123).

58. Ibid., IA.III.3.(29–30) (FC 69:136–37).

59. Ibid., IA.VI.6.(b).(43); IA.VI.2..(45) (FC 69:160, 164).

60. Ibid., IA.II.1.C.(8),(12); IA.II.2B.(b).(18) (FC 69:99–100, 103–5, 115); Mar. Vict. *Hymn*, 3 (FC 69:325).

Son. The Spirit is also identified as the Mother of the Logos in the begetting of the Son.[61]

The African Father also speaks of the Three as One in relation to the image of Word as Voice: "the Father not an empty silence, but a silent voice; the Son already a voice, the Paraclete, utterance of the voice . . ."[62] The Father is God's Being, the Son is God's Life, and the Spirit His Understanding. From Being proceeds Life and in turn Understanding.[63] In one of his hymns (III), Victorinus refers to God as Three in One like water may be source, river, and overflow, like existence, life, and knowledge are all necessary ingredients of human beings.[64] As life God is Christ, as watering He is Spirit, as the power of vitality He is Father.[65] Following up on this point, Victorinus elaborates on previous points to speak of the unity of the Three in terms of the basic unity of "to be," "to live," and "to understand." All in each one. "To be" is the Father, "to live" is the Son, and "to understand" is the Holy Spirit.[66]

Christology

As God is said to act through the Logos, the act of the Father's potentiality, so Victorinus reflects on the specific acts of Christ, what they bring about.[67] The Son of God is said to be the Son of Mary and yet before Mary.[68]

In a text filled with rich implications for contemporary concerns about women's equality, Victorinus refers to a feminine phase of Jesus, His preoccupation with giving life.[69] (The Holy Spirit is said to be the Mother of the Son.)[70] This femininity seems to emerge from the fact that the Son as

---

61. Mar. Vict. *Hymn*, 1 (FC 69:315); Mar. Vict. *Ar.*, I.B.III.B.3.57(b) (FC 69:183).

62. Mar. Vict. *Ar.*, IA.II.C.(13) (FC 69:106): "Quod omnia tria unum, pater non silens silentium, sed vox in silentio, filius jam vox; paracletis vox voicis . . ."

63. Ibid.

64. Mar. Vict. *Hymn*, 3 (FC 69:325); cf. Mar. Victor. *Ar.*, IA.VI.4.(47) (FC 69:166).

65. Mar. Vict. *Ar.*, IA.VI.4.(47) (FC 69:166).

66. Ibid., III.III.1.(4ff.); IV.II.3.B.(21–23); IV.II.3.C.(b).(25–26); IV.II.3.D.(A).(30–31) (FC 69:226–35, 284–85, 286, 291, 297).

67. Ibid., IA.II.1.A.(3–4); IA.II.3C.(a).(19) (FC 69:94, 116).

68. Ibid., IA.IV.3.(a).(35) (FC 69:147, 148).

69. Ibid., IB.II.2.B.(b).(51) (FC 69:174).

70. Ibid., IB.II.2.B.3.(a).(56) (FC 69:182–83).

life is movement. And this life as movement has a feminine power because it desires to vivify.[71]

But in a comment clearly reflecting the patriarchy of his era, Victorinus notes that Christ's Resurrection represents his masculine stage. His Resurrection is said to be a passage from femininity to masculinity.[72] Presumably this is a function of the fact that in returning to the Father one is made male.[73]

Creation and Anthropology

Implications for these doctrines emerge from Victorinus's Christology. Like St. Paul (2 Cor 4:4), he identified Christ as the image of God.[74] The image, he adds, is life-giving and the seed of all that exists.[75] Christ is like the existence of a species from which all members of the species spring. And the Father is the potentiality of being from which the species' being/essence springs.[76] In this sense, humans are not really created in the image of God, but according to the image of God.[77] The African Father uses anthropology (especially the soul) as a further means of explicating the *homoousios* of Father and Son. The soul, he notes, is simultaneously substance (his own "to be," existing as life itself) and motion (animating the body).[78]

Victorinus proceeds to elaborate on the nature of the created order as a whole in an intriguing way. He speaks of God being All in All, for God acts in all.[79] God is all things and so in all things.[80] Yet He is still above all powers and things.[81] In this sense, the African Father is in line with

---

71. Ibid., IB.II.2.B.(b).(51) (FC 69:174).
72. Ibid. (FC 69:174–75).
73. Ibid., IB.II.2.B.(b).(51) (FC 69:174).
74. Ibid., IA.II.3.C.(a).(19); IA.IV.3.(a).(35) (FC 69:115, 147–48).
75. Ibid., IA.II.3.C.(a).(19) (FC 69:116).
76. Ibid.
77. Ibid., IA.II.3.C.(a).(20); IB.V.2.C.(63–64); III.III.2.C.1.(c).(12) (FC 69:118–19, 191–93, 240).
78. Ibid., IA.VI.1.(32) (FC 69:142).
79. Ibid., IA.IV.4.(40) (FC 69:154).
80. Ibid., IV.II.3.B.(b).(22) (FC 69:285).
81. Ibid., IV.II.3.B.(b).(21) (FC 69:285–86).

the modern philosophical notion of panentheism, articulated by certain interpretations of A. N. Whitehead (process philosophy).[82]

Drawing on these notions, Victorinus claims that the universe is held together like a chain by the mutual overlapping parts—God, Jesus, the Spirit, souls, bodily parts.[83] This vision is most suggestive of modern visions of the cosmos posited by theologians seeking to engage Christianity in dialogue with evolutionary theory.

In a related image, Victorinus refers to Christ as irrigating the universe with the waters of life.[84] The whole chain of the cosmos (God, Jesus, Spirit, soul, bodies) in his view is one, all one in substance in Jesus. Yet what is created is not homoousia with Him, since He is the first to Be. But since the Father is not established in the Logos, the Father must be *homoousios* with Him.[85]

Salvation and Atonement

Victorinus describes the Work of Christ in terms of the Classic View of Atonement. Christ is said to conquer the enemies of divinity.[86] Yet such commitments do not entail Patripassianism, he insists. Unlike the Son, the Father does not proceed outside Himself on his grounds, for the Father is not in motion.[87] Besides, it is contended in a manner consistent with the Antiochene School of Christology, only Jesus's humanity suffers, not the Logos.[88]

On salvation/justification, Victorinus contends that it is through faith (alone). But although emphasizing grace like Augustine, he asserts that as we are reconciled to God the Holy Spirit strengthens love and faith. He combines this with an affirmation of Predestination, though without much clarification, quite logical given his claims for God's greatness and impenetrability.[89] Although it is not absolutely clear, the African Father could

---

82. For the most influential of such interpretations, contending that Whitehead posits a panentheist view of God, see Hartshorne, *Divine Relativity*, esp. 88-90.

83. Mar. Victor. *Ar.*, IA.II.3.F.(1).(c).(25) (FC 69:129-30).

84. Ibid., IA.VI.4.(47) (FC 69:166).

85. Ibid., IA.I.3.F.(1).(c).(25-26) (FC 69:130).

86. Ibid., IA.II.4.(28); IA.IV.3.(a).37 (FC 69:133, 147).

87. Ibid., IA.IV.1.(44) (FC 69:161).

88. Ibid. (FC 69:162).

89. Ibid., IV.I.2.B.3.(c).(16) (FC 69:276). For references to Predestination, see Mar. Victor. *Can. Ar.*, III.(2) (FC 69:60-61).

be taken as implying that love (and works) is in some sense a dimension of Justification (though in a characteristically post-Augustinian Western mode with faith and grace prioritized).

Eschatology

Victorinus's vision of the End follows clearly from his vision of the created order, with echoes of Origen ringing in readers' ears. Since all the creation is in Christ on grounds of his ontology, for He is the receptacle, at the End of the world all things will be One.[90] Without expressly claiming it, an *apokatastasis* seems affirmed. Also, we should keep in mind how in eternity with the Father, all is tranquil, for He is like the Greek universal form of life that includes all that has transpired over the aeons by all living things, and so all time is simultaneous on Victorinus's grounds.[91]

What Victorinus Can Mean for the Church Today

The richness of Victorinus's reflections on God (the Trinity) and the Lord's relationship to the world renders him a valuable resource for ministry today. It has clearly been to the detriment of the Church that his thought has been so overlooked historically. To help make the mysteries of the Trinity more intelligible and to offer the Church a scientifically credible way of describing God's interactions with the Trinity, we would do well as the famed biblical scholar Jerome did to sit at Victorinus's feet.

---

90. Mar. Victor. *Adversus Arium*, IA.IV.3.b.(37) (FC 69:150–51).
91. See notes 31 and 44 above.

18

Didymus the Blind

BORN IN ALEXANDRIA, DIDYMUS (313–398) was (the last) master of the Catechetical School in Alexandria after Origen, and so his thought is often identified with his master. As a result his work has both been praised and condemned alongside the fate of Origen's works. Many of his works were lost as a result of these condemnations (though not condemned formally at the Second Council of Constantinople where Origen was condemned, except in some official commentaries of that Council, Didymus endured condemnations by the 678 Third Council of Constantinople and by the 787 Second Council of Nicea). Though he lost his vision at a young age Didymus astonished many with his intelligence and scholarly contributions. He became a teacher of both Jerome and Gregory of Nazianzus and had a significant impact on Ambrose, who subsequently so influenced Augustine. In fact Jerome reportedly consulted with Didymus about some biblical commentaries.[1]

Theological Method

Even in his focus on the Trinity and refuting Manicheism, we begin to see hints regarding Didymus's use of a Correlationist Method and allegorical interpretation. He distinguishes the literal sense from the spiritual sense of

---

1. Jer. *Comm. Eph.*, I. Pref (*NPNF*[2] 6:498, 80).

biblical texts at some points.[2] Yet he did still refer to the divinely inspired character of Scripture.[3]

Didymus's reliance on Greek philosophical concepts further indicates his employment of the Correlationist Method of the catechetical school and its previous masters (like Origen and Clement).[4] Of course, his assertion that God subsists in a hidden way above the mind could be deemed a rejection of philosophy along the lines of Tertullian's Orthodox Method.[5] But this claim by no means connotes a rejection of the Correlationist Method, as his allegorizing of the literal sense of certain eschatologically oriented biblical texts makes clear.[6]

God and Trinity

Didymus unambiguously follows his mentor Origen in insisting that God has no body. Indeed, Didymus asserts, He is radically simple.[7] As such, God is said to be not just indivisible but also impassable.[8] God is said to show great kindness even when He threatens to act as judge.[9]

Along the lines of the Trinitarian formulation and his rejection of Arius, Didymus contended that the Son is begotten of the Father like light is begotten of light.[10] As a result, the Will of the Son is said to be identical with the Father.[11] The Holy Spirit is also described in a way that He is seen as in harmony with the First Two Persons. Thus the Spirit is said to receive His substance from the Son just as the Son receives it from the Father.[12] An early formulation of the Filioque of the Trinity (the Spirit proceeding from

---

2. Didym. *Zach.*, 12:1–3 (FC 111:290); Didym. *Spir.*, 249.

3. Didym. *Zach.*, 7:11–12 (FC 111:141).

4. Didym. *Spir.*, 35, 37; for this assessment, see Oden, *How Africa Shaped the Christian Mind*, 45.

5. Didym. *Trin.*, 3.16. There is some debate over whether Didymus wrote this text; see Ehrman, *Didymus the Blind and the Text of the Gospels*.

6. Did. *Trin.*, 3.21; Didym. *Zach.*, 10:10; 14:8–9 (FC 111:247).

7. Didym. *Spir.*, 35 [156].

8. Ibid.

9. Didym. *Zach.*, 1:3, 2 (FC 111:29).

10. Didym. *Trin.*, 3.2.8.

11. Ibid.

12. Ibid., 35, 37.

the Son as well as from the Father) seems endorsed in these comments.[13] Didymus also speaks of distinct operations of the Father, Son, and Spirit, but not a difference of nature. The Son is said to be the Hand of the Father and the Spirit His Finger.[14]

Christology and Atonement

The catholicity of Didymus's thought is further undergirded by his endorsement of the humanity of Christ.[15] Regarding the Atonement, he opts for the Classic View, speaking of Christ disarming rulers.[16] In comments most suggestive of his relationship to his native African culture and his Roman ethos, he expressly cites earlier African-related documents, the *Shepherd of Hermas* and *Epistle of Barnabas*, calling the devil black and evil ones are said to be Ethiopian/Black rulers.[17]

Anthropology

Like his mentor Origen, Didymus speaks of the nature of every rational creature as the habitation of the whole Godhead.[18] All of us have Christ in us! Didymus also embraces Greek philosophical suppositions modified, in speaking of humans as composed of body, rational soul, and spirit (which might be termed the heart).[19]

Justification and Sanctification

We have previously noted the great catechist speak of God as kind and compassionate.[20] On the relation between grace and works, he writes, "In other words, since God's truth is something great and elevated, there is

---

13. See Did. *Spir.*, 34[153], 36[159].
14. Ibid., 26, 86; see also Pelikan, *Emergence of the Catholic Tradition (100–600)*, 218.
15. Didym. *Trin.*, 3.21.
16. Didym. *Zach.*, 3:3–5; 12:9–10 (FC 111:70, 299–300); Didym. *Spir.*, 209.
17. Didym. *Zach.*, 13:7 (FC 111:313); cf. p.xxxiii, n.30, above.
18. Didym. *Trin.*, 2.6, 7.
19. Didym. *Zach.*, 12:1–3 (FC 111:287).
20. Ibid., 1:3 (FC 111:29).

need for mercy to be shown by God, the source of goodness, for people to receive it."[21]

The Holy Spirit removes hearts of stone, Didymus writes, replacing them with compliant, docile hearts that may observe God's Commandments. The Spirit works to make believers good and holy. God is said to give everything conducive to salvation.[22]

But elsewhere, Didymus writes, "When we show zeal in good works and in true and pious knowledge to be styled God's people, then it is that he for his part will be our God."[23] Similar points about those who love God receiving His gifts surface elsewhere.[24]

The apparently conflicting themes of both salvation by grace and works direct us to the familiar pattern of Eastern thought associated with deification. We noted this pattern in Didymus's mentor, Origen. Perhaps the references previously noted in Didymus's thought about God in Christ dwelling in us could be construed as a kind of endorsement of something like deification. And he does refer to the Holy Spirit as changing us into sharers in the divine glory.[25]

Regarding Sanctification, Didymus also spoke of the faithful as making progress to perfection.[26] Having become God's righteousness, the faithful are exhorted to bear fruit.[27] With God's help, good deeds can be done.[28]

Other Doctrines

Didymus deals with the doctrine of the Church. He speaks of it as the House of God, with a lamp light. Those staying and living in it are illumined by

---

21. Ibid., 8:7-8 (FC111:172: "Ἐπεὶ γὰρ μεγάλη, τίς ἐστιν χαὶ ἀνηγμένη ἡ Θεοῦ ἀλήθεια, χρεία ἐστίν ἐλεθῆναι πρὸς τοῦ Θεοῦ ὄντος πηγῆς ἀγαθοτητος, ἵνα ἀνθώποις ὑπαρχΘῆ."

22. Ibid., 7:11-12 (FC 111:144-45, 147-48); Didym. Spir., 31-37, 78, 184, 201, 236.

23. Didym. Zach., 8:7-8 (FC 111:172: "Οταν σπουζάσωμεν διὰ ἀγαθῶν ἔργω[ν χαὶ] ἀληθους χαὶ εὐσεβοῦς γυώσεως Θεοῦ χρηματίσαι λαός, [τ]ὸ τηνίκαδε χαὶ αὐτὸς ἡμῶν ἔσται Θεός οἰχειομενος ἡμῖν ἐν ἀληθείᾳ καὶ εν δικαιοσύνη."

24. Ibid., 5:5-8; 6:9-11, 12-15 (FC 111:104-5, 117, 119-20).

25. Didym. Trin., 2.12.

26. Didym. Zach., 14:9-11 (FC 111:337).

27. Ibid., 6:12-15 (FC 111:127-28).

28. Ibid., 10:11-12 (FC 111:251).

that lamp.²⁹ He also speaks with regard to the sacraments of being renewed in baptism by the Spirit.³⁰

Regarding Eschatology, the great Alexandrian theologian interprets biblical references to a cataclysmic end time spiritually and allegorically.³¹ In any case he clearly followed Origen in affirming universal salvation.³² Didymus's spiritual bents did not isolate him from social concern. One finds him on at least one occasion expressing concern for the poor.³³

Despite all the historic controversy over the validity of Origen's creative theologizing, the orthodoxy of the heritage of Origen seems solidly affirmed by Didymus his heir.

---

29. Ibid., 4:1–3 (FC 111:87–88).
30. Didym. *Trin.*, 2.12.
31. Didym. *Zach.*, 14:8–9 (FC 111:332–33).
32. Ibid., 10:10; 14:9–11 (FC 111:248, 335–36).
33. Ibid., 7:8–10 (FC 111:136–39).

19

Contemporaries of Augustine

AUGUSTINE (354–420) IS OF course the most famous and influential of all the early Church theologians, if not the greatest of all that have lived. But he had several contemporaries, or there were a number of eminent North African theologians whose career continued shortly after his ended. I have in mind especially Synesius of Cyrene and Optatus. Although both were clearly shaped in Africa, perhaps even born there (especially in the case of Synesius), there is some doubt about whether they should have been considered in this book, that their ethnicity was not necessarily African. The evidence is in fact a bit clearer for their famed contemporary.

It is true that Augustine was thoroughly Romanized, that Latin was the language of the home. But his mother Monica's name seems to have Berber origins, in the name of the Libyan/Numinidan god Mon. And Augustine himself identified with the Berber tradition in his choice of the name of the son born to him and his concubine. To name one's firstborn son Adeodatus (Godsend) was a Berber custom.[1]

Augustine's own testimony to his Berber background emerges in several of his Epistles. Writing in 390 to a friend made in his pagan days, who was critiquing Augustine's conversion to Christianity with special reference to African Catholic veneration of African martyrs, the African

---

1. For these insights, see Wills, *Saint Augustine*, 2; Brown, *Augustine of Hippo*, 32–33. T. Kermit Scott, *Augustine*, 64, adds that the significance of Adeodatus is found in this Latin name's Punic form, Iatanbaal, since Berbers sought names for their children that included the name of the god Baal. For this discussion in more detail, see my *Richness of Augustine*, esp. 8–10.

Father notes, "For surely, considering you are African, and that we are both settled in Africa, you could not have so forgotten yourself when writing to Africans as to think that Punic names were a fit theme for censure."[2]

Augustine seems to identify himself with being African in this case. In a response written in the 420s to an Italian bishop who was supporting the heretic Pelagius, the African Father wrote, "Don't out of pride in your earthly ancestry dismiss one who monitors and admonishes you, *just because I am Punic*. Your Apulian birth is no pledge over Punic forces."[3]

Perhaps the reference to being "Punic" could be taken as Augustine's admission of his Phoenician background. But recall in the Introduction we noted that the term "Punic" had come to be employed in a broader sense in the Roman Empire in this period, as a term designating all non-Romanized ethnic groups in North Africa.[4] To call oneself "Punic" in this context could very well be an endorsement of one's Berber ethnicity. There is strong evidence here that Augustine was a man of color, and quite likely indigenously African. We must be a bit more guarded about making such claims with regard to the two contemporaries of his we now consider.

Synesius of Cyrene

Of the two African contemporaries of Augustine whom we consider, we begin with the Bishop of Cyrene (ca. 373–ca. 414), an eminent student of Greek philosophy in his lifetime, who may have been of Greek (Spartan) descent. It is commonly maintained that he was born of a wealthy Cyrenian family, who, it is alleged, claimed descent from Spartan (Greek) kings. But there is not clear evidence for this claim.[5] The strongest evidence for this conclusion emerges in one of the great scholar's Epistles, where he praises the Greek language and the insights Greek philosophy affords his fellow Cyrenian citizens, claiming that nonetheless we must be content with our

---

2. Aug. *Ep.* (390), XVI (*NPNF*[1] 2:234): "Neque enim usque adeo teipsum oblivisci potuisses, ut homo Afer scribens Afris, cum simus utrique in Africa constitute, Punica nomina exagitanda existimares."

3. Aug. *C. Jul.*, VI.XVIII: "Noli istum Poenum monentem vel admonentem terra inflatus propagine spernere. Non enim qui te Apulai genuit, ideo Peonos vincendos extimes gente." Italics mine.

4. See Introduction, xxviii n. 17.

5. For this assessment, see Cameron, Long, and Sherry, *Barbarians and Politics*, 80.

context, with the Sparta fate has given you.⁶ This could be taken as an identification with Spartan/Greek culture, but not clearly so. Consequently, we proceed with our analysis of this important contemporary of Augustine.

Probably raised in a non-Christian Cyrenian home, Synesius began studying Greek philosophy as a youth. He speaks in one of his Epistles of seeking to live a life of the mind.⁷ He lived the life of the wandering scholar and political representative to the emperor, including study at Athens and Alexandria, until 410 when chosen as bishop of Ptolemais. Along the way he was mentored by Alexandrian bishop Theophilus (d. 412), known primarily for his critiques of Origen and John Chrysostom, and for purging polytheism.⁸

Theological Method

Given his pilgrimage of seeking a connection between Christian faith and Neo-Platonism, it is not surprising that Synesius's Method would reflect the agenda of seeking to translate faith into Neo-Platonic terms. In a hymn he wrote he refers to reason inviting the soul to continue its path to God. In line with the Method of Correlation he seeks a direct connection between the soul and God. In the same spirit he also posits a natural knowledge of God, claiming that all celebrate God's goodness.⁹ Even dreams are said to give revelation, providing glimpses of the unity of the cosmos.¹⁰

Other indications of the bishop's Method suggest a more conservavitve approach. In the spirit of Tertullian he claims that divine knowedge is superior to earthly matters.¹¹ And like the Orthodox theologians we have considered, he insists that he is offering no new doctrine.¹² In short, there is some dispute or lack of clarity over Synseius's Method.

---

6. Syne. *Epis.* (402), 101.

7. Ibid. (402), 140.

8. Socr. *H.e.*, V.XVI (*NPNF*² 2:126); Soz. *H.e.*, VIII.XII-XIV (*NPNF*² 2:407–8). For primary sources where Theophilus makes these points against Origen, see 180, n.1, below.

9. Syne. *Hymn.*, 1.9; Syne. *De. Reg.*, 5.

10. Syne. *Insom.*

11. Syne. *Hymn.*, 1.

12. Syne. *Epis.* (409), 105.

God and Trinity

There are evidences of the Trinity doctrine in Synesius's reflections about God. He seems to identify Father and Son.[13] Christ is called Son of God. Though poured forth, He is said to remain Himself.[14] And the Holy Spirit is referred to as a daughter.[15]

Providence

The theme of a struggle between good and evil is essential to understanding Synsesius's vision of this doctrine.[16] The soul is said to be caught up in a struggle between the gods. But instead of understanding the gods to descend to us, the Bishop of Ptolemais insits that we are to ascend to them.[17] God can bring good out of evil acts, but will employ evils when in need of avengers.[18] The determinism we previously observed in Synesius's thought seems reflected in these comments.

Anthropology

Greek philosophy clearly undergirds the Cyrenian bishop's view of human nature. A dualism is posited, and it is claimed that the soul subsequently comes into the body.[19] The purpose of humanity is said to engage in right reasoning, which includes avoiding accommodation to the brokenness of the world.[20] Of course, this is not to imply that there are no ambiguities in human life in Synesius's view. Much like his contemporary Augustine he speaks of a host of conflicting forces and passions in human beings and how passion sometimes controls us.[21] Indeed the soul can never be turned from matter.[22]

---

13. Syne. *Hymn.*, 9.
14. Ibid., 10, 3.
15. Ibid., 4.
16. Syne. *Prov.*, 1.1.
17. Ibid., 1.10.
18. Syne. *Epis.* (412), 57.3.
19. Ibid. (409), 105.
20. Ibid. (395), 137; Syne. *Prov.*, 1.10.
21. Syne. *De. Reg.*, 6.
22. Syne. *Insom.*, 5.

Christology and Atonement

Synesius does not develop full-blown treatments of these doctrines. But in two of his hymns he does affirm a fairly traditional, orthodox treatment of Jesus Christ. It is said that His life was poured out as a kenosis (an utter emptiness). He is portrayed as Mediator, who died for our sin.[23]

Justification

Synesius's endeavor to relate the Word to Neo-Platonism is evident in his treatment of this doctrine. In line with this these philosophical presuppositions he claims that we must seek to be a participant worthy of God, that the soul is journeying to be united with Him. Indeed, he adds in a Neo-Platonic manner, all nature is joined to God.[24]

Sanctification

The same Law-oriented approach is reflected in the Cyrenian bishop's vision of the Christian life. Reflecting concerns typical of previous generations of early Christians, he ruminates on how hard it is to wash out the stains (sins) that come after Baptism.[25] Of course the light of the holy is said to be available to all seekers.[26] But he does speak of being overcome by God, celebrating the sweetness of the Spirit, Who makes us joyful.[27]

Ministry

We find in Synesius's writings evidence of an internal struggle with the call to Ministry. He did not want to give up earthly amusements.[28] We know that he was married.[29]

---

23. Syne. *Hymn.*, 7, 9.
24. Syne. *Hom.*, 1; Syne. *Hymn.*, 1; cf. Plotin. *En.*, VI. Ix.1/7.
25. Syne. *Hom.*, 2A.
26. Ibid., 2.
27. Syne. *Epis.*, 57.
28. Ibid. (409), 105.
29. Ibid.

Sacraments

The bishop of Cyrene reflects the consensus we have observed among the early theologians of North Africa. Baptism is said to wash away sins if recipients are faithful. Yet Synseius did proclaim that forgiveness is possible if penitence is endured.[30]

He seems to have less to say about the Lord's Supper. About all we know about his thinking on the matter is that he associated the Sacraments with hospitality, as this becomes clear in comments about one who had been excommunicated.[31]

Social Ethics

Having himself engaged in politics (he played a leadership role as Bishop in defending Cyrenaician cities from barbarian invasions), Synesius's views on this range of issues reflect some sound realism.[32] He advises rulers to seek to build goodwill by mingling with troops and citizens.[33] Synesius oposes the genocide of ethnic groups.[34] But he supports the enslavement of conquered peoples and warns of the need to repress them.[35] He opted for patriarchalism, the man as the defender of the household while the woman works in it.[36]

Eschatology

Synsesius only focused on the future regarding Eschatology. Not surprisingly, his Greek philosophical orientation gave him a cosmic orientation and preoccupation, leading him to insist that the world will not come to a complete end with the destruction of the material cosmos.[37]

---

30. Syne. *Hom.*, 2.
31. Syne. *Epis.* (412), 58. For this analysis, see Oden, *Early Libyan Christianity*, 207–8.
32. Syne. *Epis.* (405), 125; ibid. (405), 130; ibid. (405), 132; ibid. (405), 133.
33. Syne. *De. Reg.*, 9.
34. Syne. *Hom.*, 2. See the analysis in Oden, *Early Libyan Christianity*, 186.
35. Syne. *De. Reg.*, 15; Syne. *Epis.* (395), 145.
36. Syne. *De. reg.*, 147.
37. Syne. *Epis.* (409), 105

Optatus

Optatus (who was a slightly older contemporary of Augustine) served as bishop of Milevis in North Africa. We know little of him, save his background in Greek philosophy and that he probably wrote in the late fourth century and in vigorous opposition to Donatism, mounting arguments that influenced Augustine's opposition to this heresy.[38] Donatism in his view had shattered the peace that is given to Christians. In fact he accused the heretics of fomenting mob rule, of practicing violence against practitioners of the catholic faith.[39] The Church is to be a unity in Optatus's view. He critiqued the Donatists for failing to recognize this, for acting as though it was in Africa alone (the area of Donatist concentration) that Christians could be found.[40] This commitment to unity surfaces personally in Optatus's interactions with the Donatists. He referred to his Donatist opponent as a "brother."[41]

Church and Ministry

Optatus's defense of catholicity in face of Donatism was rooted in his core vision of the Church. In his view, "The Church is one, and its holiness is produced by the Sacraments. It is not to be considered on the basis of the pride of individuals."[42] Against the Donatists, he argued that the Church is catholic, scattered all over the world, not just located in those locales where the true believers reside.[43]

Other images employed are feminine, further contributing to the conclusion that all Christians are united. He describes the Church as the Bride of

---

38. For a more detailed survey, see Mark Edwards, "Introduction," in *Optatus: Against the Donatists*, trans. and ed. Mark Edwards (Liverpool: Liverpool University Press, 1997) xvi–xviii. For Augustine's praise of Optatus for his rich background in Greek philosophy, see *Doctr. Christ.*, II.40.61 (*NPNF*[1] 2:554).

39. Optat. *Schis. Don.*, 1.1, 11; 3.4 (*OAD* 1-2, 11, 68-70).

40. Ibid., 2.13 (*OAD* 42).

41. Ibid., 1.4,6,10; 3.3; 4.2; 6.6 (*OAD* 3, 6, 10, 61, 84, 124).

42. Ibid., 2.1 (*OAD* 29): "Ergo Ecclesia una est, cujus sanctitas de sacramentis colligitur; non de superbia Personarum ponderatur..."

43. Ibid.

Christ or as our Mother.[44] She is said to be the Mother who brings Christians from the same Sacramental womb, so that all the faithful are brothers.[45]

Unity is preserved in Optatus's view by the Episcopal Chair first conferred on Peter.[46] He ascribes a primacy to the Roman See.[47]

Sacraments

Optatus offers reflections on three Sacraments. Most important of all for dialogue with the Donatists is his discussion of baptism. He begins by rejecting the Donatist practice of rebaptism.[48] In his view all the Sacraments are holy, for they belong to God.[49] Consequently, baptism must be construed as conferring grace.[50] If God is active in Baptism, the Donatist practice of discounting the Sacrament when administered by a lapsed priest must be rejected, or it seems to imply that the priest is more important than the Trinity.[51] The logic of Donatist practice implies that a lapsed priest can stop God's design in the rite.

A Real Presence view of the Sacraments seems implied in Optatus's view of the Eucharist. He speaks of Christ's Presence at Catholic altars.[52]

Optatus's treatment of the Sacraments, which is so typical of early African Christianity, reflects in his remarks about the Sacrament of Penance (Confession). He was critical of the use of the Sacrament by those who had not sinned, for in the pre-medieval era the rite was only administered to the lapsed.[53]

---

44. Ibid., 3.1 (*OAD* 57); ibid., 1.11; 2.10; 3.10; 4.5 (*OAD* 11, 40, 79, 87).

45. Ibid., 4.2 (*OAD* 85).

46. Ibid., 2.2 (*OAD* 91).

47. Ibid., 2.3, 9 (*OAD* 32, 39). For a similar interpretation, see Edwards, "Introduction," xxv.

48. Optat. *Schis. Don.*, 5.1,3 (*OAD* 96, 101).

49. Ibid., 5.4,7 (*OAD* 103, 109).

50. Ibid., 5.1 (*OAD* 97).

51. Ibid., 5.1–2, 4 (*OAD* 99, 102–3).

52. Ibid., 6.1, 2 (*OAD* 115, 118).

53. Ibid., 2.26 (*OAD* 56).

God and Sin

In a manner typical of other African theologians we have studied, there is a sense in which God is so awesome as almost to be indefinable for Optatus. He refers to God as a Spirit Who blows where He will and cannot be confined.[54] Very little else is said in the literature about the Nature of God. He does critique several heresies with implications for the Godhead or the Trinity—Arianism, Marcion, and Patripassianism.[55]

At one point, Optatus portrayed God in a legalistic mode, as a Judge.[56] And yet at other points, this Law orientation is mixed with the theme of forgiveness (see the discussion in the next section).

A similar two-sidedness is apparent in Optatus's exposition of sin. On one hand he defines sin as to err knowingly, and as we have noted he seemed to imply with regard to penance that not everyone is a sinner.[57] But in other contexts he writes more like his contemporary Augustine, as he contends that we are inherently sinful, that sin is necessary.[58]

Justification and Sanctification

Salvation and the role of grace in making it happen reflect a similarly disparate character. On one hand, Optatus can affirm something like the idea of Justification as Union with Christ, as he contends that God dwells in those who are saved.[59] The perfect sanctity that Donatists claim for themselves is not possible in his view. God is always prepared to forgive, he asserts.[60] He speaks of Donatists committing the unforgivable sin against the Holy Spirit insofar as in failing to recognize Catholic baptisms they seek to undo what God has done, claiming holiness for themselves.[61] In the same spirit the heretics are critiqued for calling the lapsed to redeem their souls by abandoning the Catholic Church, a move that in Optatus's

---

54. Ibid., 2.7 (*OAD* 38).
55. Ibid., 4.5 (*OAD* 88–89).
56. Ibid., 1.1 (*OAD* 1).
57. Ibid., 2.2 (*OAD* 32); see note 53.
58. Optat. *Schis. Don.*, 2.20; 4.6 (*OAD* 48, 90).
59. Ibid., 4.6 (*OAD* 90).
60. Ibid., 2.20 (*OAD* 48–49).
61. Ibid., 7.4 (*OAD* 143–44).

view is a compromise of Christ's redemptive work.[62] There are strong witnesses to grace here.

Regarding the Christian life, the African Father refers to discipline in the Christian life, of which peace is a characteristic.[63] Largely in response to Donatist claims and its separatism, he insisted that there is no real martyrdom if it is not accompanied by charity to all.[64]

Social Ethics

In view of his preoccupation with Donatism, Optatus does not have much to say about the Christian's role in society. But in view of Donatist use of military means to advance their cause, he insisted that the Church should support the empire.[65] He also critiqued the Donatist treatment of women, like forcing them to give up their husbands who lapsed.[66]

Augustine: The Child of His Time

Many of Augustine's characteristic agendas are reflected in the African contemporaries we have noted—a concern to keep faith and reason (especially Neo-Platonic philosophy) in dialogue and also a concern to refute the Donatist heresy. The greatest theologian of the West clearly had significant support among African thinkers in his lifetime.

---

62. Ibid., 3.4 (*OAD* 68–70).
63. Ibid., 4.4 (*OAD* 86).
64. Ibid., 3.8 (*OAD* 77).
65. Ibid., 3.3 (*OAD* 62–63).
66. Ibid., 6/4 (*OAD* 120–22).

20

After Augustine

SEVERAL EMINENT AFRICAN THEOLOGIANS of the generation after Augustine warrant attention. I have in mind especially Cyril of Alexandria and Fulgentius. We begin with the bishop of Alexandria.

Cyril of Alexandria

Cyril (d. 444) was the antithesis of a number of the great leaders of the Alexandrian church. He became its bishop despite having no formal education. (He may have gotten the job as a result of his uncle Theophilus, who himself was patriarch of Alexandria [d. ca. 412].) Like his uncle, Cyril was committed to upholding the Alexandrian understanding of Christology. Although he had been a harsh critic of Origen, including his teaching of universal salvation, a church leader ruthless in his willingness to use force against his enemies, this earlier African bishop did display some openness to forgiving those who had associated with heretics.[1]

Cyril was not as highly educated as some of the earlier Alexandrian scholars. This is evident in that he shows few signs of interest in or knowledge of science, philosophy, and history. He seems to have valued the forms, but not the content of ancient culture.[2] He was influenced by Athanasius and the Alexandrian School.[3]

---

1. Theoph. *Ad Pal.*, in Jer. *Ep.* (NPNF² 6:185); Theoph. *Pros.* (NPNF² 14:614).
2. For this assessment, see Lionel R. Wickham, "Introduction," in *CSL* xiii–xiv.
3. Cyr. *Ep. Suc.* 1, 11 (*CSL* 81–83).

Theologically, Cyril was largely a proponent of Athanasius's thinking, further extrapolating his insights. He became the champion of Alexandrian Christology. This may account for why Ethiopian Orthodoxy to this day concentrates so much attention on his works in theological education.[4] Since ancient times his works were translated into Ethiopic.[5]

Besides being an effective theologian, he skillfully functions as an ecclesiastical politician and manager of mobs.[6] His theological career was marked by controversy, not only with the emerging rival to the Alexandrian view of Christology, the Antiochene Christology, which rejected the Alexandrian belief that whatever is said of one of Jesus's Natures must be attributed to the other. Cyril also spent much of his career in conflict with Nestorius, patriarch of Constantinople, who objected to attributing the Greek term *theotokos* (God-bearer, Mother of God) to Mary, as Athanasius had done. Cyril did affirm this concept.[7]

Nestorianism was an extreme form of Antiochene Christology, holding that Christ was really two separate persons, much as two people comprise a marriage. For this reason the idea that Mary was Mother of God (*theotokos*) had to be rejected. Cyril responded with a strong Alexandrian emphasis.[8] But he did not exempt her from sin, noting that she had doubts about Christ's divinity while He hung on the Cross.[9]

The Alexandrian bishop was not a man of temperate nature.[10] Originally, the emperor sided with Nestorius, perceiving Cyril as a troublemaker.[11] Eventually Cyril persuaded Pope Celestine I to summon Council at Rome in 430 to condemn Nestorius, who was at that time patriarch of Constantiople. Cyril not only gained such papal support through the papacy's longtime empathy with Alexandrian theology, but also through Cyril's use of Alexandrian wealth to influence certain authorities.[12]

---

4. Kalewold, *Traditional Ethiopian Church Education*, 31.

5. Wickham, "Introduction," xi, 211.

6. For this assessment, see Edward R. Hardy, "Introduction: Faith, Theology, and the Creeds," in LCC 3:31–32.

7. Cyr. *Ep. Nest.* 3 (LCC 3:352–53). Cf. Cyr. *Rect. fide*, 25, 36–37; see chapter 15, note 54, for a reference to Athanasius.

8. Cyr. *Ep. Nest.* 3 (LCC 3:353, 354).

9. Cyril of Alexandria, as quoted by Schaff, *History of the Church*, 3:947.

10. For this characterization of his personality, see William Jurgens, "St. Cyril of Alexandria," in Jurgens, *Faith of the Early Fathers*, 3:206.

11. Cyr. *Ad Acac.*, 1–3 (CSL 35–39); see Wickham, "Introduction," xxii–xxiii.

12. For this analysis, see González, *History of Christian Thought*, 1:364f.

At the Council of Ephesus in AD 431 over which Cyril presided, Nestorius was deposed. But the Constantinople patriarch rallied the support of the Antiochene School to his side. In a separate Council those bishops deposed Cyril. Tensions with Antiochenes were eventually healed.[13] The climate created made possible compromises at the later Council of Chalcedon.

Theological Method

In view of the influence of Athanasius on his thought, it is not surprising that the Alexandrian bishop took positions at least by implication critical of Origen in a number of ways. In a comment about Eschatology, but with implications for Cyril's critical assessment of the spiritual utility of science, history, and philosophy, he claimed that in the future state we will jettison all corruption and its passions. We will not need these and so no returning to life again in order to have advancement (as Origen implied) will be necessary.[14]

Along the same line of thought Cyril contended that Scripture tries to make clear to us what is beyond human understanding.[15] While teaching that faith without works is dead, Cyril took a creedal orientation in claiming that excellency in action requires sound doctrine.[16] This is a clear indication of his reliance on Orthodox Method.

In line with an Orthodox Method, in some harmony with Tertullian, Cyril cautioned that there is no need to inquire into the means and methods of Creation. Such allegedly subtle doctrinal problems do not require doctrinal decisions, he claimed. It is important we not be carried away from reasonableness.[17] What Scripture does not state clearly must remain unknown and be passed over in silence.[18]

The Alexandrian bishop certainly endorsed a conservative view of Scripture, expressly referring to its inspiration.[19] But this conviction is not held without an appreciation of the authority of Tradition. In referring to the inspired Scripture's authority, though he contended that diligence

---

13. See Livingstone, *Concise Oxford Dictionary of the Christian Church*, 140.
14. Cyr. *Doct.*, 5 (CSL 199–201).
15. Cyr. *Rect. fide*, 9.
16. Cyr. *Hag. Sum.*, 2 (CSL 95).
17. Cyr. *Doct.*, 2 (CSL 187–89).
18. Ibid., (CSL 189).
19. Cyr. *Rect. fide* (CSL 97, 22).

should also be given to the Fathers of the Church and Creed.[20] This appeal to the authority of Tradition surfaces at other points. The faith of the people of God is an expression of Tradition in his view. And it is a guarantee of sound doctrine.[21]

Other hermeneutical convictions of Cyril can be identified. He sought to defend the authority of Scripture by contending that the history reported in the Bible is not outmoded. We must seek out its usefulness, he contended.[22] This seems like a qualified use of allegorical interpretation at this point. Many of the expressions Scripture uses to depict God also seem to invite allegorical interpretation. In dialogue with anthropomorphists like Audiens, Cyril contends that Scripture refers to God in human appearances as the Spirit uses expressions to speak in human terms we can comprehend.[23]

One other aspect of Theological Method that links Cyril to his Alexandrian cohorts is his endorsement of the concept of the natural law and a natural knowledge of God. He claims that we find in human beings an innate and necessary law, a spontaneous knowledge that stirs up the need to conceive of something more excellent and better than ourselves, which is God.[24] God is said to have instilled in humans a natural longing for good (including for virtue and holiness). This is the meaning of being created in God's image, Cyril contends.[25] He also refers to man as rational, with a sovereignty over all other living inhabitants.[26] Man's nature is capable of goodness, it seems.[27] It is evident, then, that though we may speak in the case of Cyril of his operating with an Orthodox Method, this is a sophisticated Orthodoxy.

---

20. Cyr. *Ad Acac.*, 6 (CSL 43).
21. Cyr. *Ep. Nest.* 2 (NPNF² 14:197).
22. Cyr. *Hayaian.*, 1.4.
23. Cyr. *Tib.*, 1 (CSL 137–39); Cyr. *Doct.* 1 (CSL 185–87).
24. Cyr. *Glaph.*, 1.2.
25. Cyr. *Doct.*, 2 (CSL 189); cf. Cyr. *Tib.*, 1, 10, 14 (CSL 139, 165, 175).
26. Cyr. *Ep. Cal.* (CSL 217).
27. Cyr. *Doct.*, 3 (CSL 193).

God and Trinity

Cyril posits a strong affirmation of monotheism, of the difference between the creator and the creature.[28] He refers to God's transcendence.[29] Relying on the language of Greek philosophy to depict God, Cyril insists that He is unchangeable and impassible.[30]

In Cyril's view it is wrong to view this ineffable God as an agent of absurdities on grounds that all things are possible for Him. God cannot do what makes falsehoods true, Cyril insisted. This will not change the evils of the past.[31] This ineffable God, he insists, does not occupy a position like created things, but fills all and exists under all.[32]

The triune Nature of God of course exhibits all these characteristics. It is said to be an ineffable substance beyond all understanding and speech.[33] With an unequivocal affirmation of the Oneness of the divine nature, it follows in Cyril's view that whatever operation (action) is suitable to it should be seen as a work of the Godhead as a whole. Thus the Son is operative in the Father's work.[34] In all divine actions, the Persons of the Trinity act together in divine harmony.[35] Whatever concerns one of the Persons of the Trinity concerns them all.[36]

The unity of Son and Father is expressed in other compelling ways. Christ is said to be begotten of the Father like light from light. Whatever the Father is, the Son is.[37] Like the Father, Christ fills all things.[38] When radiance can fall from light, then the Son will be away from the Father.[39]

---

28. Cyr. *Hag. Sum.*, 7, 8 (CSL 101, 103).
29. Cyr. *Ep. Cal.* (CSL 217).
30. Cyr. *Inc. unigen.*; cf. Cyr. *Ad Acac.*, 20 (CSL 57–59); Cyr. *Ep. Nest.* 2, 5 (CSL 7).
31. Cyr. *Doct.*, 11 (CSL 211–13).
32. Cyr. *Tib.*, 3 (CSL 147–49).
33. Ibid., 6 (CSL 157).
34. Cyr. *Rect. fide*, 41.
35. Cyr. *Nest. Dus.*, 5.6.
36. Cyr. *Doct.*, 4 (CSL 197–99).
37. Cyr. *Hag. Sum.*, 11 (CSL 105); Cyr. *Tib.*, 3 (CSL 145).
38. Cyr. *Tib.*, 1 (CSL 143).
39. Ibid., 3 (CSL 149).

The deity of the Holy Spirit was also staunchly affirmed.[40] He is one substance with the Father.[41] And He must be divine, because if the Spirit that makes us God (in deification) were of a different Nature from God, all hope would be lost.[42]

Christology and Atonement

Regarding Christology, Cyril follows the Nicene faith.[43] As God is unchangeable the Word is unchangeable, though the Logos did not reject the limitation of emptying (*kenosis*).[44]

Christ's divinity was not at all changed because of His humanity. Even when Incarnate, the Word remained exactly what it was.[45]

Cyril speaks of the Son's true union (*kenosis*) with the flesh.[46] He refers to two *prosopa* of Christ.[47] Reference is made to a hypostatic union of Word and flesh, insisting that Christ is not divided. Weaker Nestorian ways of describing this union are rejected.[48] Christ is said to be Two in One, like humans have a body and a soul.[49] Cyril speaks of a conjunction of the Two Natures into a unity.[50]

Cyril proceeds to posit the communication of idioms, that whatever is said of one of Jesus's Natures can be said of the other.[51] Consequently, Mary is referred to as the Mother of God.[52] She is the God-bearer.[53]

---

40. Cyr. *Dial. Trin.*, 7.
41. Cyr. *Hag. Sum.*, 30 (CSL 129).
42. Cyr. *Dial. Trin.*, 7.
43. Cyr. *Tib.*, 1 (CSL 139–41).
44. Cyr. *Rect. fide*, III.
45. Cyr. *Rect. fide*, XIII; Cyr. *Ep. Nest. 3* (LCC 3:350).
46. Cyr. Rect. fide, II.
47. Ibid., XXI.
48. Cyr. *Ep. Nest. 3* (LCC 3:350, 351, 352, 353).
49. Cyr. *Ep. Suc.* 2, 5 (CSL 93).
50. Cyr. *Inc. unigen.*
51. Ibid. Cyr. *Ep. Nest. 3* (LCC 3:353); Cyr. *Ad. Joann.*; Cyr. *Ad Acac.*, 13 (CSL 49–51); Cyr. *Rect. fide*, XXII–XXIII, XXVIII–XXIX.
52. Cyr. *Ep. Nest. 3* (LCC 3:353); Cyr. *Ep. Nest. 2* (NPNF² 14:198); cf. Cyr. *Ad Acac.*, 9 (CSL 45–47); Cyr. *Ep. Succ.* 1, 4 (CSL 73).
53. Cyr. *Rect. fide*, II; Cyr. *Ep. Nest. 3* (LCC 3:352–53).

Likewise, Jesus's temptation, suffering, and death can be attributed to the Logos, according to Cyril.[54] The Word suffered in the flesh, tasting death.[55] But the suffering does not affect the impassibility of the deity.[56] In fact, and in some tension with the communication of idioms, Cyril prefers not to say that Christ suffered.[57] For the Word did not change, he insists, and was not transformed into an entire man when it became flesh. Also, Cyril wants to make clear that God's Word did not actually suffer in its deity, for God is impassible.[58] Nor is Christ's Body taken up into the Trinity.[59]

In taking these positions that the Word of God suffered in the flesh, tasting death,[60] Cyril assumes an orientation more suggestive of Antiochene Christology. He would have us attribute suffering to Jesus, but not that the Word's Nature suffered. However, then more in the mode of the Alexandrian heritage, he claims that all features of the Body are to be attributed to Him.[61] It is better to say, Cyril asserts, that Christ suffered in the flesh than to say that He suffered in the nature of His humanity. The Word did not suffer blows, but in the suffering Body was the impassable Word's Body.[62]

At other points Cyril does draw the full implications of the communication of idioms. He rejects the idea that Christ contributes nothing to miracles with His Body.[63] He heals using His Body like a carpenter uses his soul.[64] If only the Logos had performed the miracles and not the Man Jesus He would be no different from the Prophets.[65]

Another way to make the point for Cyril is to say that Christ's Body is divine in the sense that a man's body is called human and in the

---

54. Cyr. *Inc. unigen.*
55. Cyr. *Ep. Nest.* 2 (CSL 7); Cyr. *Ep. Nest.* 3 (LCC 3:354).
56. Cyr. *Chr. un.*
57. Cyr. *Ep. Nest.* 3 (NPNF² 14:197).
58. Cyr. *Ep. Nest.* 2, 3, 5 (CSL 5, 7).
59. Cyr. *Tib.*, 6 (CSL 157–59).
60. Cyr. *Ep. Nest.* 3 (LCC 3:354).
61. Cyr. *Ep. Suc.* 2 (CSL 87).
62. Ibid., 5 (CSL 93); Cyr. *Ep. Nest.* 2, 6 (CSL 9).
63. Cyr. *Tib.*, 5 (CSL 155).
64. Ibid., 9 (CSL 163).
65. Cyr. *Chr. un.*

sense of being incorruptible.[66] When viewed as God, Christ knows what the Father knows.[67]

Cyril clearly critiqued Nestorian ideas, such as construing Christ as a God-bearing man.[68] Nestorius is said to have overemphasized concern to avoid confusion of Christ's Two Natures.[69]

The Alexandrian bishop also argued that the Word Incarnate has One Nature; it cannot be divided into Two Persons. The Word's Nature is not made one with men. They have not been mingled. The full humanity of Jesus has not been compromised by the union with the Word.[70]

The seeds of the modern Monophysite positions of the Ethiopian and Coptic Orthodox churches may have been sown by Cyril. He refers to the One Incarnate Nature of the Son.[71] An analogy between this union and the unity of man from two natures (body and soul) is proposed.[72]

Cyril breaks with the Apollinarian view. He insists that Christ's Body united with the Word has its own mental life.[73] No merger of Word and flesh is posited.[74]

Using language of the Classic View of the Atonement, Cyril speaks of Christ destroying the one who has the power of death, the devil. He trampled on death in order to blaze the way for our return to incorruptibility.[75] Though rich as God, Christ is said willingly to have become poor and was born like us. In this way man's nature might come to possess the lofty honors of divine majesty and put off the shame of poverty.[76] Deification is suggested here, and as we shall see is expressly affirmed elsewhere. Christ's perfection through suffering supplies us with what was lacking in our birth.[77]

---

66. Cyr. *Ep. Suc. 1*, 10 (CSL 81).
67. Cyr. *Tib.*, 4 (CSL 153).
68. Cyr. *Ep. Nest. 3* (LCC 3:353, 354); cf. Cyr. *Ad Eul.* (CSL 63).
69. Cyr. *Ad Acac.*, 11 (CSL 47).
70. Cyr. *Ep. Suc. 2*, 2–4 (CSL 87, 89); Cyr. *Ad Eul.* (CSL 65).
71. Cyr. *Ad Eul.* (CSL 63); Cyr. *Ep. Suc. 1*, 7 (CSL 77); Cyr. *Ep. Suc. 2*, 5 (CSL 93).
72. Cyr. *Ad Eul.* (CSL 63–65).
73. Cyr. *Ep. Suc. 2*, 2 (CSL 85–87); Cyr. *Ad Acac.*, 20 (CSL 57–59).
74. Cyr. *Hag. Sum.*, 15 (CSL 111).
75. Cyr. *Ep. Nest. 3*, 6 (CSL 21–22).
76. Cyr. *Rect. fide*, 4–5.
77. Ibid., 23.

Christ is also said to accomplish a general ransom.[78] At these points, which suggest something more like the Satisfaction Theory, Christ is said to offer an odor of sweet savor to the Father.[79]

Sin

Cyril seems to affirm something like Original Sin. He speaks of a penalty imposed on Adam and transmitted to us.[80] In Adam we have become corruptive because we come from a corruptible source. The endorsement of an Augustinian view of Original Sin seems qualified, though. For the Bishop of Alexandria contends that this does not mean that we are all punished for having disobeyed the divine injunction along with him.[81] But he does speak of our bodies needing deliverance from foreign corruption.[82] And he contends that it is impossible to eliminate from the flesh all desire, though he does contend that by vigilance we can prevent it from dominating the mind.[83]

Justification and Sanctification: Deification

In a manner consistent with the forgiving orientation of his uncle and mentor, we find a definite grace orientation in Cyril's thought at some points. Christ is said to justify those with faith and adorn those weakened by the old accusations. He no longer allows the severe decrees of the Law to prevail.[84] We are justified through faith in proclaiming Christ's death and confessing His Resurrection.[85] Christ is formed in us.[86]

---

78. Cyr. *Doct.*, 6 (CSL 203).
79. Cyr. *Ep. Nest.* 3, 12 (CSL 31-33).
80. Cyr. *Doct.*, 6 (CSL 201-203); Cyr. *Rom.* 5: 18.
81. Cyr. *Doct.*, 6 (CSL 201-3).
82. Cyr. *Inc. unigen.*
83. Cyr. *Tib.*, 12 (CSL 171).
84. Cyr. *Rect. fide*, 7-8.
85. Ibid., 10.
86. Cyr. *Hayaian.*, 4.2.

This last affirmation implies deification, which Cyril like his other Alexandrian colleagues endorsed.[87] Christ dyes the soul of man with the stability and unchangeability of his own nature.[88]

Elsewhere, Cyril claims that by becoming man Christ is productive of all good for human nature. This restores the image of God, so that the marks of divine nature shine in us through holiness.[89] Christ is said to elevate our life to the level of spiritual citizenship.[90] The unity that characterizes an understanding of salvation in terms of deification is reflected in Cyprian's claim about the oneness we all share in the Holy Spirit.

In another set of comments Cyril contends that Christ is being formed in us, that holiness and righteousness bring conformity to God and restore the image of God.[91] This language highlights the role of the believer in cooperating with grace.

Of course, the element of cooperation is implicit in the concept of deification. Becoming like God entails that we do something with the divine energies.[92]

Sacraments

Typical of the African spiritual ethos we have been studying, Cyril teaches that in Baptism we are reshaped in the divine image.[93] Elsewhere he referred to being baptized into Christ's death.[94]

Even more strongly Cyril employed the language of a new beginning when describing the Eucharist. In that context he spoke of a "bodily re-formation."[95] The Body received in the Eucharist was like a life-giving seed, by which the communicant was intimately joined with the Logos to be made like the Logos.[96]

87. Cyr. *Inc. unigen.*
88. Ibid.
89. Cyr. *Tib.*, 8 (CSL 161); cf. Cyr. *Doct.*, 2, 3, 6 (CSL 191, 195, 203).
90. Cyr. *Tib.*, 9 (CSL 165).
91. Ibid., 10, 12 (CSL 165–67, 171); Cyr. *Doct.*, 4 (CSL 197).
92. Cyr. *Tib.*, 10, 12 (CSL 165–67, 171); Cyr. *Doct.*, 3 (CSL 197); for deification, see Cyr. *Dial. Trin.*, 7.
93. Cyr. *Inc. unigen.*
94. Cyr. *Hag. Sum.*, 27 (CSL 127).
95. Cyr. *Inc. unigen.*
96. Cyr. *Luc.*, 22.19.

These comments presuppose that Christ is really present in the bread and the wine. Cyril refers to partaking of Christ's flesh and blood.[97] The elements, it seems, are transformed into the Body and Blood of Christ.[98] Likewise the bishop rejects the idea that the consecrated Sacramental elements lose their efficacy if a portion remains to another day.[99]

Social Ethics

We find little said about this topic by Cyril. His advocacy of the expulsion of Jews from Alexandria is the most relevant comment on this set of issues, hardly a commendable position from our modern viewpoint (though it must be granted that there had been violence exercised on both sides).[100]

Fulgentius

Fulgentius (ca. 462–527) was a monk and later Bishop of Ruspe in North Africa. Born in a wealthy family with Cathaginian roots, he was heavily persecuted by an Arian king, Thrasamund.[101] He was also a courageous champion of the Nicene way and a strong proponent of salvation by grace.[102] He even opts for the Filioque.[103] Like Augustine, he speaks of God as unchanging and not circumscribed by a particular place.[104] The Lord is also portrayed as jealous, but also merciful and loving.[105] An admirer of Augustine, Fulgentius frequently quotes him with favor.[106] He seems not to

---

97. Cyr. *Ep. Nest. 3* (LCC 3:352).

98. Cyr. *Matt.*, 26:27; Cyr. *Chr. un.*

99. Cyr. *Ep. Cal.* (CSL 219).

100. Socr. *H. e.*, VII.13 (*NPNF*² 2:159-60); also see Wessel, *Cyril of Alexandria and the Nestorian Controversy*.

101. Fer. *Fulg. Vita*, 1.5 (FC 95:6-7, 13).

102. For this characterization, see William Jurgens, "St. Fulgence of Ruspe," in Jurgens, *Faith of the Early Fathers*, 3:285.

103. Fulg. *Fide ad Pet.*, I.6; XI.54 (FC 95:64, 94).

104. Ibid., III.27 (FC 95:76-77); cf. Aug. *Conf.*, X.XXV.36-XXVI.37 (*NPNF*¹ 1:152); Aug. *Ep.* (410), CXVIII.IV-23 (*NPNF*¹ 1:446).

105. Fulg. *Rem. Pec.*, I.VII.2-I.VIII.1 (FC 95:118

106. Fulg. *Ep.* (n.d.), 12.(XV).26 (FC 95:496).

have been Black himself, as in one text he calls attention expressly to a Black man from Ethiopia.[107]

Theological Method

Fulgentius writes that we can study our hearts in light of Scripture. The Bible is said to reveal who we are and ought to be. Its study in meekness and humility is urged.[108] It is said to be divinely inspired.[109] An Orthodox model of theology is quite obviously advocated here. Regarding ontology and his view of human nature, the African Father operates with the usual body-soul dualism of Greek philosophy.[110] Like earlier African theologians, Fulgentius also affirmed creation out of nothing.[111]

God, Christology, and Atonement

The bishop teaches a rigorous affirmation of the full humanity of Jesus, yet also claims His humanity was aware of His divinity.[112] This entails at least by implication an Alexandrian Christology is in operation in his thought. Mary bore God. God is said to be the Son of the Virgin Mary.[113] Yet he qualifies this point subsequently, not wanting to say that Jesus's soul has full knowledge of the Trinity as if it were One Nature with the Trinity.[114]

The Trinity, though, is vigorously affirmed, along with the Filioque.[115] This God fills the whole creation.[116] With interesting insight Fulgentius compares the Father and the Son to a person and his cloak or to a person and the air he breathes. The air and the cloak are both in and of the person

---

107. Ibid., 12.(I).2 (FC 95:476).
108. Ibid. (n.d.), 6.12 (FC 95:353).
109. Fulg. Rem. Pec., I.CII.1 (FC 95:117).
110. Fulg. *Fide ad Pet.*, III.35 (FC 95:82).
111. Ibid., III.25-27 (FC 95:75).
112. Fulg. *Ep.*, 14.26 (FC 95:535); cf. Fulg. *Fide ad Pet.*, II.11-14, 17 (FC 95:66-68, 70).
113. Fulg. *Fide ad Pet.*, II.17 (FC 95:70); cf. ibid., XVIII.61 (FC 95:96-97).
114. Fulg. *Ep.*, 14.31 (FC 95:542).
115. Fulg. *Fide ad Pet.*, I.3-5 (FC 95:61-63); ibid., II.7; XI.54 (FC 95:64, 93-94).
116. Ibid., III.27 (FC 95:77); Fulg. *Ep.*, 14.5 (FC 95:503).

wearing the cloak and breathing, but when exhaled and removed they are independent.[117]

Jesus must be divine, Fulgentius contends, for human nature would not be sufficient for taking away the sin of the world.[118] Christ bore the weakness of our souls.[119] He offers a sacrifice, presumably to the Father.[120] However, the language of the Classic View of the Atonement also appears, as it is claimed that Christ swallowed up death.[121]

As Fulgentius puts it elsewhere, the mortality of our humanity was absorbed by his immortality.[122] Yet the African Father does not thereby make God vulnerable, insisting instead that He is Himself impassable, that only as flesh is Christ born.[123] He clearly operates with an Antiochene Christology.

Justification/Predestination and Sanctification

Like his mentor, Augustine, Fulgentius endorsed the idea of sin as concupiscence, contending that sin is transmitted to children through concupiscent sexual intercourse.[124] He claims that even a just man's good work is rendered void by the defect of Original Sin.[125] But he did distinguish venial and mortal sin.[126]

Fulgentius does speak of the significance of penance as an opportunity to win eternal life. We gain mercy in conversion.[127] But repentance is only fruitful in the Catholic Church, he contends.[128] Mercy takes up and frees the converted in this context.[129] Grace is prevenient, and it is said to lead to

---

117. Fulg. *Ad. Mon.*, III.II.3–5 (FC 95:261–62).

118. Fulg. *Ep.*, 17.9.

119. Ibid., 18.9.

120. Fulg. *Fide ad Pet.*, III.25; XIX.62; XXVU.69 (FC 95:75, 97, 100).

121. Ibid., II.13 (FC 95:67).

122. Ibid., II.12 (FC 95:67).

123. Ibid., II.7–8 (FC 95:65).

124. Ibid., II.16; XXV.69–XVI.70 (FC 95:69, 99–100); Fulg. *Ad. Mon.*, XX.1 (FC 95:213–14).

125. Fulg. *Rem. Pec.*, II.VIII.6 (FC 95:159–60).

126. Fulg. *Fide ad Pet.*, III.45 (FC 95:90).

127. Ibid., III.39 (FC 95:84); Fulg. *Rem. Pec.*, I.XII.2–3 (FC 95:124–25).

128. Fulg. *Fide ad Pet.*, III.39 (FC 95:85); Fulg. *Rem. Pec.*, II.I.2 (FC 95:147).

129. Fulg. *Fide ad Pet.*, III.41 (FC 95:86).

perseverance in the Christian life.[130] Then Fulgentius adds that no one is able to attain forgiveness of sins if he neglects the duty of good works and does not hold fast to faith.[131] Salvation is not given to the wicked, he asserts.[132]

This Pelagian-like language is strongly balanced by assertions of the role of grace in saving us. The African Father contends that in every sinner who makes use of his free will, grace begins to work through the conversion of the heart.[133] God is said to pour the light of true conversion into those whose sin He forgives.[134] There is a (prevenient) grace of conversion.[135] Faith is the beginning of salvation, he claims.[136]

We have already noted Fulgentius's teaching of prevenient grace, and it is frequently evident in his corpus.[137] He even affirms salvation by grace without works.[138] This fits his strong doctrine of Providence and affirmation of Predestination.[139] He taught that the Will of God is always fulfilled, because His Power is never defeated.[140]

Fulgentius compares human freedom's need for grace to the eye needing light in order to see.[141] There is no faith in his view if not given by God. Nor can we will good without the assistance of grace.[142] Without faith, he claims, all human effort is empty.[143]

On the question of how grace relates to free will, when dealing with Sanctification or sloth in the Christian life, the African Father anticipates the medieval Western Catholic tradition, claiming that works that are the fruits of grace in us merit eternal life.[144] There is no forgiveness of sins if one

---

130. Fulg. *Rem. Pec.*, I.IV.1–2 (FC 95:114).

131. Ibid., I.V; II.XXI.3 (FC 95:115, 183).

132. Ibid., II.VI.1 (FC 95:151–52).

133. Ibid., I.XIV (FC 95:127).

134. Ibid., I.XV.1 (FC 95:128).

135. Ibid., I.XV.2 (FC 95:128–29).

136. Fulg. *Fide ad Pet.*, 1 (FC 95:60).

137. Fulg. *Ep.* (n.d.), 6.12 (FC 95:353); Fulgentius, *Rem. Pec.*, I.XXIV.1; I.VIIII2; II.3 (FC 95:140, 119, 149).

138. Fulg. *Fide ad Pet.*, III.43 (FC 95:88).

139. Ibid., XXXV.78 (FC 95:103).

140. Fulg. *Ep.*, 15.15.

141. Ibid., 15.5.

142. Ibid., 17.47; ibid., 14.4, 5 (FC 95:502).

143. Fulg. *Rem. Pec.*, II.IX.2 (FC 95:160).

144. Fulg. *Ep.* (n.d.), 7.2, 11–12 (FC 95:297–98); cf. Council of Trent, *Decretum de Justificatione* (1547), V–VII.

negelcts the duty of good works.[145] If unwilling to be changed he will not be changed by God.[146] Fulgentius even refers to earning merits for eternal life.[147] At one point he even claims that God grants access to those who knock, but enkindles the desire to seek Him.[148]

Fulgentius very nicely represents the Augustinian heritage, helping clarify whether he and the Church teach salvation by grace alone or by grace and works. In a comment rich with ecumenical significance, Fulgentius contends that it ultimately does not matter as long as grace plays the prior role:

> You may perhaps say that a man is saved by God's mercy alone; and others will say that unless a man's own will accompanies and cooperates with that mercy, he will not be able to be saved. And both views may rightly be held, if a proper order of divine mercy and human will be observed, so that the one comes before and the other follows after. The beginning of salvation is conferred by God's mercy alone. With that mercy the human will then becomes the cooperatrix.[149]

Grace is not given to all.[150] Like Augustine, Fulgentius seems to affirm Double Predestination. We have already noted how he expressly teaches Predestination at points.[151] He offers a response to those contending that there is an injustice in this, pointing out that since we have sinned voluntarily it is fitting that those damned are destined for it.[152] The fact that evil emerges is not caused by God, but by our own will. Invoking Augustine, he claims that we are predestined to damnation, but not to evil.[153]

---

145. Fulg. *Rem. Pec.*, I.V (FC 95:115).

146. Ibid., II.XIII.3 (FC 95:168).

147. Ibid., II.X.4 (FC 95:163-64).

148. Fulg. *Ep.*, 14.1 (FC 95:499).

149. Ibid., 15.11: "Quod autem vos dicitis, sola Dei misericordia salvari hominem, illi autem dicunt, nisiquis prepria voluntate cucurrerit et elaboraverit, salvus esse non-poterit, *digne utrumque tenetur*, si ordo rectus servetur divinae misericordie et voluntatis humanae, ut illa praeveniat, haec sequatur: sola Dei midericordia initium salutis conferat; cui deinde voluntas hominis cooperatrix suae salutis existat ut midericordia Dei praeveniens voluntatis humanae dirigat cursim et humana voluntas obediens . . ."

150. Ibid., 10.

151. Ibid., 17.67; cf. Fulg. *Fide ad Pet.*, III.42; XXXIV.77 (FC 95: 87, 102-13); Fulg. *Ad. Mon.*, I.III.1-4; I.V.1; I.XIII.1 (FC 95:192-93, 194, 204); Fulg. *Ep.*, 15.15.

152. Fulg. *Ad. Mon.*, I.XIX.4 (FC 95:213).

153. Ibid., I.VI.1 (FC 95:194).

Continuing to affirm the priority of prevenient grace and our freedom from works of the Law, Fulgentius asserts that works of the Law cannot justify.[154] But this does not preclude his attention to sanctification.

By grace we are saved, he asserts, but then we learn to leave behind the evil life. He speaks of receiving perseverance.[155] Perseverance is even enjoined.[156] In a similar vein he contends that those who truly love God obey His Precepts. Among these include strictures against marital excess.[157] But in Augustinian fashion he adds that such obedience is because they are changed by God's Word, that there are no good works unless given by God.[158]

Sacraments

Along with Augustine and most of the early African tradition, Fulgentius taught that in baptism we are made members of the Body of Christ.[159] Not only is baptismal regeneration taught, but Christ's Presence in the Sacrament is also affirmed.[160]

Baptism is said to entail salvation for children.[161] But in accord with Cyprian of Carthage he contended that there is no salvation if baptized outside the Catholic Church.[162] Only in the Catholic Church is forgiveness of sins received and given, he asserted.[163] Fulgentius's contention that there is no salvation outside the Church[164] is related to his insistence that it is necessary to receive penance in order to gain eternal life.[165] The African Father depicts the Eucharist as an upbuilding of the Body of Christ in love, rendering the faithful a holy priesthood to offer spiritual sacrifices.[166]

---

154. Fulg. *Ep.*, 17.52.

155. Fulg. *Rem. Pec.*, I.XXIII.1; I.XXIV.1; II.II.3 (FC 95:140, 149); Fulg. *Ad. Mon.*, I.VIII.1 (FC 95:197).

156. Fulg. *Rem. Pec.*, II.VIII.5; II.XXII.3; II.IX.1 (FC 95:159, 183).

157. Fulg. *Fide ad Pet.*, III.45 (FC 95:90).

158. Fulg. *Rem. Pec.*, II.XII.1 (FC 95:165–66); Fulg. *Ad. Mon.*, I.IX.3 (FC 95:199).

159. Fulg. *Ep.* (n.d.), 12.26 (FC 95:496).

160. Ibid., 12.25.26 (FC 95:494, 496).

161. Fulg. *Fide ad Pet.*, XXX.73 (FC 95:102).

162. Ibid., XXXVIII.81; III.45 (FC 95:104, 88).

163. Fulg. *Rem. Pec.*, I.XIX.1 (FC 95:133).

164. Ibid., (FC 95:136); cf. ibid., I.XXII.1; II.I.2 (FC 95:138–39, 147).

165. Fulg. *Fide ad Pet.*, XXX.73 (FC 95:101).

166. Fulg., *Ad Mon.*, II.XI.1 (FC 95:250).

Ministry

Fulgentius did establish lifestyle standards for priests. A holy life and sound doctrine are said to be necessary for teachers of the Church.[167] We have already noted Fulgentius's espousal of the concept of the priesthood of all believers.

Church

Fulgentius refers to the Church as the Christian's Mother.[168] There is good and bad in the Catholic Church (including clerics), he contends. Yet he urges that the good not be deserted on account of the bad.[169]

Social Ethics

Although on the African Father's grounds we cannot do works without grace any more than the body can function without the soul, Fulgentius does not rule out the possibility that sinful human beings can do civilly righteous deeds (practice justice).[170] He writes, "Certainly such people [unbelievers] can possess a certain kind of goodness, which pertains to the justice of human society, but because it is not the product of faith in God and of love of God, it is not able to assist them."[171]

We are all capable of such civil righteousness because all of us naturally know the Law of God (the natural law).[172] And he makes clear that such righteousness includes feeding the hungry and clothing the naked.[173]

---

167. Fer. *Fulg. Vita*, Pro. (FC 95:4).

168. Fulg. *Rem. Pec.*, I.XXI.1 (FC 95:136).

169. Fulg. *Fide ad Pet.*, XLIII.86 (FC 95:105); Fulg. *Rem. Pec.*, XVIII.1 (FC 95:133).

170. Fulg. *Ep.*, 17.47.

171. Ibid., 17.51: ". . . quibis aliqua quidem bona, quae ad societatis humanae pertinent aequltatem, in esse possunt. Sed quia non fide et caritate Dei flunt, prodesse non possunt."

172. Ibid., 17.52.

173. Fulg. *Rem. Pec.*, II.XIV.2 (FC 95:169).

Summary

The post-Augustinian African theologians we have considered illustrate the history of the Church since Augustine. For all of Augustine's impact on the West his theology has not been unanimously endorsed—and even when it has, the diversity in his thought continues to reflect in his followers. Consequently, we find in Cyril a decidedly non-Augustinian Eastern way of doing theology, reflected notably in his soteriology, which resembles so many of the pre-Augustinian theologians considered in this book. While with Fulgentius, a follower of Augustine, we can identify his endorsement of prevenient grace. Similar differences exist between these post-Augustinian Fathers on Theological Method. Post-Augustinian African thought offers us a rich diversity for ministry today.

Conclusion

Using Early African Theology Today

IF READERS HAD ANY residual, cultural doubts prior to picking up this book, it should be obvious by now that Christianity in Africa is not a European thing, but an "indigenous faith" of the Continent. Even in those regions (especially west and south Africa) where European and American missions were responsible for planting churches after the colonial era began, we should not forget that many of these missionary agencies relied heavily on African-American missionaries. It is well to be reminded of the Black American Presbyterian William Henry Sheppard, who worked in what is today Zaire in the nineteenth century and of Kelly Kemp, an African-American missionary with the United Brethren for Christ mission in Liberia, just to name a few. Nor should we forget the missions planted by African-American denominations like the African Methodist Episcopal Church and the National Baptist Convention.[1]

Why does it matter to learn that Christianity is not a White thing? Relearning that Christian faith and practice are deeply indebted to early African theological insights gives the Church a crucial resource for speaking against the paternalism and racism that continue to plague American life and global society.

How else can we use early African theology today, in addition to employing these insights in the project of social reconstruction in interests of more justice? This has been a book about legacy—about recovering the

---

1. For a summary of these developments, see Ellingsen, "Changes in African American Mission: Rediscovering African Roots."

ancient roots of Christianity not just for people of African descent, but also recovering the legacy of the Church catholic. Let's review in closing precisely how ancient Africa continues to impact us all.

Formation of the Canon and Theological Method

We cannot give ancient African Christianity all the credit for the formation of the biblical canon. But we have already noted Athanasius's contribution in formulating the oldest list of books of the Bible that corresponds to the canon as we have it today (including the Apochrypha). Of course, Athanasius does not get the credit for formulating this list. He was merely functioning to summarize what had been standard among all his fellow North African bishops. But their collective influence on the canonization process is apparent not only in the overlap between Athansisus's list and the Church catholic's consensus, but also insoar as it was in Councils of the African church (in Hippo in 393 and in Carthage in 397, both acting on an earlier statement of the Council of Laodicea) that the Church finally formalized its consensus.

Regarding Theological Method (how theology is done with regard to one's starting point and use of sources other than Scripture as well as the sense in which the Bible is deemed authoritative), it is true that debates over this topic have roots in the different approaches of the different biblical authors. But it is significant that major models of Theological Method (the dispute over whether to employ Philosophy or some other conceptuality as the starting point in doing Theology, or whether these should be shunned in favor of exclusive concentration on the Word of God) have their roots in the African theology of the first centuries, and that it is in that context that controversies over the options first emerged.

Monasticism

We have already made the case for the contribution of ancient North African Christianity to monasticism. In many ways Africa is the mother of monasticism and the great impact it has had on Catholicism and the Eastern churches. The importance of monastic piety for African spirituality continues to this day. Following a long-standing tradition, all bishops of the Ethiopian and Coptic churches must have been monks. Monasticism breeds spiritual leaderhip for these churches. And in the West, we should not overlook the role of women in monasticism—how many of the nuns over the centuries of Christian history, including the early African Christian Mothers, serve as significant models for women's leadership in the Church today. In addition, the growing interest in monastic spirituality by some Protestants represents another example of the how the contributions of the ancient African Mothers and Fathers still matter today.

Polity, Worship, and Liturgy

To this day, denominations that have a polity that includes bishops are in line with the polity of early African Christianity. The Catholic and the Eastern churches come to mind immediately as informed by this polity, but vestiges of it remain in several Protestant bodies. They all opt for a polity with roots in African Chrstianity.

Likewise, these same churches share with ancient African Christians liturgical worship. We have already noted that the oldest postbiblical manual of worship, *The Didache*, may well have had its roots in Africa. And it has been most influential on the development of other liturgies. In this connection it is relevant to note the development of a distinct African liturgy, the Liturgy of St. Mark, whose oldest manuscript dates only in the twelfth century, but whose origins may be as ancient as the first centuries. Still the dominant worship style of the Ethiopian and Coptic churches, it displays many characteristics of the dominant Eastern and Western liturgies.

Trinity and Christology

The impact of early African Christianity on these two ecumenical doctrines is even more clearly recognized. We have already noted that among the first to endorse this concept were Clement of Alexandria and Tertullian in the late second century. More data can be provided for the conclusion that the Trinity is indebted to, if not actually rooted in, ancient African spirituality. The influence of Alexander of Alexandria on the Council of Nicea is significant. Perhaps even more so is Athanasius's role in defending the Nicene formula, finally convening the Synod of Alexandria, which first officially endorsed the doctrine. In addition, the numerous concrete images for understanding the Trinity among the African theologians considered in this book, not to mention Augustine's insightful treatment of the doctrine, provide some impressive and helpful contributions for reflecting on the Trinity today.[2] Ancient African Christianity can contribute to the Western church's recovery of a Trinitairan piety (which has been on the wane in this part of Christendom at least since, if not before, the 1054 East-West Schism).

With regard to Christology, we have noted that the concept of Two Natures and One Person has roots in Tertullian. And one of the two dominant Christologies of the catholic heritage, Alexandrian Christology, has its roots in the ancient African church. We have much to learn from ancient African Christianity regarding how we talk about Jesus Christ.

Creation and Providence

The catholic concept that God created out of nothing with no mediator emerged as an affirmation that the Church needed to make while in dialogue with Greek philosophy and Gnosticism. While the Greeks had posited demiurges as the agents the gods used in creation, we have noted that Clement of Alexandria insisted that God alone made creation without a demiurge, by the mere act of the Will, and Tertullian also taught creation out of nothing in repose to Gnostic ideas that God relied on pre-exsitent evil matter in creation. The contributions of Alexander of Lycopolis to the critique of dualisms in understanding creation are also still relevant.

Although the dominant model of the pre-Augustinian Fathers and Mothers for Providence was to affirm human free will, Dionysius of Alexandria's reflections on God as energy that regulates all things, yet not without some free will of the created order, is most suggestive of what we know about modern physics (the Big Bang Theory) regarding how the cosmos was formed and continues to operate (the role of energy in creating matter). This ancient African bishop can, then, be a valuable resource for engaging in dialogue with Science today.

Soteriology and Sanctification

Although it is only with Augustine that we can unambiguously speak of African Christianity's role in the formulation of the doctrine of Original Sin, there are significant precedents for Augustine's formulation of this

---

2. For an extended discussion of Augustine's treatment of the Trinity, see my *Richness of Augustine*, 47–49.

concept in the African theologies of the first centuries of the Church on this continent.[3] Thus we find Cyprian of Carthage referring to infant sin as he advocates infant baptism.[4] And Commodianus equated sin with desire, much as Augustine construed sin as concupiscence. Pseudo-Macarius also spoke of sin this way.[5] Although he taught free will, Athanasius also spoke like Augustine did later of the insatiable desire to sin.[6]

To be sure, as we have noted, the pre-Augustinian African church leaders we have considered in the book have most in common with Eastern conceptions of soteriology (teaching deification sometimes, and always the simultaneity of grace and works in contributing to Justification). Protestants and even Catholics on the whole must look to Augustine for inspiration for their commitment to the prevenience (priority) of grace in saving us. But readers of these Western traditions can find some insights from the pre-Augustinian African leaders that resonate with their commitments. Optatus, Fulgentius, and at some points (though inconsistently) Cyril of Alexandria as well as Cyprian of Carthage prioritize grace.

In this connection Protestants can find some instances in which they share similar sentiments with early African theology regarding the Christian life. We have noted how Dionysius of Alexandria sometimes spoke of the spontaneity of the Christian life and Macarius even claimed that Christians are intoxicated by God. While Lutherans can find their own heritage in such commitments, Methodist-Holiness proponents of striving for perfection have allies in the literature attributed to Macarius and to Theognostus of Alexandria.

Social Ethics

A rich diversity on the proper relation between church and state, a debate that continues in the Church to this day, reflects among the African theologians considered in the book. Some like Origen, Theonas of Alexandria, and Lactantius posited a friendly relation between church and state and others like Tertullian, Fulgentius, as well as the Desert Mothers and Fathers, insisted

---

3. For Augustine's formulation of the concept of Original Sin, see his *Nupt. et concup.*, I.XXV (*NPNF*[1] 5:275).

4. Cypr. *Ep.* (n.d.), LXIV/LVIII.5 (*ANF* 5:354).

5. Comm. Instr., LXIV (*ANF* 4:215-16); Mac. *Hom. IInum.*, 16.4; 17.6; 26.2 (*PM* 130, 137, 164).

6. Ath. *Log. Eoan*, 5 (*NPNF*[2] 4:38-39).

on keeping them in tension, contending that a Christian society is not possible, and so Social Ethics is to be based on reason and the natural law.

What It All Means

The issues raised by an appreciation of the rich diversity of the thought of the ancient African Christian Mothers and Fathers clearly prefigure many of the ongoing theological disputes in the Church catholic. No doubt we can gain more clarity about these perennially disputed issues as we study their origins (in ancient North Africa).

While working through the book's chapters, it should also have become clear to readers (Protestants, Catholics, and Eastern Orthodox Christians) how many of their denominational distinctives are rooted in ancient African Christian theology. Gaining clarity from the African Mothers and Fathers on these disputes can continue to stimulate theological reflection today.

Of course the study of the thought of the ancient African Mothers and Fathers is a sort of pleasant homecoming for Eastern Orthodox Christians. So much of the Eastern Orthodox heritage and its practices are rooted in ancient North African ways of living out the Gospel. But exposure to the theology of the ancient African Mothers and Fathers can be of real theological benefit to Western Christians and Protestants in particular. From these Mothers and Fathers we might be able to recover a stronger foundation for clerical authority along with a more self-consciously Trinitarian piety, convictions that may be essential to the Church's survival in our postmodern ethos, with its cynicism about authority and its attempt to reduce all that is distinctively Christian to the realm of private spiritual values. The Christianity of Africa may help us to get in touch more faithfully with the Apostolic witness to the Lord.

Secondary Source Bibliography

(See Abbreviations for Primary Sources)

Anatolius, Khaled. *Athanasius: The Coherence of His Thought*. New York: Routledge, 2004.
Atiya, Aziz S. *A History of Eastern Christianity*. London: Methuen, 1968.
Baker, R. A. "Was Saint Athanasius of Alexandria a Black Man, the 'Black Dwarf'?" *ChurchHistory101.com*, http://www.churchhistory101.com/feedback/athanasius-black-dwarf.php.
Barnes, Timothy D. *Athanasius and Constantius*. Cambridge: Harvard University Press, 1993.
———. *Tertullian: A Historical and Literary Study*. Oxford: Clarendon, 1958.
Barth, Karl. *Church Dogmatics* III/2. Translated by G. T. Thomson et al. Edited by G. W. Bromiley and T. F. Torrance. Edinburgh: T. & T. Clark, 1960.
Bediako, Kwame. *Christianity in Africa: The Renewal of a Non-Western Religion*. Edinburgh: Edinburgh University Press, 1995.
———. *Theology and Identity: The Impact of Culture upon Christian Thought in the Second Century and in Modern Africa*. Oxford: Regnum, 1992.
Benedict XVI, Pope. *Church Fathers: From Clement of Rome to Augustine*. San Francisco: Ignatius, 2008.
Benson, E. W. *Cyprian: His Life, His Times, His Work*. London: Macmillan, 1897.
Boersma, Gerald P. "The Logic of the Logos: A Note on Stoic Logic in *Adversus Praxean* 10." *Journal of Early Christian Studies* 22 (2014) 485–98.
Bregman, Jay. *Synesius or Cyrene, Philosopher-Bishop*. Berkeley: University of California Press, 1982.
Brent, Allen. *Cyprian and Roman Carthage*. Cambridge: Cambridge University Press, 2010.
Brinton, Crane, et al. *Civilization in the West*. Englewood Cliffs, NJ: Prentice-Hall, 1964.
Brown, Peter. *Augustine of Hippo: A Biography*. Berkeley: University of California Press, 1969.
Budge, E. A., ed. *The Book of the Saints of the Ethiopian Orthodox Church* [Mashafa Senkesar]. 4 vols. Cambridge: University of Cambridge, 1928.

SECONDARY SOURCE BIBLIOGRAPHY

Burns, J. Patout, Jr. *Cyprian the Bishop*. London: Routledge, 2002.

Cameron, Alan, and Jacqueline Long, with a contribution by Lee Sherry. *Barbarians and Politics and the Court of Arcadius*. Berkeley: University of California Press, 1993.

Chadwick, Henry. *History and Thought of the Early Church*. London: Variorum Reprints, 1982.

———. "Pachomius and the Idea of Sanctity." In *The Byzantine Saint: University of Birmingham Fourteenth Spring Symposium of Byzantine Studies*, edited by Sergei Hackel, 11–24. Crestwood, NY: St. Vladimir's Seminary Press, 2001.

Clendenin, Daniel B., ed. *Eastern Orthodox Theology: A Contemporary Reader*. Grand Rapids: Baker, 1995.

Courtois, Christian. "Saint Augustin et le Problème de la Survivance du Punique." *Revue Africaine* 94 (1950) 259–82.

Crouzel, Henri. *Origen*. Translated by A. S. Worell. Edinburgh: T. & T. Clark, 1989.

Digeser, Elizabeth DePalma. *The Making of a Christian Empire: Lactantius and Rome*. Ithaca: Cornell University Press, 2000.

Dunn, Geoffrey D. *Tertullian*. London: Routledge, 2004.

Earle, Mary C. *The Desert Mothers: Spiritual Practices from the Women of the Wilderness*. Harrisburg, PA: Morehouse, 2007.

Ehrman, Bart. *Didymus the Blind and Text of the Gospels*. Atlanta: SBL, 1986.

Ellingsen, Mark. "Changes in African American Mission: Rediscovering African Roots." *International Bulletin of Missionary Research* 36 (2012) 136–42.

———. *The Richness of Augustine: His Contextual and Pastoral Theology*. Louisville: Westminster John Knox, 2005.

Frend, W. H. C. "A Note on the Berber Background in the Life of Augustine." *Journal of Theological Studies* 43 (1942) 188–94.

Gauche, William. *Didymus the Blind: An Educator of the Fourth Century*. Washington, DC: Catholic University of American Press, 1934.

Gelzer, Heinrich. *Sextus Julius Africanus und die Byzantinische Chronographie*. Leipzig: B. G. Teubner, 1880.

Getty, Marie Madeleine of Jesus, Sister. *The Life of the North Africans as Revealed in the Sermons of Saint Augustine*. Washington, DC: Catholic Univeristy of America Press, 1931.

Glancy, Jennifer. *Slavery in Early Christianity*. Oxford: Oxford University Press, 2002.

Gonzalez, Eliezer. "Anthropologies of Continuity: The Body and Soul in Tertullian, Perpetua, and Early Christianity." *Journal of Early Christian Studies* 21 (2013) 479–502.

González, Justo. *History of Christian Thought*. Vol. 1. Nashville: Abingdon, 1970.

———. *The Story of Christianity*. 2 vols. San Francisco: HarperSanFrancisco, 1984.

Greenslade, S. L., ed. *Early Latin Theology: Selections from Tertullian, Cyprian, Ambrose, and Jerome*. Library of Christian Classics 5. Philadelphia: Westminster, 1956.

Gumerlock, Francis X. *Fulgentius of Ruspe on the Saving Will of God: The Development of a Sixth-Century African Bishop's Interpretation of 1 Timothy 2:4 during the Semi-Pelagian Controversy*. Lewiston, NY: Mellen, 2009.

Hanson, R. P. C. *Origen's Doctrine of Tradition*. 1954. Reprint, Eugene, OR: Wipf & Stock, 2013.

Harmless, William. *Desert Christians: An Introduction to the Literature of Early Monasticism*. Oxford: Oxford University Press, 2004.

Harnack, Adolf von. *The Mission and Expansion of Christianity in the First Three Centuries*. Translated and edited by James Moffatt. 2 vols. New York: G. P. Putnam, 1908.

Hartshorne, Charles. *The Divine Relativity*. New Haven: Yale University Press, 1948.

Harvey, Susan A., and David G. Hunter, eds. *The Oxford Handbook of Early Christian Studies*. Oxford: Oxford University Press, 2008.

Isichei, Elizabeth Allo. *A History of Christianity in Africa: From Antiquity to the Present*. Grand Rapids: Eerdmans, 1995.

Jaeger, Werner. *Two Rediscovered Works of Ancient Christian Literature: Gregory of Nyssa and Macarius*. Leiden: Brill, 1954.

Jenkins, Philip. *The Lost History of Christianity: The Thousand-Year Age of the Church in the Middle East, Africa, and Asia—and How It Died*. New York: HarperOne, 2008.

Jurgens, William, ed. *The Faith of the Early Fathers*. 3 vols. Collegeville, MN: 1970–79.

Kalewold, Imbakom. *Traditional Ethiopian Church Education*. Translated by Menghestu Lemma. New York: Teachers College Press, 1971.

Kant, Immanuel. *Critique of Pure Reason*. Translated by Norman Kemp Smith. New York: St. Martin's, 1965.

Kaplan, Steven. *The Monastic Holy Man and the Christianization of Early Solomonic Ethiopia*. Wiesbaden: F. Steiner, 1984.

Kierkegaard, Søren. *Training in Christianity; and the Edifying Discourse Which "Accompanied" It*. Translated by Walter Lowrie. Princeton: Princeton University Press, 1944.

Latourette, Kenneth Scott. *A History of Christianity*. Vol. 1, *Beginnings to 1500*. Rev. ed. Peabody, MA: Prince, 1997.

Layton, Richard. *Didymus the Blind and His Circle in Late-Antique Alexandria*. Urbana: University of Illinois Press, 2004.

Livingstone, E. A., ed. *Concise Oxford Dictionary of the Christian Church*. 2nd ed. Oxford: Oxford University Press, 1977.

Lyman, R. J. *Christology and Cosmology: Models of Divine Activity in Origen, Eusebius and Athanasius*. Oxford: Clarendon, 1993.

Maddox, Randy L. "John Wesley and Eastern Orthodoxy: Influences, Convergences, and Differences." *Asbury Theological Journal* 45 (1990) 29–53.

Maier, Harry. "Clement of Alexandria and the Care of the Self." *Journal of the American Academy of Religion* 62 (1994) 719–45.

Maloney, George, trans. *Pseudo-Macarius: The Fifty Spiritual Homilies and The Great Letter*. Translated and edited by George Maloney. New York: Paulist, 1992.

Martens, Peter. *Origen and Scripture: The Contours of the Exegetical Life*. Oxford: Oxford University Press, 2012.

Meijering, E. P. *Orthodoxy and Platonism in Athanasius: Synthesis or Antithesis?* Leiden: Brill, 1968.

Meyer, Marvin, and Richard Smith, eds. *Ancient Christian Magic: Coptic Texts of Ritual Power*. San Francisco: HarperSanFrancisco, 1994.

Oden, Thomas C. *Early Libyan Christianity: Uncovering a North African Tradition*. Downers Grove, IL: InterVarsity, 2011.

———. *How Africa Shaped the Christian Mind: Rediscovering the African Seedbed of Western Christianity*. Downers Grove, IL: InterVarsity, 2007.

Osborn, Eric. "Arguments for Faith in Clement of Alexandria." *Vigiliae Christianae* 48 (1994) 1–24.

SECONDARY SOURCE BIBLIOGRAPHY

———. *Tertullian: First Theologian of the West*. Cambridge: Cambridge University Press, 2003.
Outler, Albert, ed. *John Wesley*. New York: Oxford University Press, 1964.
Patrick, Theodore Hall. *Traditional Egyptian Christianity: A History of the Coptic Orthodox Church*. Greensboro, NC: Fisher Park, 1996.
Pearson, Birger, and James Goehring, eds. *The Roots of Egyptian Christianity*. Paperback ed. Minneapolis: Augsburg Fortress, 1992.
Pelikan, Jaroslav. *The Emergence of the Catholic Tradition (100–600)*. Chicago: University of Chicago Press, 1971.
Rankin, David. *Tertullian and the Church*. Cambridge: Cambridge University Press, 1995.
Robinson, James, ed. *The Nag Hammadi Library in English*. 3rd rev. ed. San Francisco: HarperSanFrancisco, 1990.
Russell, Norman, trans. *The Lives of the Desert Fathers*. Kalamazoo, MI: Cistercian, 1981.
Sauneron, Serge. *The Priests of Ancient Egypt*. Translated by David Lotson. Ithaca: Cornell University Press, 2000.
Schaff, Philip. *History of the Christian Church*. 3rd rev. ed. 8 vols. Reprint, Peabody, MA: Hendrickson, 2002.
Schleiermacher, Friedrich. *The Christian Faith*. Edited by H. R. MacKintosh and J. S. Stewart. 2 vols. New York: Harper & Row, 1963.
Scott, Mark. "Guarding the Mysteries of Salvation: The Pastoral Pedagogy of Origen's Universalism." *Journal of Early Christian Studies* 18 (2010) 347–68.
Scott, T. Kermit. *Augustine: His Thought in Context*. New York: Paulist, 1995.
Seyr, F. "Die Seelen- und Erkenntnislehre Tertullians und die Stoa." *Commentationes Vindobonenses* 3 (1937) 51–74.
Shaw, Mark. *The Kingdom of God in Africa: A Short History of African Christianity*. Grand Rapids: Baker, 1996.
Shortt, Charles De Lisle. *The Influence of Philosophy on the Mind of Tertullian*. London: E. Stock, 1933.
Surhone, Lambert M., Miriam T. Timpledon, and Susan F. Marseken, eds. *Tertullian*. Betascript, 2011.
Swift, Louis J. "Arnobius and Lactantius: Two Views of the Pagan Poets." *American Philological Association* 96 (1965) 439–48.
Tillich, Paul. *Systematic Theology*. Vol. 1. Chicago: University of Chicago Press, 1951.
Torjesen, Karen Jo. *When Women Were Priests: Women's Leadership in the Early Church and the Scandal of Their Subordination in the Rise of Christianity*. San Francisco: HarperSanFrancisco, 1993.
Torrance, T. F. *Divine Meaning: Studies in Patristic Hermeneutics*. Edinburgh: T. & T. Clark, 1995.
Tracy, David. *Blessed Rage for Order*. New York: Seabury, 1978.
Trigg, Joseph Wilson. *Origen: The Bible and Philosophy in the Third-Century Church*. Atlanta: John Knox, 1983.
Tzamalikos, Panagiōtēs. *Origen: Cosmology and Ontology of Time*. Leiden: Brill, 2006.
Veilleux, Armand, trans. *Pachomian Koinonia*. 3 vols. Cistercian Studies Series 45–47. Kalamazoo, MI: Cistercian, 1980–82.
Vivian, Tim. *St. Peter of Alexandria: Bishop and Martyr*. Philadelphia: Fortress, 1988.
Volz, Carl. *Faith and Practice in the Early Church*. Minneapolis: Augsburg Fortress, 1983.
Ward, Benedicta, trans. *The Sayings of the Desert Fathers*. Kalamazoo, MI: Cistercian, 1975.

Weinandy, Thomas G. *Athanasius: A Theological Introduction*. Burlington, VT: Ashgate, 2007.

———, ed. *The Theology of St. Cyril of Alexandria: A Critical Appreciation*. Edinburgh: T. & T. Clark, 2003.

Wessel, Susan. *Cyril of Alexandria and the Nestorian Controversy*. Oxford: Oxford University Press, 2004.

Wilhite, David E. *Tertullian the African: An Anthropological Reading of Tertullian's Context and Identities*. Berlin: de Gruyter, 2007.

Wills, Gary. *Saint Augustine*. New York: Viking, 1999.

Zahn, Theodor. *Athanasius und der Bibelkanon*. 1901. Reprint, Whitefish, MT: Kessinger, 2010.

Index

Abraham, 6
African Methodist Episcopal Church, 198
African Religions, Indigenous, xxv, xxvi, 2n2, 34–35, 52, 65–66, 117, 133–34, 144, 170
Agaton, 11
Alexander of Alexandria, xi, xxvi, 122–24, 130, 131, 200
Alexander of Lycopolis, xi, 116–18
Alexandria, Synod of, 200
Alonius, 9
Ambrose, 165
Ammonas, 10
Amoun of Nitria, 22
Anatolius of Alexandria, xi, 100
Anthony, xi, 1, 2, 3, 4, 6, 9, 10, 11, 12–15, 23, 131
Anthropology (Human Nature), xxiv, 14, 37–38, 55, 69, 110–11, 119, 122, 127, 135, 141, 145, 146, 162, 167, 173, 183
Anti-Semitism, 190
Apollinarus, 187
Apphy, 4
Arianism, 11, 68, 90, 101, 102, 119, 124, 130, 131, 155, 166, 178, 190
Aristotle, 107n33, 108
Arminium and Selucia, Council of, 132–33
Arnobius, xi, 104, 125–29

Athanasia, 25, 29
Athanasius, xi–xii, 3, 8, 10, 11, 112, 12–14, 15, 122, 122n1, 124, 130–41, 180, 181, 200, 202
Athenagoras, xii, 30
Atonement, xxiv, xxxv, 3, 14, 19, 37, 54, 56, 71, 90, 111–12, 117, 123–24, 128, 137, 138, 144, 147, 163, 167, 174, 185, 187–88, 191, 192
   Classic View, xxxv, 3, 14, 19, 37, 54, 71, 90, 112, 123, 128, 144, 147, 163, 167, 187, 192
   Governmental Theory, 54, 123–24
   Moral Influence Theory, 111, 112, 128
   Satisfaction Theory, 54, 117, 123, 147, 188, 192
Audiens, 183
Augustine, xii–xiii, xxiii–xxiv, xxviii–xxix, xxxi, xxxiv, 8, 10, 22, 111, 118, 127, 138, 141, 155, 163, 165, 170–71, 173, 176, 179–80, 190, 194, 195, 197, 200–201, 201–2

Barnabas, The Epistle of, xxxii, xxxiii, 167
Barth, Karl, 51
Berber, xxvii, xxviii–xxix, xxxiv, 170–71
Bessarion, 23
Big Bang Theory, 201
Biblical Canon, 131–32, 199

INDEX

Caecilian, Bishop of Carthage, xxxiv
Calvin, John, 88, 140
Cappadocians, 15
Carion, 23
Carthage, Council of, 199
Carthage, Seventh Council of, 86
Carthage, Synod of, 83
Catechetical School of Alexandria, 30, 63, 95, 101
Celestine I, 181
Christology, xxiv, xxxii, xxxv, 11–12, 13, 25–26, 31, 36–37, 54, 55, 66, 67–68, 70–71, 89–90, 101, 111–12, 117, 119, 123, 128, 132, 135–37, 138, 139, 141, 147, 156, 159–60, 161–62, 163, 174, 181, 182, 185–87, 191, 192, 200–201
   Alexandrian, 36, 54, 71, 123, 137, 181, 185, 186, 191, 201
   Antiochene, 123, 163, 181, 182, 192
   Monophysite, 11–12, 71, 187
Church
   -Polity, xxiv, xxxii–xxxiiii, xxxiv, xxxv, 43–44, 58–59, 73, 80, 84, 85–86, 87, 89, 90, 94, 97–98, 120–21, 140, 143, 168–69, 174, 176–77, 195, 196, 200
   Apostolic Succession, 59, 73
   Papacy, 177
   Priesthood of All Believers, 44, 73, 196
Clement of Alexandria, xiii, xxxi, 30–47, 63, 107, 156, 166, 200, 201
Commodianus, xiii, 78–81, 202
Constantine, 104, 131
Constantinople, Second Council of, 64, 165
Constantinople, Third Council of, 165
Corpes, 10–11
Creation, xxiv, 37–38, 55, 68–69, 78, 96, 109, 119, 135, 136, 138, 141, 153, 162–63, 182, 201
Cyprian of Carthage, xiii–xiv, xxxiii–xxxiv, 81, 82–94, 106, 202
Cyril of Alexandria, xxxi, 131, 180–90, 197, 202
Cyrus of Alexandria, 10

Decius, xxxiii
Demetrius, Bishop of Alexandria, 63, 64
The Didache, xxxii, xxxiii, 200
Didymus the Blind, xv, 165–69
Dionysius, Bishop of Alexandria, xv–xvi, 95–99, 201, 202
Docetism, 37
Donatism, xxxiv, 176, 178, 179

Ephesus, Council of, 143, 182
Eschatology, xxiv, 3, 4, 14–15, 17, 37, 38, 44–45, 49, 59, 71, 74–75, 80, 98, 113, 141, 147, 153, 164, 169, 175
   Apokatastasis, 72, 74–75, 147, 164, 169
Ethiopian Orthodox Church, 181, 187, 200
Eucharistus the Secular, 22–23
Eudeman, 23
Eupraxia, 25–26
Eusebius of Caesarea, xvi, xxvi, 119
Eusebius of Nicomedia, 130

Felicitas, xxxiv
Ferrandus, xvi
Fortunatianus, xxxi
Frumentius, xxvi
Fulgentius, xvi, 180, 190–197, 202–3

Gnosticism, xxv, 2, 7, 20, 23, 31, 32, 37, 38, 40, 42–43, 49
God
   -Trinity, xiv, xxxii, 33, 35–36, 52–54, 61, 67–68, 89, 96, 99, 101, 102, 108–9, 117, 124, 126–27, 131, 134–35, 141, 144–45, 155, 156–61, 165–66, 172, 173, 178, 184–85, 191–92, 200–201
Gregory of Nazianzus, 142–143, 165
Gregory of Nyssa, 64, 142–143, 145

Hartshorne, Charles, 163n82
Heraclitis, 49
Hippo, Council of, 199
Holy Spirit, xxiv, xxxi, xxxii, xxxiv–xxxv, 49, 51, 56, 57, 59, 66, 68, 72, 101, 102, 108–9, 139, 143, 144, 147–48, 149, 150, 153, 154–56,

INDEX

160–61, 163, 165–66, 169, 173, 183, 185
Tongues, Speaking in, 128

Isaac of Cells, 9, 10
Isaac the Theban, 5

Jaeger, Werner, 142, 143
Jerome, xvi–xvii, 8, 48, 155, 165
John the Short, 25
John Cassian, 5
John Chrysostom, xxxi, 172
Julian the Apostate, 130
Julius Africanus, xxxi
Justification, xxiv, xxxii, xxxiv, xxxxv, 3, 10–11, 13–14, 16–17, 18, 24–25, 25–26, 29, 38, 39–41, 56–57, 62, 71–71, 79, 90–91, 97, 101, 112–13, 115, 118, 120, 121, 128, 138–39, 144, 147–50, 151, 152–53, 163–64, 167–68, 174, 178, 188–89, 192–94, 195, 202
    Deification, 13–14, 16–17, 40, 72, 138, 139, 144, 147–48, 149, 150, 151, 152–53, 188–89
    Forensic, 148
    Union With Christ, xxxii, xxxv, 178

Kant, Immanuel, 9, 207
Kemp, Kelly, 198
Kierkegaard, Soren, 50, 207
Kyria, 22

Lactantius, xvii, 104–15, 125, 202–3
Liberius, xxxi
Longinus, 10

Macarius of Alexandria, 6, 15, 142–43
Macarius the Egyptian, 6, 15–17, 24, 101, 142–55, 202
Manicheism, 110, 116, 117, 118, 165
Marcion, 37, 49, 50, 178
Marriage, 60
Mariology, 26, 123, 181, 185, 191
    Mother of God, 26
Martyrdom, xxxiii–xxxv, 12, 41, 48, 63, 76, 91, 92, 103, 170, 179

Mary the Egyptian, 23, 26–27, 29
Matoes, 9–10
Messalians, 142, 143–44, 154
Minucius, Felix, xxxi
Monasticism, 1–29, 80, 101, 141, 145, 153–54, 199–200, 202–3
Montanism, 48, 49, 51, 57, 59
Moses the Negro, 5, 6, 17–18

National Baptist Convention, 198
Nestorianism, 181, 182, 187
Nicea, Council of, 122, 131, 134, 155, 200
Nicea, Second Council of, 165
Nicene Creed, 66
Nilus, 15
Nisterius the Great, 9, 15
Novatian, xxxiv, 82–84, 88, 98
Novatus, 82

Oden, Thomas, ix, 207
Ontological Argument, 51–52
Optatus, xvii, 170, 176–79, 202
Origen, xvii-sviii, 9, 11, 21–22, 23, 31, 36, 63–77, 95, 99, 101–2, 105, 141, 147, 164, 165, 166, 169, 172, 180, 182, 202–3

Pachomius, xviii, 2,7
Pambo, 6
Pantaenus, 30
Paphnutius, 23
Paul, 2, 6
Paul The Simple, 16
Pelagianism, 10, 29, 79, 193
Perpetua, xxxiv–xxxv, 29
Peter of Alexandria, xviii, 119–21
Phileas, xix, 103
Philo, xix, xxx–xxxi
Photius, xix
Pierius of Alexandria, xix, 64, 101–2
Plato, xxv, 33, 34, 65, 107–108n.33, 108, 114
Plotinus, xix, 156
Poemen, 9
Pontius, xix
Praxeas, 52

INDEX

Predestination, 38, 39, 40, 149, 163, 192, 193, 194
Priesthood of All Believers, See Church
Providence, xxiv, xxxv, 7, 12–13, 29, 37, 69–70, 89, 95, 96, 97, 99, 109–10, 112, 115, 117, 126, 127, 135, 136, 144, 146, 173, 193, 201
Punic, xxvii, xxviii–xxix, 170–71

Racism, 198–99
Rome, Council of, 181

Sacraments, xxiv, xxxii, xxxiii, xxxv, 4–5, 26, 27, 44, 57–58, 73–74, 83, 84, 86–89, 90, 103, 140, 143, 153, 174, 175, 177, 189–90, 195
  -Baptism of Infants, 87, 202
Salaminius Sozomen, xix
Sanctification-Christian Living, xxiv, xxxiii, xxxv, 3, 4, 6–7, 9, 10, 13, 14, 16–17, 18, 19, 24–25, 25–26, 27, 28, 29, 41–43, 47, 56, 57, 63, 72–73, 80, 91–93, 97, 98, 101, 102, 103, 112–13, 118, 120, 125, 128, 129, 138, 139, 144, 147–53, 167, 168, 174, 179, 188–89, 192, 193, 195, 201–202
  Perfection, 14, 17, 19, 41, 42–43, 101, 153, 182, 202
  Perseverance, 195
Sarah, 27–28, 29
Schleiermacher, Friedrich, xxxi, 31–32
Sexism/Patriarchalism, 20–21, 22, 23, 42, 46, 60–61, 76, 78–79, 98, 175, 179
Shenoute of Atripe, 6
The Shepherd of Hermas, xix, xxxii–xxxiii, 167
Sheppard, William Henry, 198
Simeon Stylites, 6
Sin, xxiv, 3, 5, 9–10, 18, 19, 40, 55–56, 69–70, 78–79, 87, 89, 97, 111, 112, 120, 127, 137–138, 141, 146–147, 178, 188, 192, 201–202
Slavery, 93
Social Ethics, xxiv, 3, 12–13, 15, 17, 19, 36, 39, 45–47, 60–62, 76, 80, 86, 93–94, 98, 113, 114–115, 129, 140, 154, 169, 175, 179, 190, 196, 202–203
Poverty, Concern for, 3, 15, 17, 19, 36, 45–46, 62, 80, 86, 93, 113, 140, 169
Socrates Scholasticus, xix, 142–43
String Theory, 106
Stoicism, 2, 42, 54, 108, 126
Syncletica, 28–29
Synesius of Cyrene, xix–xx, xxxi, 170, 171–75

Tertullian, xx–xxi, xxxiv–xxxv, 23, 32–33, 36, 48–62, 84, 106, 110, 118, 126, 141, 155, 166, 172, 182, 200, 201, 202–3
Theodora, 24–25
Theognostus of Alexandria, xxi, 64, 101, 202
Theological Method, xxiv, xxxi, xxxii, 9, 12, 15, 19, 28–29, 30–35, 47, 49–52, 64–67, 76–77, 78, 84, 95–96, 98, 100, 104–7, 115, 116, 125–26, 129, 132–34, 141, 144–45, 155–56, 165–66, 172, 182–83, 191
Theonas of Alexandria, 102, 202–203
Theophilus, xxi, 24, 172, 180
Tillich, Paul, xxxi, 31–32, 208
Tracy, David, 33n24, 208
Tradition, Authority of, 50–51, 133, 182–83
Traducianism, 55, 110

United Brethren for Christ, 198

Victorinus, Caius Marius, xvii, 155–64

War, 61, 76, 93, 115, 129, 140, 175
Wesley, John, 42, 154
Whitehead, Alfred North, 162–63
Wisdom of the Elders of Ethiopia, 4, 8, 11, 23
Worship, xxxiii, 200

Zacharius, 6
Zeno, 49

www.ingramcontent.com/pod-product-compliance
Lightning Source LLC
Chambersburg PA
CBHW031808220426
43662CB00007B/565